Praise

'A great depth of reading and thinking here, and the whole thing thrums, right at the back of it, with a contagious sadness; a contagious anger; a contagious grief . . . This is a brave and necessary book'                                               Sam Leith, *Guardian*

'Personal revelations are expertly woven into interview material, social history, and theorising by psychologists and other writers . . . Renton deserves praise and attention for disturbing our equanimity about this tradition'
                                    Miranda Green, *Financial Times*

'[He] brilliantly deconstructs the myth of the British stiff upper lip'                                    Rod Liddle, *Sunday Times*

'Shocking, gripping and sobering . . . impassioned, candid and thoroughly researched'    Rupert Christiansen, *Sunday Telegraph*

'Enormously valuable'                        John Preston, *Daily Mail*

'By the end of this thoughtful and sensitive indictment of one of the cornerstones of the British establishment, it's very hard to conclude anything except that generations of children have been emotionally damaged on a truly shocking scale'
                                        Andrew Anthony, *Observer*

'Gruelling and gripping'        William Moore, *Evening Standard*

'Renton has the thirst for truth, and for exposing depravity, of a Gitta Sereny'            Ysenda Maxtone Graham, *The Times*

'Impressive in its breadth and depth'
                                        Harry Hodges, *Daily Express*

'This is a fascinating book'                        Ian Irvine, *Prospect*

Alex Renton is an award-winning journalist whose career has ranged from theatre criticism to food writing to the investigation of child abuse, and as war reporter in the Middle East, Africa and the Balkans. He is also the author of *Planet Carnivore*. He was educated at Ashdown House and Eton, and lives in Edinburgh with his wife and two children.

www.stiffupperlip.org.uk

# STIFF UPPER LIP

## Secrets, crimes and the schooling of a ruling class

### ALEX RENTON

WEIDENFELD & NICOLSON

A W&N Paperback
First published in Great Britain in 2017
by Weidenfeld & Nicolson
This paperback edition published in 2018
by Weidenfeld & Nicolson,
an imprint of Orion Books Ltd

1 3 5 7 9 10 8 6 4 2

A CIP catalogue record for this book
is available from the British Library.

ISBN 978 1 4746 0101 6

Typeset by Input Data Services Ltd, Somerset

Printed and bound by CPI Group (UK) Ltd, Croydon, CRO 4YY

www.orionbooks.co.uk

For Ruth Burnett, who understands

# Keep a Stiff Upper Lip

*There has something gone wrong,*
*My brave boy, it appears,*
*For I see your proud struggle*
*To keep back the tears.*
*That is right. When you cannot*
*Give trouble the slip,*
*Then bear it, still keeping*
*'A stiff upper lip'.*

*Though you cannot escape*
*Disappointment and care,*
*The next best thing to do*
*Is to learn how to bear.*
*If when for life's prizes*
*You're running, you trip,*
*Get up, start again —*
*'Keep a stiff upper lip!'*

*Let your hands and your conscience*
*Be honest and clean;*
*Scorn to touch or to think of*
*The thing that is mean;*
*But hold on to the pure*
*And the right with firm grip,*
*And though hard be the task,*
*'Keep a stiff upper lip!'*

*Through childhood, through manhood,*
*Through life to the end,*
*Struggle bravely and stand*
*By your colors, my friend.*
*Only yield when you must;*
*Never 'give up the ship',*
*But fight on to the last*
*'With a stiff upper lip'.*

Phoebe Cary (1824–71)*

* Cary was a well-known American poet and an early advocate for women's rights. The first recorded use of the phrase 'stiff upper lip' was in the United States in 1815.

# Contents

# Author's note

## Prep and public schools

In Britain we say 'public schools' when we mean private, secondary ones – an example of the confusing codes the stiff-upper-lip tendency likes to employ. The term dates from the time of the ancient scholastic institutions, such as Winchester, Westminster and Eton, set up by statute. Like much else, 'public' was adopted by the new nineteenth- and twentieth-century fee-paying schools to show that they emulated the older ones in ethos and exclusivity. In 2017 there were 282 schools that called themselves 'public' in the British sense.*

This book uses the term 'public school' to denote any private school from the late nineteenth century onwards that was fee-paying, traditional in regime and existed for children aged between eleven and nineteen. 'Preparatory school' is the same though for younger children. I use 'state school' to denote ones that really are for all the public, without barriers of class or income.

* Until 1871, only nine were recognised as 'public schools'. Since then only members of the Headmasters' and Headmistresses' Conference, a self-selecting association of the 'world's leading independent schools', call themselves public schools.

## References and additional material

Full references to sources, further footnotes and some additional material can be found online at www.stiffupperlipbook.com. The site also contains resources for people seeking help in the aftermath of child abuse, mental and physical.

I welcome any comments or questions about this book and the wider issues: please contact me through the same website.

# Introduction

## Zombie stories

Many a lad who leaves an English public school disgracefully ignorant of the rudiments of useful knowledge, who can speak no language but his own, and writes that imperfectly, to whom the noble literature of his country and the stirring history of his forefathers are almost a sealed book, and who has devoted a great part of his time and nearly all his thought to athletic sports, yet brings away with him something beyond all price – a manly straightforward character, a scorn for lying and meanness, habits of obedience and command and fearless courage. Thus equipped, he goes out into the world, and bears a man's part in subduing the earth, ruling its wild folk, and building up the Empire . . .

The Rev. T. L. Papillon, 'The Public Schools and Citizenship'

This is not a book about me, but it starts with something that happened to me. In 1974, aged thirteen, I left my hated 'prep' school, where I had boarded since the age of eight. It had done its job: I got into a famous 'public' school and thus on to the escalator to achievement and security that members of Britain's privileged class have organised so neatly since the nineteenth century. But the experience came at a price, and with side effects. One was that I didn't become the sort of citizen pictured by the Reverend Thomas Papillon.

Like many of the million Britons alive today who experienced the boarding school system, I spent the years after leaving forgetting what had happened to me there. I didn't send my own children away to school at eight, or at thirteen. But at Christmas 2013, my school and all it stood for came back into my life. The memories rose, as badly buried things will. There was a headline in the *Daily Mail* – 'Boris school at the centre of probe into sexual abuse' – and when I found it I wept. The story said that a group of men (though not Boris Johnson) were beginning a civil case over 'horrific attacks' by two former teachers at the school. A police investigation had begun. 'The effects of this abuse,' went a statement from twenty former Ashdown children, 'has damaged a number of pupils long into adulthood and it is felt among us that, as part of the healing process, it is important for us to take our power back and take action against such damaging and horrendous actions.'

They were all a couple of years younger, but I had known them, and I knew the teachers they were talking about. I spoke to my mother, who remembered other things that I had forgotten. I went with Ruth Burnett, my wife, to Sussex to visit the school, for the first time since leaving. It was changed – they all are – but in its essentials the same. Seven-year-olds still board. We saw one, who, diffident and teary, made it all look very stark: he was 'having trouble settling in'. He would get over it soon, we were assured by the headmaster. Like a surgeon's saw or a dentist's pliers, boarding school was and is a tool: simple, practical and sometimes brutal.

A couple of months later I published an article in the *Observer*'s magazine about my experience of abuse – physical and emotional – at Ashdown House. I was not the first to have done this. Many ex-boarding school writers have spilled the beans; for some of us it is the most obvious therapeutic act. But perhaps because the story also looked at the current deluge of allegations about abuse in care institutions, or perhaps because my astute, ex-boarding school editor at the *Observer* invited readers to send in their stories, the article got an extraordinary reaction. The social media postings garnered thousands of shares and comments. In twenty-five years of investigations and campaigning journalism, I'd never had such a response.

Most of it was sympathetic. Some readers were quick to point out the ironies in a story of 'posh abuse' – people who'd paid for it. ('Sometimes we do not truly realize how blessed we were to be born into poverty,' said one commenter.) Others asked: So what? Who's surprised? Auberon Waugh, ex-public school boy and satirist, was quoted, on the upper and upper-middle classes' time-honoured habit of sending their offspring into the care of paedophiles at boarding schools: 'Of course, the English are famous throughout the entire civilised world for their hatred of children.'

Others made a fair complaint: nearly a quarter of a million children are sexually abused in the UK every year, according to the Children's Commissioner, so why should these old stories take up our – and the police's – time? But the counter-view was important: if this was how the ruling class cared for its children, no wonder the public institutions of Britain that they went on to run – from the BBC to the NHS – seemed so careless, so arrogant and so prone to cover-up. We needed to find out what went wrong in the schools of the elite, as much as in Stoke Mandeville Hospital.

Many people told what had happened to them, stories

often full of a lifetime's sorrow. The newspaper's moderators were busy deleting posts that made allegations against specific schools and teachers. But even after that winnowing, the comment streams and my inbox had several hundred credible stories of apparent criminal abuse by adults at boarding schools, private and state.

I read all the mail over the following weeks. It was not easy. Some accounts were dozens of pages long; there were honed chapters of planned books and plangent streams of emotion. Many began: 'I've never spoken of this to anyone . . .' After a few days of reading these I began to have crude and obvious nightmares. I was asleep, but aware that something was amiss – many-limbed things were scuttering around the room, crawling out from under the bed and on to it.

Many of the people who sent me their stories got an Out of Office response – a promise to read and respond within a few weeks. Often the robot text would get a reply; the mere fact of having told the story had opened doors. 'Don't worry, I imagine you're overwhelmed with sob-stories from the ex-boarders. You don't need to reply. After I sent that email to you I showed it to [a partner], and we started talking. Better late than never . . .'

Other accounts were not as easy to handle. Some people demanded interventions that were beyond me – for a start, the newspaper did not have the funds to sponsor long investigations of rich, potentially litigious institutions, though we did tackle one, Gordonstoun School. But there were people who clearly needed help that I was not qualified to give. There were suicide risks, and victims with details of predatory sex offenders still working in institutions. Most got a standard response. It suggested a series of steps: talking therapy, campaigning, the law. But it was pretty clear too that seeking legal redress wasn't necessarily a good idea. There is value for the soul in revenge, but often the long and dreary process gets people already prone to anger even more riled and unhappy. When it came to getting abusers to court, the emails told far more stories of failure and frustration than of resolution. In March 2017 Martin Haigh, a science teacher at Ashdown House when I was in my last year there, received a 12-year sentence for serious sexual assaults on four boys at the school, one of them only eight years old. This was a wonderful result for those men, now in their 50s, and an inspiration to many more who have suffered at the hands of predators who thought themselves beyond the law. Yet it was all horribly slow: the conviction came 42 years after the first parents complained about Haigh, and 15 years after the first Ashdown ex-pupils went to the police.

What left victims most angry was Haigh's evidence that Ashdown's then headmaster had sacked Haigh in 1975 for sexual abuse of the children, after two sets of parents complained, but that, seemingly, Haigh had not been reported to any authority. Kent police are now investigating allegations from pupils at a school where Haigh taught five years after he left Ashdown. Clive Williams, who was joint headmaster of Ashdown House at the time, says he had no involvement in Martin Haigh's departure in 1975 and had no knowledge of his crimes. The other co-headmaster, Billy Williamson, is dead.

But English civil law was changing. The principle had been that compensation for personal injury can only be claimed in the three years after the event – not much use to child abuse victims, who tend not to report the offences against them for many years. But the victims of Jimmy

Savile had got a change – in cases of severe abuse, the judge may extend the limitation. So putting together groups of victims from the schools to mount civil actions started to make sense. Many of them work in banking or financial services – they are ex-public school pupils, after all – and they have faith in punishments that hit the pocket. If schools' insurers could see an added liability risk, they would put on pressure to toughen up the schools' child protection systems. A well-known financier from one group told me he would be putting any compensation money he got straight into a charity that provides trauma counselling for children in state schools. 'Not that there isn't a need in private schools, too.'

In the end, doubtful about my abilities as an email counsellor, fearful that I might make someone's pain worse (and conscious that I was over-stretching my own emotional capacities), I reverted to being a journalist. I made a database of the allegations I'd been sent and started to find patterns. When I compared my data with that of other journalists, we realised that as many as half of the schools of the privileged had harboured adult sexual abusers, and perhaps many more. I realised I needed to look back to the beginning of the modern private school system, in the mid nineteenth century, to see how this had come about. We were not alone. In 1989, a group of officials representing police, social services and the charity Childline told a conference on institutional abuse that they thought 75 per cent of residential schools had had at least one case of sexual abuse.*

---

* Jack O'Sullivan, 'Sex abuse "at 75 per cent of boarding schools"', *Independent*, 9 December 1989

People didn't write to me because they had been happy, of course. I only inspired a dozen people in some 800 accounts to tell me what great times they'd had at school; even then, half of those sunny stories were given in order to provide contrast with a story of a friend or relative who had been miserable. As I processed the information, other things I had not known became clear. One was how many women had stories of serious abuse to tell, physical as well as psychological – they made up nearly a quarter of the total. The next was just how rife the problems of violence, sexual assault and neglect were in the schools, right up to the twenty-first century. Linked to that was the fact that teachers accused of criminal acts almost always got away with it; until recently, the normal sanction was a discreet sacking, often with a reference enabling the offender to continue their careers. Abusers went from school to school, in both the private and state sectors: this was an industry with a culture of employing paedophiles and sadists. But the most important realisation for me was the extent of the abuse that was not criminal.

The stories that led me to write this book are those of children abandoned by their families into the care of strangers, often astonishingly early. The usual entry age to the system in the 1960s and 1970s was around seven or eight years old.* The communities these children arrived in were not normally kind or caring. The British, we know, have always been both sentimental and violent to children in a way that sets them apart from other European nations. But in the boarding schools cruelty and bullying,

* A 1966 study of a sample of 2,794 sixth formers in boarding schools found that a majority boarded before eleven and more than a third before eight. At the time 1.7% of all British schoolchildren boarded.

by children and adults, was a function of the system: not a disciplinary practice but an ingredient in the magic of that unique education. Neglect, as we would see it today, was normal. Even if the schools had been as comfortable and cuddly as a nursery, the stories I was sent made it clear that the shock of that abrupt separation had had extraordinary, lasting effects on the adults that emerged from early boarding. Some still thought it was their fault they had been sent away, some felt their parents' 'betrayal' had soured the future: all of them had learnt, very young, the limits of love.

Naturally, some thought that was all to the good. Here's a man who was sent, at eight, a month after his father's death: 'Now looking back that was the making of me. What it made was an incendiary mix. Too dangerous to be either employed or ignored. But it works.' Others try hard to find good moments amid the sad, for balance. But many of them were still struggling with the notion that their parents had colluded with the schools – that they knew their loved child would suffer yet thought that good. When I first started considering the rotten parts of the private boarding school industry, I thought I was looking at a breath-taking fraud that had been carried out, for over a century, on some of the most powerful and educated people in the country. That of course was far too simple. The truth was more complex and more disturbing.

Anthropologists know of many societies that ritualise the abuse of their children. Tradition and the 'hardship is good for you' trope justify it. In some cultures children are provably loved and cherished, but also deliberately hurt. There are Amazon tribes who scald their children with hot water or scrape their skin with sharks' teeth to teach them to deal with the pain that life inevitably brings. But there is a key difference with the British elite: it ritually sends its children away, very young. Alone in the world, these parents withdraw love and security in order to educate their child. Only they sacrifice their own happiness, forgo the joy of seeing and helping their children grow and develop, for the cause of future privilege. What follows is an attempt to explain how an entire class, briefly one of the most powerful the world has known, decided that its children needed to suffer to become useful citizens.

Researching this story has been fascinating and troubling. My first problem lay with the evidence. Memory is fallible and fluid: we edit our stories of our childhood all our lives, to extract from them what is useful, and also what we can bear to live with. That problem is all the harder when trying to research a class that is schooled in self-protection and secrecy, that prides itself in not saying what it truly thinks, and, like any ruling elite, always has a variety of views available on the same issue, some for outsiders and some for insiders, for the elect and for the masses.

I have relied on many sources to tell this story, starting with my own memory of what I think happened to me and to my family. I have also used published accounts, because the literature and drama of boarding schools has always addressed the cruelty of the system, even if chiefly for entertainment. Very occasionally I've been able to use contemporary accounts of children who boarded. But the most useful resource has been the correspondence from readers of that first article, and I am profoundly grateful for the frankness and honesty of those hundreds of men and women who decided to revisit some of their darkest days in order to help me. I hope it helped them.

# PART ONE

# Leaving Home

# 1. Dropped off aged eight

On attaining the age of eight, or thereabout, children
fly away from the Gardens and never come back . . .
The boys have gone to Pilkington's. He is a man with
a cane.*

J. M. Barrie, *The Little White Bird*

One September day at the end of the 1960s, when I was
eight and a half years old, my parents delivered me to preparatory school. I wore grey corduroy shorts, new and rigid
as cardboard, knee-high grey woollen socks and shiny
black Start-rite shoes. The shorts were much too big, but
I had an elasticated belt with a silvered clasp like an S on
its side: a snake, I thought. Under the grey school jumper,
over a grey shirt was one line of colour: a blue tie whose
knotting my father had helped me master. In the photo
taken before we got in the car, my face is solemn, my
blond hair tamed. But I was excited: only a few weeks earlier I'd sat up all night to watch Neil Armstrong set foot
upon the moon. Now I was leaving my younger siblings
on the planet of Home and adventuring to a new world.

Ashdown House is not far from our family's house in
Sussex. The twenty-five minutes of the journey there

* Pilkington was a prep school headmaster: he became the model for
the villainous Captain Hook of *Peter Pan*.

remain imprinted nearly half a century later – we were to do it twenty times or more every one of the next five years. I can play the drive out in my mind: each hamlet, each curve of the road, the Mars Bar that we stopped to buy at one village shop for a treat, my mother stifling tears, her songs and her brave attempts at jokes: 'Let's see if we can keep a stiff upper lip, and our chins up, and our brows set, and our socks pulled up *and* our best feet forward, all at once.' This didn't diminish her pain. Nor did it do much to soften the lump of compounded fear and sorrow that seemed to have occupied the place where my lungs and stomach were supposed to be. As term followed term, those grim, too short journeys got no easier. I recall thinking – Why are you upset? You're going home.

I remember, that first time, my father stopping the car at the school's gate. He said it was best that kisses and hugging be done now, not at the school. That I sort of understood, more than I did his advice, given in a man-to-man talk a few days earlier: 'Remember, if any of the older boys try to take you into a bush, just say "No".'

We pulled up on the gravel by the columned portico of the grey stone building. It seemed very grand. I remember watching my trunk and my tuck box disappear into the dark and noisy interior. At the steps was Billy Williamson, the headmaster; huge, with a monkish frill of hair round his jowly head. I had to wait to shake hands with him: he was busy with a short woman in a checked coat who was presenting a curly-haired boy even smaller than me. This was Princess Margaret and her son David. The headmaster, when he had done with the royals, rumbled pleasantly at us from high above. 'He seems very nice,' said my mother.

The parting I don't remember. I know my mother showed me to my dormitory, five iron hospital beds with candlewick spreads in a bare room under the eaves. Two of the other beds also had new boys assigned to them. My mother unpacked a few of my things and tucked the cloth piglet that had been my comforter since toddlerhood under the pillow. No doubt she asked the dormitory captain, a boy a year or two older, to be kind to me. Later that evening he explained to us some school rules. One was that crying was not allowed. Any crying that occurred would be punished by him and his deputy with a beating. He thwacked the bed with his unfurled belt: the same snake buckle that I'd thought was so cool now looked like it would hurt.

My arrival story is ordinary, except that I don't remember saying goodbye. The moment of separation stays vivid for most people who were dispatched at an early age into institutions, whether paid for or state-run. I have heard from hundreds who have told stories of their days at boarding schools: quite a few of them were not even fully aware of what was about to happen when they arrived. Of course, the younger the child, the more that seems possible, and in the twentieth century tens of thousands of children were packed off aged just six and some as young as four. It was a common experience: at the peak of the system, in 1967, 43,000 children were boarding at prep or primary school.*

My arrival was civilised. It wasn't unusual for children to be dragged from the family car. Quite often the parents simply lied to their offspring – 'We'll see you later!' – and bolted. A friend sent to board at eleven remembers running down the school drive after her parents' car: 'At one

* In 2016 there were 4,809 children at primary level boarding schools in the Independent Schools Council, which represents 80 per cent of them all.

point, it braked, and I thought they were stopping for me, but it was just for a corner. I don't think until then I really knew I was going to have to stay.'

Some of the saddest stories of the drop-off come from children who were spectators. Younger siblings who went along for the ride remember the misery overtaking a brother and sister as the school got closer, the tension between the mother and father, sometimes a forced removal from the car: 'his fingers levered off the headrest one by one'. Bear Grylls, now a professional adventurer, remembers the shock of seeing his father, an Army officer, in tears in the car on the first trip to Ludgrove House: 'I felt confused as to what part of nature or love thought this was a good idea. My instinct certainly didn't; but what did I know? I was only eight.' Grylls hated his time at the school.

A woman who grew up at the prep boarding school where her parents worked remembers those partings:

> I saw at first hand the sadness and trauma boarding can cause. I remember the sobbing mothers, and the stiff-upper-lip fathers telling their distraught sons to 'be a man and grow up'. And I remember wondering why they'd had children in the first place, when they so obviously wanted to get rid of them. My mother and father tried to soften the sadness of the younger ones in particular – teddies allowed on beds, bright homely dormitories, bed-time stories – but my kind and gentle mother knew it couldn't make up for what they'd lost, no matter how hard she tried . . . One boy used to cry, so hard, at the beginning of each term. He was bullied for that.

Many people tell of watching in disbelief as the family saloon disappeared behind the rhododendrons; then turning to face the tumult of children, noise-filled corridors, strange smells and unloving adults, and feeling, in a way that never left some, utterly lost. 'The end of my childhood,' concludes a friend who went through this at nine.

Another feature of the arrival stories is the child's clear-eyed observation of parents' strange behaviour. Mothers are brittle or weepy; most fathers – if they went along – brisk or even joyful. Auberon Waugh wrote of his father's 'undisguised glee at the prospect of getting rid of his children'. He held an end-of-holiday party: 'Papa would dress in white tie and tails. His speech was always some variation on the theme of how delighted he was that we were going back to school.' Most mothers, then and now, are upset: 'I cried buckets, every time I took them back,' one modern mother told me. 'I drove away as fast as I could because I knew I would embarrass them: eventually I got the au pair to drive them to school.'

Of course, it is not easy to think of a good way to deliver a young child into the hands of strangers for an amount of time that will seem oceanic to a seven- or even a twelve-year-old: 'We'll see you at half-term, darling!' As any parent who uses day-care knows, most children will object to the idea at first, even if they understand that the separation is only to be for a matter of hours. Combing through the accounts of arrival there are few that are not traumatic, though of course a happy transition is not the stuff of gripping autobiography, and not likely to have been sent to me. They are, in any case, recollections of events that happened decades before, often mediated in therapy or smoothed and rounded by repeated telling. That does not make them worthless: they are revealing, vivid and often tragic. 'Robin', who was at my school, Ashdown House, wrote this to me:

> I was eight nearly nine and without exaggeration can remember the day as if it were yesterday when I experienced my major trauma. I remember being left at the top of the driveway near the School Gate and waving goodbye to my Mum as a young boy and being overwhelmed by a feeling of abandonment. Wondering why I was left in the countryside prep school with adults I knew nothing about, also with their Christianity and at times 'scatty or unconventional behaviour'! After leaving my childhood behind and actually being in England that first term when my youngest sibling was born. She was born in Hong Kong. I felt replaced.

Robin has spent more than a quarter of his life in mental institutions. He sees the fracture at the gates of Ashdown as the moment his life took the turn that brought him, unwilling, to where he is as a middle-aged man: ill and incomplete, 'unable to trust, unable to love'. For others, luckier, the horror of the break marks the beginning of similarly extraordinary lives, some more happily lived. But the shock remains and reverberates. So does the anger at the careless adults who chose a child's iron fate in a fit of whimsy. Here's Rupert Everett in his autobiography saying goodbye to his mother at the age of seven:

> 'Darling,' she said, as she unprised my hand from hers, her voice carefully casual, 'we'll probably go while you're having tea so I'll kiss you goodbye now.' She stumbled into the car and shut the door. I looked down at the

tears splashing on to my shoes: new sandals from Start-rite. Last week I had loved them, but now they were just another part of the plot against me. I couldn't look up. I didn't want to see the betrayal in my mother's eyes . . .

'What are you looking at darling?' She was crying and her mascara had run.

'My shoes,' I said. And I looked up, but the car had already moved off.

The first boarding school boy to describe the arrival was the novelist William Thackeray. In 1817, aged five and accompanied by his four-year-old cousin, he left his parents in Calcutta to go to boarding school in Southampton. This was quite normal practice for the children of British colonials; in the 1930s my aunt and her sister, also in India, were dispatched to board at the ages of four and six. In 1860, with dozens of new boarding schools opening, Thackeray was still ruminating on the effect of sending young children away from home.

> Perhaps I recollect driving down (with a certain trunk and carpet-bag on the box) with my own mother to the end of the avenue, where we waited – only a few minutes – until the whirring wheels of that 'Defiance' coach were heard rolling towards us as certain as death. Twang goes the horn; up goes the trunk; down come the steps. Bah! I see the autumn evening: I hear the wheels now: I smart the cruel smart again: and, boy or man, have never been able to bear the sight of people parting from their children.

Thackeray used his experiences at a succession of brutal

schools in his fiction. In private letters, he told of years
where his only hope lay in dreams of his mother. 'That
first night at school – hard bed, hard words, strange boys
bullying, and laughing, and jarring you with their hateful merriment – as for the first night at a strange school,
we most of us remember what THAT is,' he wrote in a
magazine article. I wonder if some of the fathers who
avoided taking their children back to school did so not
through indifference, but for fear of the memories the trip
might trigger.

The first insult remains vivid, just as key to the narrative
as the first arrival. Like being strip-searched on arrival in a
prison or the initiation rituals for Army recruits, a violent
affront to justice or normality drives the transition from
the familiar to the new. 'I think the school knew our spirit
had to be broken,' a correspondent writes. Often, the stories are of the shock of bad food – the clot of cold fat, the
incomprehensible meat, outraged hunger. These are usually told, looking back, as comedy. But familiar, edible food,
as any parent knows, is central to a child's comfort.

The first bedtime stands out, too: at home it was a time
of stories and hugs, of warmth and security. At Ashdown,
bed was not safe or warm. After lights-out that first night,
the dormitory captain explained that the belt would be
used not just to punish for crying, but for any noise at all,
including a creak from a bedspring. It is not just the fear
but the affront that adults remember. 'I arrived at Hazel-
grove House preparatory school in 1958, aged eight years,'
writes one of my correspondents. 'My first-night highlight
was having all the toy cars I had put on my dormitory
bed to share and play with thrown out of the window. Another "new boy" started on the same day as me, with a

bed-wetting problem. A little sympathy would have helped him . . . The matron angrily ripping his urine-soaked sheet off his bed one morning, rubbing his tear-stained face in it, though, did not help.'

The adults were often more avid than the children in the ritual of shocking the novices. The actor Selina Cadell told me of her first day at Bedales in 1961, aged eight.

My first memory, as I watched my parents drive away, unsure when I would see them again, was of the Matron of the Girls' Dorms handing me a tall glass of milk. Minutes before this my mother had answered her question: 'Is there anything Selina doesn't like?' with the simple word 'milk'. Assuming of course that she had somehow misunderstood, I gently explained that milk made me sick.

'I don't care what it does, you will not leave this room until you drink it,' came the response.

I started to drink, slowly. To my surprise the Matron produced a pair of scissors at this point and started to cut off my hair. It was quite long. She cut it quite short. I was sick on the carpet. I had to clear up the mess, the vomit and my hair, before I was taken to my dorm.

I cried all night, that first night. But the abuse I received and the threat of violence from the bullies in my dorm soon altered that. My crying went inside.

Thackeray's memoir stands out, not just because he was the first to tell the story, but because, unlike many of the others, he stood by his experience. Most memoirists of schooldays use the harsh stories of their first days or years as an antiphon, the necessary prelude to happier times. It makes for a neat plot, and tells how we matured and learned not to complain, to despise self-pity. But Thackeray never used the wry humour and self-deprecation that colours so many of the accounts. He does not gloss his misery, or turn it into something useful.

There are some stories of children bouncing into the school with a joy that never deflated. But it seems clear that there were few children for whom the first separation was not an elemental shock. The parting is a necessary rite in life's journey, obviously enough. A door closes, another opens. Separations are the pivots in the great Victorian novels that fed the imaginations of twentieth-century British children. For the many people who now look back in pain or wonder at childhoods spent with strangers, that initial forced severing is the beginning of a story that, decades later, many, including me, are still trying to unravel and understand.

# 2. The rise of the prep school

The most common driving factor is tradition – obeying it, or buying into it. I come from a long line of boarders. Eleven generations of my mother's family, hereditary chiefs of a Scottish clan, have left their valley in Ayrshire to seek an education; until my generation came along any other course would have been unthinkable to the class that ran Scotland, then Britain and then the Empire. My father's family – just three generations of boarders – are more typical. They were of the aspirational class of newly wealthy Britons who seized on the private boarding school system with such certain enthusiasm a century or so ago.

At the beginning of the nineteenth century the Rentons were shopkeepers in Edinburgh's Canongate and their children attended the city's day-schools; at the beginning of the twentieth, my grandfather and his two brothers were at fashionable English boarding preparatory schools, being 'prepared' for Harrow. Like thousands of others, the family had prospered in the age of British industrialisation and imperial wealth; clever investments in Ceylon tea plantations had transplanted them from Edinburgh's Old Town to an estate in Bedfordshire and a house in London's Knightsbridge. My great-grandfather James Renton became wealthy and powerful planting and selling tea, but he retained the strong Edinburgh accent that betrayed his beginnings. Like many others, he turned to the schools to add polish that would ease the children up the social ladder – though, for my great-uncle Noel that brought no more than a lieutenancy in a fashionable regiment followed by death on the Western Front in 1915. He was not quite twenty-one.

Private boarding schools as we know them today were born in a nineteenth-century boom fuelled by this vast new middle class: people like the Rentons. Between the 1840s and the 1870s the ancient schools used by the British elite – Rugby, Eton, Harrow, Winchester and a few others – were forced into a series of gradual reforms that would make them into a model for education in Britain – and far beyond – for the next century or more. All of these were practical. The most important was the introduction of age limits, rules and entrance exams, a way to put some order into institutions that were then notorious for violence, anarchy and remarkably high death-rates. In the 'bearpit' that was eighteenth-century Eton, six-year-olds often lived and learned alongside man-pupils as old as twenty. The school's youngest-ever student, the illegitimate child of the Earl of Pembroke and a lover, Kitty Hunter, started aged four in 1766. The boy was entered as a pupil under the name Augustus Retnuh Reebkomp. It cannot have taken the older children long to decipher the anagrams of his parents' names.

These systems became standard when state education began to be formalised in Britain at the end of the century, giving us the primary and secondary school system that operates in most of the world. Meanwhile, in the latter half of the nineteenth century, dozens of new fee-charging secondary schools – Liverpool College, Brighton College, the Glasgow and Edinburgh Academies, Fettes, Marlborough and Radley – had started, largely because there was not room in the more ancient ones for the newly rich middle class that wanted to buy their sons – and a few daughters – entry to the establishment. These were instant ancient institutions. They deliberately aped the structures of the grand old schools in their rituals, discipline and even their architecture. They too needed a supply of 'prepared' thirteen-year-olds.

To get to one of the 'public' schools – so called because they had been set up by statute, and were recognised in law – it was necessary to have been made ready; hence the preparatory or private schools, private because anyone could open one. In the 1920s, 240 such schools prepared boys for entry to the naval colleges, where they would become cadets and then officers. Until the 1960s both prep and public schools, with the exception of a few urban ones like West London's St Paul's, were almost entirely for boarders.

Sleeping and living at the schools came about by necessity. Most of the class that used them, before the great expansion of the nineteenth century, lived in ancestral homes spread across rural Britain. The children had either to be tutored at home or to go away. But the separation soon became hallowed practice, and the new junior schools demanded the same. They had to 'prepare' children for both the demands of the curriculum and the rigours of communal, single-sex boarding life. Besides, boarding made money for the teachers who supplied the beds and food; even in the most expensive schools, staff were appallingly ill-paid up until the late twentieth century. Throughout their history the schools have shown genius in turning what makes economic and practical sense into ethos, the ingredients of the magic formula for educating the British elite. Thus recruiting older children to do the job of keeping control of the younger gave rise to the time-honoured roles of prefect and fagmaster. Cost-saving solutions became the means of instilling virtues such as bravery, resilience and – a much-used term – 'manliness'. Hence the use of fear and violence to ensure discipline became as much a part of the spell as freezing dormitories and disgusting food – all good for shaping the man to be.

The private school business was a goldmine. It was an easy way for a man with an education and some talent at charming parents to set himself up. By the late nineteenth century there were 700 recognised preparatory schools feeding the public schools, both new and old, though only 11 of those existed for girls. In 1981 there were reported to be 570, typically with a hundred or so pupils each, most of them boarding.

The Fergussons, my mother's ancient family, sent their children off to ensure the family's continued membership of the establishment. James Renton and many others – then and now – sent his children away to acquire the social polish that would allow them to join it. It would not do to have the children enter the public schools with a rural accent, the most vivid signal that they were from outside the Upper Ten Thousand, as the late Victorian elite liked to call themselves. Why were the newly rich business-men of the Lancashire mills sending their children south to expensive schools, wondered the Taunton Commission, set up by the government in 1864 to examine the public schools. It was so that 'they may lose their northern tongue . . . and be quite away from home influences'.

There were other, less-voiced concerns. Not least was the threat Victorians called 'beastliness'. The historian Jonathan Gathorne-Hardy writes that the period of great growth in prep schools coincided with a panic about morality in the public schools: 'it seemed imperative to remove from the lustful hands of eighteen-year-olds the lovely little boys of nine and ten'. But just as strong was another 'moral' pressure: to remove boys from the 'softening' influence of mothers and home.

The task was not all about forming the 'character' of the young girls and boys, though that word comes first in the headmasters' treatises. There was work to be done in the classroom, especially as the public schools began selective entrance exams. Mathematics was of some importance, sciences were not. The children chiefly needed to know the Bible and the ancient languages. Education at the public schools – and many of the grammar schools that aped them – remained primarily a matter of learning Latin and Greek until the 1950s. It was still important in getting scholarships until the 1980s.

It was generally held, and certainly so at Ashdown House when I was there, that unless you started Latin at eight or nine you had no chance of progressing through the system. Ancient Greek began a year later, and was also compulsory. One account of preparatory schooling in 1817 has boys being taught Latin at five years old and Greek at six. At Ashdown, we in the top form being prepared for scholarship exams at twelve were expected to be able to translate, flawlessly, any piece of English into Latin – and have a go at verse, too. Friday's Latin prose classes, taken by Billy Williamson, were punctuated by the furious thwacking of his cane on our desks, and sometimes on us.

Latin made Winston Churchill's first day at St George's, Ascot, aged seven, a terrifying one. After his mother had gone, a master took him to a room, gave him a book and ordered him to learn the first declension of the noun *mensa*, a table. The year is 1882. The future prime minister

had never read or spoken Latin before, but he nevertheless memorised what was set out before him, a familiar
litany to many of his readers: *mensa*, a table; *mensa*, O table;
*mensam*, a table; *mensae*, of a table; *mensae*, to or for a table;
*mensa*, by, with or from a table.

When the teacher came back the young Winston gab-
bled this off, and then asked, as any bright seven-year-old
might, 'What does it mean, sir?'

'It means what it says. Mensa, a table. Mensa is a noun
of the First Declension. There are five declensions. You
have learnt the singular of the First Declension.'

'But,' I repeated, 'what does it mean?'

'Mensa means a table.'

'Then why does mensa also mean O table?'

'Mensa, O table, is the vocative case . . . you would
use that in addressing a table, in invoking a table . . .
You would use it in speaking to a table.'

'But I never do,' I blurted out in honest amazement.

'If you are impertinent, you will be punished, and
punished, let me tell you, very severely,' was his conclusive rejoinder.

Such was my first introduction to the classics from
which, I have been told, many of our cleverest men have
derived so much solace and profit.

Like many a boarding school memoirist, Churchill is wry:
his biographers verify that the severe punishment was a
real threat. Churchill was whipped for damaging the headmaster's hat and for taking sugar from a pantry. 'Flogging
with the birch in accordance with the Eton fashion was a
great feature of the curriculum,' he wrote, explaining that
two or three times a month the whole school was made to

gather to listen to the screams of one or more offenders being 'flogged until they bled freely'. Other pupils from the time told tales of the sexualised sadism of the head-master, the Reverend Henry Sneyd-Kynnersley. He is said to have died, aged just thirty-eight, while flogging one of his charges.

The young Churchill was truly miserable. In his memoir he writes of a 'life of anxiety': after two years he was taken away, ill, perhaps after a nervous breakdown. One report has it that the rescue came after his nanny saw the purple marks from a flogging on Winston's bottom, and, out-raged, showed these to his American mother, Jennie.

Lord and Lady Churchill had chosen St George's for their boy because it was 'the most fashionable and expen-sive' school in the country – criteria that still count for much today. My parents selected Ashdown House. Years later, I asked them why. Because it was not too far away, they said, and because some neighbours' children had done well there. It had, too, a reputation for getting children into Eton, where my father had been a scholar. The school's entry in the Public Schools Yearbook for 1973 boasts of winning 150 scholarships in thirty-two years, and offering, as extras, carpentry, archery and boxing and an outdoor swimming pool. It was also smarter – and more expensive – than most.

The 1960s were the high age of the boarding prep school: in 1967, over 60,000 children, a quarter of them girls, were attending them. Most of the schools were private companies, usually owned by the headmaster, until the late 1980s, when independent inspection at last became some-thing near rigorous. One prep school teacher who served in the 1960s and 1970s told me that inspections were all about the head's relationship with the local education authority; if that was smooth – and it was easy to make it so, with gifts to the inspector – warnings were given to the school well ahead of the day, giving time to polish up the premises and the pupils. The system demanded a lot of trust and complicity from its customers, the parents.

Ashdown House is typical. It was founded by William Randall Lee in Brighton in 1843, two years before the town's own public school, Brighton College, opened, with a firm rule of accepting only 'gentlemen'. The same family, and their spouses, ran the school until 1930. The Lees were successful. Arthur Lee, William's son, taught 'peers innumerable', according to the obituary of him published in the *Morning Post* in 1897, along with the children of generals and the Duke of Genoa. Lee did well enough to move the school in 1886 from a terrace in Brighton to the Georgian house beside Ashdown Forest that I first saw in 1969. It had been put up, in 1794, on top of a Tudor manor house, by the architect who would build Washington's Capitol Building and the columned front of the White House. The elegant portico that welcomed us into the school spoke of grand democratic credentials.

Traces of the earlier Ashdown House School are few. A couple of memoirs from the 1930s talk of a small and 'brutal' establishment, with a number of 'possible sadists' as teachers, including Arthur Evill, the headmaster. He wielded a three-foot cane on the boys. In his autobiography, the journalist Hugh Massingberd says that his father had been 'emotionally scarred by the sadistic cruelty of the appropriately named Mr Evill'. None of this stands out from the average account of boarding school life at the time. Evill's descendants were children at the school when I arrived in 1969.

In those accounts, the school and its activities sound just as they were fifty years later. Boys played on the school golf course 'among the cowpats', the swimming pool was cold and slimy, the teachers got the best food. An ex-sergeant took the children for physical jerks twice a week and piled them in tiers to form human pyramids while delivering 'moral lectures'. One of his homilies stuck with the writer and adventurer Desmond Fitzgerald, who went aged eight in 1925: 'Duty is duty and duty must be done,' said the sergeant.

Like so many of the memoirists, Fitzgerald is keen for us to know how cruel the regime was and how frightened he had been. But, equally, readers should not think this did him any harm. He despises those who attribute 'their sub-sequent errant behaviour' to brutal boarding schools and sadistic teachers. 'I confess to some irritation at the current fashion to blame everyone and everything but yourself for your faults.' Arthur Evill, he says, despite his practice of 'wigging' the boys by tugging the short hair in front of their ears, succeeded in doing what he was paid to do: 'get the boys into public school'. Fitzgerald went on to Wellington College, where he usually had to stay at school during the holidays as well, 'my family being in Kenya'. He went home once in ten years of boarding. If you believe his memoir, this was just fine.

The man I met on the gravel in 1969, Billy Williamson, had taken over Ashdown shortly after the Second World War. One of his pupils in the early 1940s, when he taught at a school called Wellesley House, was the publisher Anthony Blond. In a memoir, he described Williamson as a 'magic man', a brilliant teacher. Blond says Williamson was 'in love, as teachers have to be (without being prac-tising pederasts) if they are to stay sane, with the concept of "boy" – and some specimens more than others.' Williamson was a keen flogger of their 'bare bottoms', but the pupils liked their master no less. He married the mother of one of the Wellesley House pupils, and, with her money, bought Ashdown from its previous headmaster's widow.

By the time my parents met him, Ashdown's numbers had doubled and it had a waiting list, though the private company was still, as Williamson's successor told me, always on the edge of bankruptcy. This, he explained, was why such poor-quality teachers were so often hired – 'we were desperate!' In my time, these men would often leave abruptly, amid shocking gossip. However shaky the finances, Ashdown charged well above the average for the time, and my parents were also planning to send my four younger siblings to boarding school. In 1969, a year there cost £600 (£9,500 in 2017 terms). But today full boarding at Ashdown House costs over £26,000.

# 3. 'What were the mothers thinking?'

> It's going to really, really crucify me but I feel that it's a sacrifice I'm making and I'm hoping that in the future it will prove to be for April's benefit.
>
> Sandra Ross tells a 2010 TV documentary how she feels about her eight-year-old's departure to boarding school, subsidised by the British Army

If you tell these stories today, outside the milieu that used and still uses the boarding schools, it is the mothers that people wonder about first. How could they have done it? How could they part with children so small, give them up to the care of strangers? And then ignore their distress? Today, when maternal love is seen as absolute and inviolable – at least in contrast to men's unreliable instincts – it is near-unthinkable that educated, empowered women could abandon a young child voluntarily.

Yet, in the nineteenth and twentieth centuries, hundreds of thousands of middle-class mothers did, and there is no shortage of explanations. Culture, a dominant patriarchy, social pressure and the lack of education for so many women, even in the middle and upper classes, are all blamed. I've been told that previous generations of women did not love children as we do today, or that the upper class had sentimentality bred out of them. I have heard an eminent Jungian psychoanalyst – an Old Etonian and

a specialist in ex-boarders with psychological problems
– account for it all with the Oedipus myth and women's
'underlying hatred of their sons'. That seems inadequate.
For a start, what about the girls? Fifty thousand were
boarding at the height of the industry in the late 1960s.

Many mothers will pass the blame for the decision to
board to their children, even today. 'I just couldn't bear the
idea – I'd hated my boarding school. But she just insisted,' the mother of a ten-year-old at a smart Midlands prep
school told me recently. 'Harry Potter did it, of course.
And while I was in bits, still am really, she has never
looked back. Desperate for the start of each term. It's quite
hurtful!' Children have begged to go to boarding school
ever since *Tom Brown's School Days*, the first propagandis-
ing novel, was published in 1857. But, equally, parents
plant thoughts in children's minds; we help them come
round to what we really want them to do. And if they have
agreed, that helps with the parental guilt, should anything
go wrong. Naturally, children who have been told they are
going to have a lovely time at a holiday camp with a few
lessons find it very hard even to tell the most kind and
open mother or father that they got it wrong.

Some parents seem simply to have abandoned their children. That cruelty bites deep. One of my correspondents,
Clare, told me: 'I went to boarding school aged seven in
the sixties and after receiving no letters from my parents
most of the first term plucked up the courage to ask to see
the Head. I asked her if my parents had died and no one
had told me. She explained they had busy lives. As they
lived abroad I saw them at most ten weeks a year thereafter. I never forgot that: learning how unimportant I was to
them.'

Even today, prep school teachers tell of having to cater

for those left behind at holidays, the children whose parents were overseas and unable to make arrangements, or those that had simply been forgotten. A man who went to Ashdown in the 1970s told me recently that his mother only ever came once to take him out. 'She didn't think it was necessary; she was tough and thought we should be too. I was her third child and I think she just wasn't very interested in me.' On the sole occasion she did come, she opened the car door to a similar-looking boy, said, 'Come on, hurry up and get in,' and drove off with him. It wasn't until she reached the end of the school drive that the child was able to tell her she'd made a mistake. He laughs heartily as he tells the story: 'Of course, when she came back, it was all my fault.'

From the other side of the school door, it is not hard to find some dry-eyed scepticism about parents and, indeed, the strength of parental love. Boarding school housemasters and housemistresses – or houseparents, as they're now often known – generally don't send their own children to board before thirteen, at least. They know what significant numbers of parents use the institution for: 'a dump for something that has got in the way' and 'long-term child care' are just some of the terms I've heard from the teachers. The daughter of an eminent boarding school headmaster told me that often parents just failed to turn up to collect their offspring. She would see her father patiently explaining on the phone to the parents that they were really needed. 'Well, we can look after them for a few days, but after that we really have to go on holiday ourselves.' 'Selfishness is almost always the real, hidden reason why people send their children away to board,' concludes the novelist William Boyd, who endured ten years of 'penal servitude' at Gordonstoun.

The writer Bella Bathurst went to board at eleven. She remembers being forgotten, more than once. 'It'd be half-term, and there'd be some muddle. Eventually I'd be rescued. Staring out of the window, waiting, watching all the other girls leave . . . you do contemplate what looks like the truth: nobody loves me. That memory stays with you.' Another woman was sent at the age of three to join her sister, boarding in a Belgian convent. Her memory is blurred, of course, but she is left with the perception that she didn't go home more than once a year. 'When I asked the nuns why I was there, they said my mother didn't love me because God didn't love me.' A vivid memory is being locked in a coal cellar to pray when she had been disobedient. When I asked her how this affected her adult life, she laughed: 'Not at all – it was nothing like as bad as an English boarding school!' She and her English boarding school-educated husband sent their own children to board at one of those, though not at three years old.

There are pressing reasons why parents may have to send their children away. In many accounts a child goes to board because a family is in crisis, through death, illness or break-up. Often, careers have to come first. The reason the British government still spends £80m a year on boarding schools is to enable armed forces children, largely those of officers, to attend them while their parents are serving the country. But many parents still make – or allow – their children to sleep away from home even when they live close by the school.

The culture is strong. The chief reason my parents sent me and my siblings off at eight years old was because everyone else they knew did it. The possibility of alternatives did not occur to most parents with boarding school history in their own families, if the money for fees was available. But still, extraordinary choices were made. Bella Bathurst's mother followed her other siblings to board. But she went at only six years old, very young for a girl in the 1930s. 'I think Granny just had to do it, it was during the war, and she couldn't cope.'

Often parents roll out the happy memories of their own schooldays as one of the reasons for continuing the tradition. The psychotherapist Nick Duffell recalls his mother telling 'wonderfully mendacious stories about how fabulous it all was; not till near the end [of her life] did she reveal how scared she had been'. Here is Alison Collett, one of my correspondents:

> I never felt that my parents repented of what they had done and even now my mother will defend her decision partly on the grounds that she 'loved' the public school she went to at nine and that I am 'so much more fortunate than my father' who was put in an orphanage at four. I have never told my story – always a short non-self-pitying version – to anyone who has not been appalled, so it's hard to understand my parents' denial.

But other parents, provably loving, were subject to processes now explicable through modern psychology. A common reaction to past trauma is to 'normalise' it – render it into something explicable and regular, and so learn to live with it. What could be better proof to yourself that your boarding experience had been good than to send your beloved children to do the same? There is another, more abstruse effect that may be explained in the newer science of epigenetics. This posits that our DNA changes very fast under stress from environmental factors. It enables us to adapt, and our children to cope: it might – possibly – provide a part of the explanation as to why the boarding school class handed the habit on to the next generation.

Eleven generations of my mother's family have gone off to board: the habit was well ingrained, for the boy children. For the Fergussons, boarding worked. They are unglamorous, impossibly ancient Scots nobility, chiefs of the clan Fergusson. Some of the Fergusson ancestors arrived from Ireland a thousand years ago or more, married some of the conquerors from Normandy, and took land in south-west Scotland. They have lived there ever since, the estate and the family's fortunes waxing and waning with the centuries. The Fergussons were on the winning side – the English one – in the wars of the seventeenth and eighteenth centuries and they earned titles and more land as a result. They became richer through sugar plantations in the West Indies, using slave labour. They helped build and rule the British Empire in the nineteenth and twentieth centuries, and sold much of the land to pay for the glory and the adventures. There are dozens of similar families in Scotland.

A bought education was always a necessity to such people. It brought connections and some protection from the English aristocracy's prejudice against Scots. Two of my line of Fergusson grandfathers studied sciences and agriculture. They worked to improve their land and the lives of people on it. But most of my ancestors studied as gentlemen were supposed to – classical Latin and Greek with a smattering of History, the Bible and some Mathematics. These things were – as many of them complain in their letters, stored in the family archive – tedious and near-useless, especially in the dawn of the industrial age. But this experience shaped them into the men the family needed for it to prosper: men who could thrive in the Army or the law courts, who would pass with ease into the drawing rooms and clubs of the upper class, who could marry to advantage, both in terms of genetics and the acquisition of wealth. This education was difficult to arrange, sometimes distressing for parent and child, and expensive. Until the mid nineteenth century, the Fergusson boys travelled to schools in the English Home Counties by ship from Leith. Each boy's fees cost more than a skilled worker's annual wage. It was a significant expense but a proven investment.

I say 'man' and 'boy' because few women of this class then went away to school, and those that did went in their late teens for 'finishing'. It was not until the twentieth century that the Fergussons began sending some of their girls to boarding school. My mother, who grew up in the house during and after the Second World War, was taught – along with various cousins and other local girls – by a governess, while her brothers went to prep school and then to Eton. They were not poorly educated: my mother is a published author and has been a successful businesswoman. The letters and journals that survive show the Fergusson women to be the intellectual match and more of the men; some, like my fearsome great-grandmother, dominated house and husband. But only one of the girls ever went to boarding school: my great-great-great-aunt Elizabeth in 1846.

In the family archives are letters and diaries that show that my ancestors were not short of love for their children: they missed them, visited them, wrote weekly and were overjoyed when they came home from England for the holidays. In 1845 my grandfather's grandfather, Sir Charles Fergusson, spent days arguing against his fifteen-year-old daughter Elizabeth's plan – backed by her mother – to go to board in Brighton. This is from his journal:

I, on the other hand, now seeing how excellent and delightful Elizabeth is at present, feel anxious, lest, in seeking for accomplishments, & what is called improvement & cultivation of mind, some of this freshness should be lost. Also, the long time – 2 Years – with merely the breaks of the holidays, – is a very painful part of it. Only God knows what is best, & I only now desire to be enlightened as to what is best – and that, whatever has been resolved on, may be defeated if it is not for the Eternal good of my beloved Child, Amen.

He gave in.

My grandfather is said to have been unhappy at prep school, but only twice in all those generations have boarding schools gone demonstrably wrong for the Fergussons. In 1746, aged sixteen, my ancestral uncle John Fergusson abruptly quit his Northamptonshire school, to his mother and father's horror. He had decided to join the English army marching to fight Bonnie Prince Charlie and the Highland rebels, then threatening London. It turned out to be a good call – the Fergussons prospered from backing the winning side – though John stayed in the army, never going back to school.

Much worse came with a later generation. In 1894 my great-great-uncle Alan Fergusson, a gawky, much-bullied sixteen-year-old, was placed at Glenalmond College, having run away from Rugby School. A few weeks later he set fire to a wing of that Gothic pile in rural Perthshire, causing £2 million of damage, in modern prices. This caused an international sensation: his father, Sir James, the sixth baronet, was an MP and former governor of New Zealand. Despite the family's efforts to have him declared mentally incompetent, he was tried and jailed for a year for arson. Nonetheless, both my brother and several cousins took their places at the rebuilt Glenalmond when their time came.

It's often said that in no culture other than wealthy Britain are children voluntarily separated from their families so young. That was true, at least until the 1960s, when the Soviet Union began a massive boarding school programme on the grounds that parents were ideologically untrustworthy. (At its height it catered for 2.5 million children.*) When anthropology became a popular science – especially for ex-public school adventurers – there was excitement at the news that many traditional cultures separated children from their families in order to celebrate initiations and train them to survive. British colonialists in Kenya were entranced by the independent-minded Maasai, romanticising them as an African version of King Arthur's knights. Comparisons were made between the boarding schools and the Maasai custom of sequestering an entire age-set of adolescents, *morani*, to live together and learn the skills necessary to become an adult warrior.

Yet in all these societies the ritual separation happens around or after puberty, and only for a matter of months. Nowhere – in societies traditional or modern – are the children separated from their blood relatives for eight or more months of the year for ten years, from the age of seven or

---

* This is few compared to modern China, where, according to a 2011 survey, 33 million children board, some as young as three. This is not ideological, but driven by the central government's policy since 2000 of closing village schools to save expense: now 53 per cent of children in rural Western China are at state-run boarding institutions, often in gruesome conditions.

eight. Even in the warrior cult of ancient Sparta, whose legendary hardening of children was so admired that several schools took Spartan sayings for mottos,* the separation was for days, not months.

Until the Second World War, in the boarding school class most children were first brought up by domestic servants and governesses, inside the family home. But the dominant theory of the science of child development, 'attachment', concludes that what a growing child needs is a reliable loving figure and a sense of continuity and security. A paid mother might do it, but what no school gives is hugs.

From the mid-eighteenth century a debate went on about the role of mothers and the use of schools. A vast succession of practical books on household management and child-rearing were published, often by women. Usually these emphasised to mothers how important their role was, especially in raising sons. By the mid nineteenth century they were being warned not to let servants do the job. Women's morality, it was suggested, was superior to men's, mother's love pure and redemptive, and the job of instilling Christian beliefs into the growing child of vast importance. The role was not humdrum but heroic, and well worthy of an intelligent woman. 'The hand that rocks the cradle is the hand that rules the world' is a much-quoted line from the American poet William Ross Wallace, the poem published in 1865.

But tough love was prescribed at home, too. Many Victorian mothers, like Victorian schoolmasters, believed in beating as a moral instrument. One of the popular Victorian

---

* Loretto School uses *Spartam nactus es, hanc exorna* ('Sparta is yours, adorn it').

lady's periodicals, *The Queen*, ran a series of articles and letters in the winter of 1866 under the headlines 'Discipline for Young Children' and 'Infant Discipline'. The letter that began the debate, from a mother, 'I.M.L.', starts by quoting a friend who recommends corporal punishment even for the youngest, instructing that the miscreant should be sent to collect the rod from a drawer 'as it makes the child more humble'. But, I.M.L goes on, 'My heart fails at the thought of whipping my Violet of five . . . Will some mother who, like me, remembers the penalty of whipping being inflicted often on herself for trifles, help me in some way to sparing my children, and yet making them good?'*

Other voices addressed maternal instincts, and guilts, directly. They are ancestors of today's critics who question mothers who work rather than look after their children. In 1899 an anonymous writer in the *Westminster Review* – then a voice of liberal proto-feminism – condemned women who 'hand over their most powerful function to the nurse, governess and schoolmaster . . . chancing altogether the most dangerous part of the moral character in their boys: expecting, on a mere supply of cash, a finished and flawless article to be supplied to them'. In the same magazine in 1896, under the title 'The Making of Woman', another essayist pronounced: 'The woman who prefers school to home education confesses herself either unable or unwilling to assume the responsibilities of motherhood.' The social historian Claudia Nelson believes that behind these strictures lay profound fears about sex; masturbation and

* In his book *The English Vice* the historian Ian Gibson argues that much of the copious correspondence on corporal punishment in *The Queen* and other late Victorian household journals is hoax material written and submitted by male, ex-public school flagellomaniacs for their entertainment.

homoeroticism, known to be a feature of single-sex boarding school life, were dangerous vices a mother's presence
might prevent.

But this literature was for the emerging middle class,
who for the first time had options to consider when deciding how a child should be educated. A contradictory
current ran in upper-class thinking, then and well into
the twentieth century. Here it was believed that mothers
should keep a distance from their children. The work of
child-care was unseemly, menial, or – even worse – boring.
Children, who should be seen and not heard until they
reached adolescence and the age of reason, tended to be
displayed to their parents and grandparents at breakfast
and before bedtime. Most of their days were spent apart.
These practices went hand in hand with another belief:
that motherly love could be a very damaging thing.

This was clearly widely believed in the later Victorian
age, where much time and thought was spent on worries of
how to instil morality, 'manliness' – and guard against its
dreadful opposites, like 'the sin of Oscar Wilde'. Charlotte
Guest, wife of the industrialist and Member of Parliament
Sir Josiah Guest, had awful qualms about sending her
three boys off to prep school. She was particularly worried
about swearing and 'bad influences', with good reason. But
she was overcome after taking the advice of clergymen and
the headmaster of Harrow, the boys' ultimate destination.
Lady Guest wrote in her journal in September 1845: 'It
seems a sad prospect but everybody says it is the only way
to bring up boys; and what is to be done? How can I, a poor
weak woman, judge against all the world?' It seems absurd
to suggest (though it has been) that male-dominated culture prevented all upper-class women from having a say
in a child's education. Generations of Fergusson mothers

played a major part in choosing their children's schools. Sometimes mothers, like Churchill's, released their children and took them home. But it must have been difficult to rebel, especially in families where, demonstrably, the fathers and the brothers had all the arguments of tradition and success to back up their view.

Besides, by the late Victorian period, the debate on a mother's role seems to have come to a consensus: the moral and physical health of their children was at risk if kept at home. The message was sent with thundering solemnity by the great band of clergymen-headmasters who ran the schools and wrote copiously in the periodicals. In the early twentieth century the poet laureate John Masefield (who had been a very unhappy boarder at King's School, Warwick in the 1880s) was fulminating against the cult of motherhood, saying children should be taught by men. Indeed, he would make it a criminal offence for mothers to attempt to impose on children. 'The world has gone steadily downhill in all manly qualities since the "mother's personality" became what is called a "factor in education".'

So, the pressure to send the children away became immense: for the wealthier families it remained almost unarguable until late in the twentieth century. A mother's suffering at the early loss of her children – as real, I am sure, in the nineteenth century among boarding school parents as it is today – became ennobled. It was a sacrifice, done selflessly for the children's good. There are anthropological parallels. Chinese mothers supervised the crippling of their daughters well into the early twentieth century, in foot-binding rituals. It is mothers, not fathers, who supervise and direct the mutilation of their daughters' genitals in the cultures where that is practised. Male demands may direct the cruelty to the child, but women's active participation is required. The truth is that maternal instinct, far from being adamantine, is easily trumped by culture. 'I hate my mother for sending me to board. I will never forgive her: she never listened, she was a bitch,' one woman told me. Yet she and her husband, an Army officer, sent their boys to board too – subsidised by the state.

# 4. The brick parent

> I wouldn't send a dog to boarding school at age seven.
>
> Child development psychologist John Bowlby, 1973*

The first thing that a child psychiatrist or a psychotherapist looks at today, when taking on a troubled child as a patient, is their 'attachment pattern'. It's a simple principle of bonding between an infant and a trustworthy carer that is the core to modern beliefs about how to grow an emotionally healthy person. 'Attachment to a primary figure is essential to good childhood development: without, worry and anxiety tend to rule the psyche,' says a standard textbook. If the child has been in and out of care, or parents have been absent, violent or unreliable, a diagnosis of avoidant or disorganised attachment may be made. Because it's a well-acknowledged problem – the theory of attachment has dominated child development science for fifty years – there is much that can be done. The first step is to enable the child to talk about their anxiety or their anger, to understand what triggers them to hit children in the playground, or fear going home.

Not making a good attachment can be catastrophic. 'Insecure attachment is a lifelong risk factor for problems with learning, relationships, later parenting and career

---

* Bowlby boarded at that age himself.

choices, as well as for issues with emotional and mental well-being,' says Robin Balbernie, a psychotherapist who advises government on early years policy, and has served on the front line in local Child and Adolescent Mental Health Services – the people who step in and do something when a child starts smashing up the classroom, or arrives on Monday covered in bruises.

Unlike most in his profession, Balbernie uses vivid language, even in formal submissions to parliamentary committees. 'In the very worst case of insecure attachment the child's personality becomes organised around survival rather than love. This "disorganised" attachment is the most severe type of insecure attachment. There is no coherent internal working model beyond a hair trigger stress response, just messy sediments of past grief, fear and confusion.' With inmates of prisons, the care system or mental institutions, poor attachment in early life is almost always an issue. Depression and substance dependency are linked too.

There are those who challenge the overwhelming dominance of attachment theory, especially as revelations about genetics tell of more and more character traits that are 'coded' into us at birth, indicating that nature may be more important than nurture. But new advances in neuroscience are also giving more weight to attachment. It is already widely accepted that children who have suffered abuse and related trauma will show differences in the volume of their brain from the normally treated child; these have been spotted by neuroimaging in parts of the prefrontal cortex, the amygdala and the hippocampus. Another technique has shown neural network abnormalities.

A new discipline – neuropsychology – has arisen from this work. Neuropsychological studies of the children damaged in these ways found 'suggestions' of a range of problems: 'deficits in IQ, memory, working memory, attention, response inhibition and emotion discrimination'. The last resonates with attachment theorists – 'poor emotional regulation' being a classic symptom of disorganised attachment. The advanced brain-imaging techniques, like those used by Usha Goswami at the Centre for Neuroscience in Education in Cambridge, seem to show differences in the brains of infants according to whether they have had 'poor' or 'good' attachment, irrespective of whether they have been abused.

Clearly, attachment science is of great interest to those in psychology who look at boarding school and its after-effects. Later I will look more at the work of Nick Duffell and Joy Schaverien, two psychotherapists who have pioneered the now busy field of treating 'boarding school syndrome' in adults. They see the abrupt breaking of attachment that happens at the door of the boarding school as unique, and provably damaging. A key issue is that the child suffers the catastrophe with the knowledge that their trusted primary carers thought this was good for them. So if school is not good, the child has to decide that either he or she, or the carer, is wrong. This may be very traumatic. The boarding school door is often the place when a child realises that adults' love has its limits.

Psychologists talk about the limited emotional intelligence, the paucity of the coping mechanisms of children who have suffered 'disorganised attachment'. But it's a poor and dry jargon for something so elemental and so devastating: learning that love is not reliable. That trust may be betrayed. Being told you are loved does not count: the one who loves you has to prove it.

You might argue that a parent so emotionally ignorant as to dispatch a seven-year-old to board can hardly have the mindset that would do a good job in infancy. But in fact, the class and culture I grew up in generally provided reasonably good attachment: these were more emotionally literate people than their forefathers, especially after most of the upper middle class stopped using servants to keep the children away. Children who have had good attachment in early life are resilient, research shows, so perhaps we were better able to withstand the shock of being sent away to school. Many psychologists write of those who start off with secure attachment having the capacity to 'self-repair'.

There is a significant problem with using attachment theory to criticise the boarding school system. It is that there is no clinical research on sudden attachment fracture in mid-childhood. Most of the academic work looks at infants, and a little of it at adolescence. So, despite the many practitioners now working with what Duffell has called 'boarding school survivors', there is still little more than anecdote to back up their diagnosis of attachment problems, which may differ from those of younger children whose attachment issues are generally about long-term neglect, not the sudden separation and total abandonment to strangers. This is odd, given that perhaps a million Britons alive today went to boarding school. Some analysts I've spoken to warn against assuming too much about the risks of mid-childhood separation. A huge amount of character development has already occurred by the age of seven. William Meredith-Owen, sceptical of 'boarding school syndrome', says: 'Challenges can be beneficial.' He adds a caveat: 'But I don't think anyone would say unhappiness could be good for a child.'

So we are left with stories. These, as we'll see, are powerful. There is a body of first-hand accounts going back to the nineteenth century with ample evidence from both parents and children that something momentous happened at the first separation. 'I never felt he was mine again,' says a mother; 'the school took him from me.' 'I never again had a proper relationship with them,' says an ex-boarder; 'for me, love and childhood, all that stuff, ended when I was eight.'

I have found no boarding school that considers attachment theory important or relevant. The Boarding Schools Association is not able to produce any psychologist who can rebut the clutch of adult emotional problems now known as 'boarding school syndrome'. Yet the drive and power to 'attach' were crucial long before the theory was voiced by John Bowlby. Core to the British boarding school system – and to its brilliant effectiveness – was the realisation that if you took a child away at an early age from its family, like a puppy from a litter, their emotional needs and demands would be transferred to the school: their teachers, their fellow pupils, to the institution itself. The last becomes what psychiatrists looking at institutionalised patients call the 'brick mother'. As Balbernie writes, in the course of human evolution, the natural methods of attachment behaviour – the learning of social skills, the forming of identity, confidence and self-esteem – have often been put to the task of building 'group cohesion'.

The school was the 'right mother of men' – as a line from Glenalmond College's school song has it. Many ex-boarders have said that it became the family. Some thought this was a good thing: 'Better than my family,' remarked a recent Cheltenham Ladies' College pupil I heard in a debate on the value of boarding school. (Many in the audience, at

Edinburgh University in 2014, groaned in dismay.) 'Give me a child until he is seven and I will give you the man,' said the founder of the Jesuit order, echoing Aristotle. Family bonds are strong material: breaking them awakes powerful instincts. If you were to design a mechanism for building a life-long loyalty to a team and an ideology, boarding early would seem a smart way to begin.

# 5. Ideal upbringings

> Your home might be far from perfect, but at least it was a place ruled by love rather than by fear, where you did not have to be perpetually on your guard against the people surrounding you. At eight years old you were suddenly taken out of this warm nest and flung into a world of force and fraud and secrecy, like a gold-fish into a tank full of pike.*
>
> George Orwell

Everyone seems to know what an unhappy childhood is. But there is not much agreement about what makes a happy one. While researching this book, I asked every expert I spoke to – child psychologists, psychotherapists, trauma and abuse experts, psycho-neurologists, child development writers and, of course, teachers – for a definition and got no good answer. One eminent psychologist said that the only valuable answer you can get is from children themselves. So I asked mine their formulas for a happy childhood: the younger one, then aged ten, said: 'It is knowing that you are loved and feeling safe and having enough of what you want.' The older, sixteen, said: 'Having an excellent Wi-Fi connection.'

* 'Such, Such Were the Joys', published in the American *Partisan Review* magazine in 1952. For fear of libelling the headmistress, Orwell's essay was not published in the UK until 1967.

Child development science is, you realise, inexact. Not only is the shape of a good childhood hard for the experts to agree about, the notions of what it might be are under continual change. So is how important a happy childhood is to becoming a happy adult. And then there's the problem over where good and happy coincide with effective, or if they do at all. In Rachel Cusk's novel, *Outline*, a character repeats his mother's wisdom about the bitter-sweetness of life: 'There was no such thing as an unblemished childhood, though people will do anything to convince you otherwise.' This thought lies alongside a belief that an efficient, productive childhood needs a dose of hardship, some tough love. Here lie echoes of pre-Victorian notions of the innate evil of children, before reason and God have been beaten into them. A headline over a recent piece in the women's section of the *Daily Mail* ran: 'Why a happy childhood can make you an unhappy adult', with the writer blaming her comfortable suburban upbringing for her failures later. She quotes the broadcaster Kirsty Young: 'I don't want my children to be "happy" . . . They will be bloody lucky if they glimpse it now and again. I want them to be content and have self-worth.'

I have asked many parents who were unhappy boarders why they sent their own children to board. The ancient notion of the benefits of hard knocks underlies much of their reasoning. A psychotherapist would have no problem deconstructing that – the patient needs to process their traumas in a positive way in order to come to peace with them. Thus a horrible experience slowly transmutes into a necessary one and then perhaps to a positive one – so positive that their own dearest possession, their child, must be put through the same.

Another thing parents will say – often alongside the

above — is that things won't be *so* tough: the schools have
changed since their time. Winston Churchill was the first
of many to deride this adult cliché: not reassuring, given
how hideous his school turned out to be. The simplest line
is that a modicum of misery is normal and necessary. 'We
knew you were unhappy. But so was your father,' said my
parents, as did many others. That is often considered explanation enough: 'Look at your dad — he did all right.'
But through the ages children have been made to do many
barbaric things we would not now contemplate with the
same justification: some miniature chimney-sweeps grew
up all right.

Clearly, pragmatic adult concerns dictate how a childhood should be. If we believe that the lessons learnt in
childhood shape most of our adult behaviour, then we need
first to decide what behaviour we want to see. But those
beliefs shift all the time. Research done over the last fifty
years shows interesting changes in the shopping list of
parental hopes for the moral qualities of their offspring.
Honesty used to come top, with obedience, good manners
and respect for their betters following. But over this period
obedience has slid down the list while qualities implying
autonomy — independence of thought and self-reliance —
have gone up, especially among middle-class parents. Even
honesty is not nearly so popular as it once was.

Memories of a happy childhood are not just subject to
shifting definitions but also to the vagaries of recall. Many
researchers in the field are highly dubious about adult
memories of childhood, which can be selective, or glossed,
cleaned up or darkened according to the story that the
adult has decided best fits him or her. Many of my correspondents say, quite frankly, that they don't remember
much of their schooldays, apart from a few vivid moments.

That's a common reaction to long-term trauma, but it may mean they were bored more than miserable. One academic review of the body of research in this area drily concludes: 'A reconstruction of childhood based on the adult's script is by definition incomplete and inaccurate.'

Some go further. Valerie Sinason is a psychoanalyst specialising in 'development disorder' and a theorist in the hotly debated area of false memories. She writes: 'Attachment research has shown that those with good-enough family backgrounds are able to remember positive and negative incidents in childhood, whilst those with more problematic experiences cannot bear to think of any negative experience. "I/they had a wonderful childhood" is the surprisingly common statement of depressed parents and of abusing or depressed parents concerning their children. Could it be . . . that a happy childhood is the most common false memory?'

Not for the first time, the outsider is left ruing how unproductive a trip into the depths of academic psychology is, in terms of the gold that can be brought back. None of this is of much use either to the survivors of boarding schools or indeed to the schools' defenders. It doesn't matter what happened, you have to conclude, so long as you remember it as happy. Underlying this problem is the father of psychology's own uncertainties about memory and indeed about the notion of normality – 'an ideal fiction', Sigmund Freud said.

There's ample research to show that bad childhoods, even those involving abuse and trauma, don't necessarily mean that the rest of a life will be flawed. The longest and most thorough research on male adult happiness, the Harvard Grant Study, concludes – with most of its original subjects now departed – that the important thing is that you believe you had a happy childhood, not least a good relationship with your mother. But the study, which has followed 268 men since 1938, also shows they are capable of rewriting their past completely: a bloody war record becomes a happy one, a Christian adolescence is changed to one of complete agnosticism, an abusive parent morphs with the years into a gentle and decent one. There is also copious research to show that some provably terrible childhoods – featuring emotional and sexual abuse – can produce remarkable and high-achieving adults, just as they may produce quite ordinarily happy ones.

This leads back to the arena of definition-debating. In 1977 a book on the Harvard Grant Study defined a happy life as 'a successful career and a fulfilling marriage'. It is a materialistic view that few would formulate so brashly today. But while the Victorians might have thrown in phrases including 'virtue' and 'duty', the Grant Study formula is probably a good distillation of the aspirations of the middle class during the 150 years of the modern boarding school system.

That system has not altered much; what has changed is our idea of what happiness is, and how to achieve it. But the Grant Study's most notable conclusion is that people who come to believe they had a happy childhood – even when the study's own records show that belief was only acquired in later life – do better, both in career or financial success and in their personal lives. George Vaillant, who directed the study for three decades, concluded his analysis of mountains of data gathered over seventy-five years with the disarmingly simple formula: 'Happiness is love. Full stop.'

# PART TWO

# Settling in at Prep School

# 6. 'The end of childhood'

It seemed very English to try to pass off an emotional
state as a sort of stomach bug.

Rachel Cusk on homesickness, *Outline*

Once inside the doors, parents' car gone, the prep school
children took their first steps into an alien world. There
are no credible accounts that I can find of anyone below
the age of eleven enjoying those first days or weeks. Many
ex-boarders talk of confusion, exhaustion and what we'd
now call stress; all brought on by the need to learn geog-
raphies, codes and rituals from scratch in an atmosphere
dominated by fear and lacking any privacy. The induction
of prisoners into jails seems a fair comparison.

One woman was sent to England to board at the age
of nine because her parents' work kept them abroad – a
common justification then and now. She wrote to me of
the long list of new rules and customs that confronted and
confounded her. For one, it was not done – 'virtually pun-
ishable' – to weep out loud. 'To this day at the ripe old age
of sixty-four if I am very upset about something I go to the
toilet. A survival behaviour that was established all those
years ago, the toilet was the only private place I could go
to and give expression to my sorrow without risk of being
ostracised.'

Some talk of this period as, simply, 'the end of childhood'.

Others say: 'I never felt safe again.' Many single out a lone and paltry mistake – getting in the wrong meal queue, using a Christian name, bed-wetting – as the beginning of a life-long social disability. These memories, of moments when doors slammed shut, have been reshaped over the years, and it is hard to find any contemporary accounts. But there are some.

When I was eleven, excused games because of illness, I was ordered to remain in the school library at Ashdown House. I was – so the term reports say – the school's most bookish boy, but this time I started writing a novel about the first days at a prep school. It is clearly my school: 'Brierly House' has the same address, the same headmaster: just the names changed. Reading it back now, I am shocked by the need I had felt even then to tell the story.

There are seven pages of close, neat handwriting in a foolscap book preserved by my mother. I wrote about a new boy, first through the eyes of his mother. 'Well, I'm sure it's a very good establishment,' she muses as she drives away, wiping a tear. Left behind, the boy is shocked by how huge and noisy everyone is, by the cold and dirty dormitories, the rituals of discipline and the threat of violence. The terrifying headmaster looms biggest in the jungle: his jowls, his monk's hairdo and his attacks on any sign of timidity or weakness, his 'childish prejudice' against a German child . . . 'If a boy, in his opinion, deserved teasing, he did it mercilessly.'

But the story begins with the arrival. There's 'an intense feeling of obscureness' in the new boys as they are first led into the school by the matron:

A pathetic huddle, of children, torn away from the comfort and serenity of their home lives, to become an object for processing in the huge, strange, preparatory school machine . . . The tear was so complete in all their minds that 'Home-sickness' had not yet taken its grip on them, at the moment they were too amazed by this new world to long for the other.

I hope that I would have introduced some fun to the novel, had the seven pages gone any further. Anger is what dominates the pages: about power unfairly reserved to bullies and flawed adults, about the denial of the basic right to choose one's own destiny. You can hear the same complaints in Winston Churchill's account of his 'hated' prep school, St George's in Ascot, written forty years after he left:

I was no more consulted about leaving home than I had been about coming into the world . . . It appears that I was to go away from home for many weeks at a stretch in order to do lessons under masters . . . After all I was only seven, and I had been so happy in my nursery with all my toys. I had such wonderful toys: a real steam engine, a magic lantern, and a collection of soldiers already nearly a thousand strong. Now it was to be all lessons . . .

Churchill, like so many, felt torn from childhood's heaven and sent to a hell. The word doesn't seem too strong: it was somewhere not just without toys, but without love.

St George's is now an exclusive girls' public school: its website mentions the Churchill connection, but quotes him only on how modern and fashionable the school was. Most of the accounts, those sent to me or in published memoirs, attempt to look for good among the unhappiness. But those who – like Churchill – have decided that the experience doesn't need gloss or context, tell stories that are often angry and incredulous. One correspondent remembers the children at his Home Counties school, popular with wealthy British expatriate families living in Africa. The time is the 1970s:

> They were often very young, at least six, and, looking back, often profoundly traumatised, one indication being the way a number of them would regularly shit in their underwear and wet the beds, which in itself attracted ridicule. I can remember carrying one boy back to the school from the games pitches during winter as he was so cold he really couldn't manage on his own. [Another] – no older than my son now – kept getting told off for sleeping in bed with his brother because he missed his mother so much. The thought sickens me still.

It is not just anger but the pain of adjustment to an unfair world that rings through the accounts. Ultimately, as the child gives up hope of rescue – a process well mapped in some of the more convincing psychology – these feelings metamorphose into deeper emotions. Children accept the hard notion that their trust in those who first cared for them may have been a misjudgement. Their energies turn to coping and survival: new patterns of behaviour that will shape their future selves, and indeed their lives.

My first term at Ashdown was no more or less harsh than most of the accounts. It was violent, shocking and I survived it: I learnt. In my dormitory there were three of us new boys, and two others who had been at the school a year or two. We were seven or eight years old; they were nine or ten. My first vivid memory is of the two older boys addressing us all once we had climbed into those cold hard beds – a story that is in my twelve-year-old's attempt at a novel.

As dormitory captain and vice-captain, they said, they had the right to whip us for infringing any rules. Failing to fold the counterpane corners into triangular 'flaps' when we made our beds was one. The instrument for the beating would be 'a whippy bamboo with a split in the end so when it flies through the air it opens and pinches you to give extra pain!' says the dormitory captain in my novel. 'It's very sore.' But in fact the boys used the regulation belt, the one with the snake for a buckle.

I don't think the older boys beat us with it that night, but they did over the next few weeks. That buckle hurt, but it was the very fact of violence that was most shocking – the rare spanking my mother gave offered no comparison. The chief rule that we broke was the one against making noise after lights out – for which Billy Williamson himself would beat whole dormitories, if he were drunk enough. Perhaps that's why our dormitory officers were so severe about the rule. But they extended 'making noise' from talking to letting one's bedsprings squeak or crying.

I remember lying with the pillow hard over my face to stifle the snuffles of homesickness, while also lying still as stone in order to keep the rusty old bed quiet. All three of us new boys were in the same bind. The relief when the officers found another boy crying and pulled his sheets back to beat him with the belt was enormous. The noise he made during the operation was cover for you to move your stiffened limbs in the bed and perhaps take the opportunity to sob a bit, too. Stories of concealing grief come up again and again. 'Over time I trained myself,' a friend told me, laughing. 'I started by saying I was only allowed to cry every other night. Then only once or twice a week. And so on. By my second year I was absolutely fine!' He is a qualified psychotherapist and firmly in the 'never did me any harm' school.

I don't remember much else from those first weeks. Few people do. Looking back, most of my correspondents recall the early confusion and the lack of privacy more than any bullying or physical abuse. C. S. Lewis, author of the Narnia novels, wrote vividly of early boarding school life and its confusions:

> From my point of view the great drawback was that one had, so to speak, no home . . . In and out of school hours one spent one's time either evading or conforming to all those inexplicable movements which a crowd exhibits . . . The bare brick passages echoed to a continual tramp of feet, punctuated with catcalls, scrimmages, gusty laughter. One was always 'moving on' or 'hanging about' – in lavatories, in store rooms, in the great hall. It was very like living permanently in a large railway station.

# 7. Unreliable memories

Finding wholly credible stories is not easy. Given the remodelling time and experience do to memories, a genuinely reliable account obviously needs to have been given as close as possible to the event. There are very few of those. The schools learnt a long time ago that outsiders generally brought a sceptical eye and that the children, however well drilled in loyalty, can be devastatingly frank. Allowing inquisitive writers open access to boarding schools is a bit like allowing them into abattoirs, in terms of ensuring the future of the meat trade. It was always thus: in a discussion of public school education in 1857, an article in *The Times* stated: 'Parents may well abstain from looking into the process, and content themselves with the result.'

The best material on children's experiences in residential education dates from 1968, in Royston Lambert and Spencer Millham's celebrated book on boarding schools, state and private, *The Hothouse Society*. Lambert was a pioneer in sociological investigation, who was to become a guru of alternative education in the 1970s. Millham had a longer career in social policy for children, helping bring an end to the brutal 'approved schools' used for young offenders. Both Lambert and Millham were working class in background, going to state day schools before Oxford University. They remain some of the few outsiders to consider the totality of the system; Lambert was also the first

commentator to see that the fact of boarding was very significant to children, whether at a state institution or the
hallowed ancient public schools.

The government paid for the research that led to *The
Hothouse Society*: a team of researchers spent months observ-
ing, interviewing and collecting written accounts inside 66
secondary schools (no child under eleven was interviewed).
The institutions ranged across the spectrum of state and
private, from remedial to traditional to progressive. The
children's accounts were edited to provide a balance of
opinions that reflected the overall range of viewpoints.

Overall, the negative stories comprise about 30 per cent
of the hundreds of quotes. But the book is even-handed,
Lambert and Millham's tone unjudgemental. They are
only occasionally shocked, though what they uncover is
often shocking. 'Bullying is a major sport at [a state-run
boarding school],' they write, ahead of a heart-jolting
selection of small boys' accounts of physical abuse; 'sport'
is a rare lapse from the clinical.

But the children's ghost voices ring with passion and insight. It's hardly surprising that a storm of protest greeted
*The Hothouse Society*. This was mainly over what was seen
as salacious reporting of accounts of homoerotic contacts
between the schoolboys (Lambert was known to be gay
himself). The greater challenge was that children's opinions should be taken seriously by policy makers – a wholly
novel notion. Lambert's career as a government-sponsored
sociologist came to an end with the publication of *The
Hothouse Society*, but he had already agreed to become headmaster of the experimental and markedly liberal boarding
school Dartington Hall.

The bulk of the stories in *The Hothouse Society* start unhappily and improve. An eighteen-year-old looking back

reports that he was 'lost at first': 'the first few days I didn't
have any friends . . . I was so bad I kept wanting to run
away, but it did get nicer after a bit.' Or, after an account
of long misery, beating, extortion and bullying, the inter-
viewers hear 'but now I am on a perfectly even keel'. This
may be what psychologists call 'habituation' – becoming
accustomed enough to deny the validity of their initial response. The problem is that the child comes to believe he
or she was at fault in not liking the experience, too weak
or too sensitive, when all they were in fact was innocent.

Survival in an unkind environment demands some kind
of acceptance, because the body and mind cannot live
with prolonged stress and anxiety. But 'getting used to
it' encompasses a great range of actual reactions. Here is
a fifteen-year-old girl at a 'progressive' school that she'd
entered two or three years earlier:

> I remember my first evening at school after my mother
> had dropped me off; I was wandering around the school
> by myself behind a great tall boy and we were just about
> to pass through some swing doors, I didn't know wheth-
> er to turn round and run in the opposite direction rather
> than risk having a great heavy door swing in my face. I
> made up my mind to be brave and have never been more
> surprised than when this boy stopped and held the door
> open for me. I have never been homesick since.

This written account is from an eleven-year-old 'new
boy', still not 'settled', as the teachers would put it:

> [School] is a shitty dump. Is bluddy fucking prison
> camp made to look like a palace out side and prison
> inside. I hate it and I have only been here 7 weeks. Its

bloddy awful. The food is SHIT. I really hate it no kid-
ding. We only allowed out three times a week and Mr
Tomkins is a SEX omo!

Habituation is also about finding a narrative that suits
others. I found a letter to my eldest sister from Ashdown,
written perhaps when I was nine or ten. Two years younger
than me, she and I were close, and I had told her what I felt
unable to tell my parents. She worried awfully. This must
have made me feel guilty, not least because I knew she too
would soon be dropped off at boarding school.

> Dear Chris
> School isn't nearly as bad as I always think it is. It's
> always much better once you get back. I am in a Senior
> dorm actually but it's not nearly as bad as I thought
> it would be. In fact it's quite fun. How are the guinea
> pigs?
>     Love Alex xoxox etc

It's interesting that Royston Lambert seems predis-
posed to believe that the elite of ancient, paid-for 'public
schools' (which he separates from 'ordinary' private
boarding schools) were happier. When he introduces one
fourteen-year-old's story of homesickness and shock at the
viciousness and dishonesty of his peers, he says, 'Neither
do the public schools always escape criticism . . .' before
telling a story of the system of licensed bullying and exploitation called 'fagging', a feature of life at Eton until
1980 and at many of its cohorts until more recently. As
was common at the time, Lambert makes a case for fagging
– where older boys could use younger ones as unrewarded
labour – as a good thing, in that it 'is an important method

of assimilation' to the school for new children.

Yet other accounts make no case for a difference. There were (and are) good and bad schools in both private and public ownership, just as there are children who adapted easily and those who didn't. Of course, many of the systems of schools that flourished in the twentieth century were modelled on the private ones of the nineteenth. The culture of licensed abuse that was at the core of the discipline and teaching system in most of the schools of the rich was faithfully replicated in the schools for everyone else, whether children slept at home or not. It was not Royston Lambert's job to examine that, though the conclusions of his research led him to suggest that the state and private schools should merge, as many academics and politicians had been arguing since the 1940s. Clearly his public school interviewees told fewer tales of hardship. Was that because they were genuinely better-treated, or because the code of not complaining had been better drilled in?

# 8. The puppies

'I really, really, really didn't like it,' says an eleven-year-old at Hawtrey's prep school, remembering his first term. 'I remember seeing the bars on the windows that first night and thinking, "Oh flip!" I really, really felt like I was just being dumped here . . . It's not quite so bad now.' He's being interviewed in a gripping fly-on-the-wall film broadcast in 1994 by the BBC, *The Making of Them* (the title quotes one of the breezy mothers as she justifies dispatching her eight-year-old). It is perhaps the rawest, least censored account of young private school children talking frankly about their lives.

The eleven-year-old, Alexander, is relaxed on camera in his wire-rim glasses, tweed jacket and tie. He chuckles at the memories of his misery aged seven, like an old gent reminiscing over tough times in war. 'I only had one friend, I'd only met him once before. We just sat together. But he knew some of the other people. I was left on my own. One of the older boys caught me – well, not caught me, but found me – crying behind one of the lockers . . . Most people don't like it that much when they come here but they get used to it. I've forgotten who it was but there was someone who really, really hated it here. He actually decided that he wouldn't come back the next term. But his mother and his father actually had to just about drag him back to school. Well' – another chuckle – 'now it's fine.'

At a later point in this film, we hear what may be the original of this story from Alexander's father. Swigging a brandy and soda at home on a sofa, he tells us of a contemporary who had to be 'heavily sedated' in order to 'be dragged back to school'. He chortles as he goes on: 'I don't know what upset him about the place. He hated it . . . Perfectly normal chap now.'

The film lives on through YouTube. It caused little fuss at the time, though some parents did remove children from Hawtrey's, one of the two schools featured. But few independent schools would make the mistake of allowing a film-maker free access (and final cut) again. Colin Luke, the director, told me how the shoot was done. He employed the youngest, most boyish cameramen he could get, in order to calm the nervous headmaster. He asked them to film everything – the great Georgian porticos, the boys, the teachers, the corridors – from a crouch, so we saw it all from the children's height.

When the children pause in their interviews, Luke's cameramen don't stop filming. This can produce stark insights into the real workings of these children's minds – moments that leave you thinking, 'Oh God, they're so young.' One gap-toothed blond child, nine years old, is asked what boarding school has done for him:

It has changed me . . . When I'm older, something like twenty, if I become a businessman I'm going to need to be able to manage by myself. Being at boarding school is quite a lot about being able to manage and handle yourself, without help from other people . . . Going to boarding school for me's an achievement, it's made me more grown up . . . it gives you a responsibility, it really has changed me quite a lot.

He is solemn, putting emphasis on each long noun, like an adult making a speech: like the adult who made that speech, perhaps. When at last he has run out of steam the cameraman asks him how old he is. Then the boy reverts, a happy grin spreads across his face, and he tells us all about his birthday party – 'I had a clown birthday cake, and it was really nice, and on the nose it was that really yummy stuff, and it was red, and I had the nose all to myself and it was really nice . . . !'

One of the strengths of the film is that, without ever stating its purpose, it is entirely about the pains of separation, and children's and parents' adaptation to that. No violence or bullying is shown: there's lots of talk of boys comforting others who are crying over homesickness. Their society functions adequately, as a prison one can. But other accounts I have had reveal that both the schools in the film had at other times in their history suffered the usual problems of institutions that tolerated violence and incompetent teachers.

I don't remember much of that long first autumn, or indeed of the ones that came after. Letters from home. Small joys – mainly related to food, of which there never seemed to be enough. Punishments. Williamson's rages. Small tragedies – I cried, for a whole night, it seemed, when a stick of lip-salve my mother had given me broke in my hands. Rare kindnesses stand out from the grey, like peaks in a cloudscape. I remember looking for excuses to hang out in the linen room, the matron and her assistants' domain, attracted by the warmth of women's voices and laughter. It is no wonder that schooldays memoirs are full of stories of under-matrons or cleaning ladies 'with whom the whole school was in love'.

Psychotherapists talk of the trauma young children

must suffer in a regime where physical affection and reassurance were impossible. It wasn't something you thought of then, of course. But I remember one evening, when the others were out of the dormitory, wrestling and then hugging one of the other new boys. We were shivering, both naked from our communal bath, and I remember that his skin was still tanned from the summer holidays, smooth and beautiful. But we were only eight: I think that the episode was about hunger for physical contact as much as any pre-sexual experimentation.

David Cornwell (the writer John le Carré) has written, in fiction and journalism, of his miserable schooldays, which were a double abandonment – his mother left his violent father and the family, so he and his older brother went to board. Cornwell was only five when he started at a succession of schools: the beginning of 'sixteen hugless years'. He too sought comfort in the arms of other boys. 'For love, at dead of night, we had one another's trembling little bodies, which stole from bed to bed like sticky frogs in search of a pond,' Cornwell wrote in a 1977 memoir. I remember that after I'd hugged my dorm-mate and he'd hugged me back we still called each other Smith and Renton, as the code demanded.

It was and remains widely believed that contact with loved ones risks interrupting the healthy hardening-up process. A 1920s schoolmaster put down an enquiring mother keen to visit her newly boarding child in characteristic fashion: 'If you had a puppy, would you cut off its tail an inch at a time, or do it all at once?' Other headmasters forbade letter-writing, reports historian Vyvyen Brendon, until boys 'got over the first feeling of soreness'. Even today, many schools, prep and public – Oundle is one, Ashdown

House another – advise against visits, or even phone conversations with home, for a new child's first weeks as a full-time boarder. Weaning is tough, for puppies and children.

The first relief for all the prep school boys and girls was the exeat or half-term, the initial weekend break that came six weeks into the autumn.* That first respite is as vivid an experience as the first arrival. It is clear from many of the accounts that some younger children thought the release would mean rescue. Once they returned, the all-seeing adults who loved them would spot that an awful mistake had been made. They always had before. So harsh disappointment was in store. Often, families had moved on. Some children found their bedroom had been reassigned. My family celebrated when I came home. They all seemed to have missed me a lot. But I remember thinking, on that first half-term, that my place had been taken by a new kitten that everyone was very keen on.

The psychoanalyst Joy Schaverien says that many of her ex-boarder clients made the decision not to speak to their parents: she speculates that they actually lacked the vocabulary to express their suffering. They may have shown their feelings in physical complaints – car-sickness or a stomach ache on the trip back to school. My correspondents often say they didn't tell their parents because they did not want to disappoint them. 'After all, they'd scrimped and saved. They wanted me to have a good time. I couldn't tell them they'd made a terrible mistake.'

Some parents listen only to what they want to hear and

---

* Our ancestors spent much more time at school: at Eton there were only two terms per year. Sir Arthur Conan Doyle, who boarded at nine, got only six weeks holiday a year from the Jesuit school Stonyhurst in the late 1860s and 1870s. He did not enjoy the experience.

they ask questions that will get the answers they need. A telling example of this comes in *The Making of Them*, when the fathers and mothers pull up in their cars at half-term and start quizzing their offspring. 'Well, are you having a great time?' are the first words from a jolly mother with Farrah Fawcett hair. (We've previously seen her at home, saying she doesn't want to talk to her boy on the phone, because children tend to lie when they ring up and say they are unhappy.) 'Is it wonderful, is the food good?' There's a moment while her son looks at her, wondering how to answer. 'Very,' he says. 'Is it? Oh good!' she says, with a big smile.

An adult ex-boarder in the film makes the point that what the child therapists call 'disclosure' – a child reporting an abuse – becomes more and more difficult because the child will start to accept his experience. If there is something not 'wonderful', it may be the child's fault. 'If I'd been asked aged nine or ten how I was doing, I would have said, "Well, I was homesick at first. I've settled down a lot, thank you. You know, you can't be attached to your Mum's apron strings for ever. It's jolly good fun in the dorms, you know." You learnt to be who you had to be. You had to be a good chap, getting on with it, part of the system. But I went on missing my home terribly.'

I don't remember my parents asking me during that first trip home if I was happy. If they did, it clearly was not possible for me to tell them what was happening in my dorm: either how I lay in bed rigid for fear of being beaten for making a noise, or about the naked wrestling. What I did tell them was things that I could show – that I had chilblains from the cold, that the backs of my knees were red and the skin broken from eczema or some other affliction. My mother provided what I needed, cream and a little sympathy. But I never showed her the marks the beatings made. That would have crossed a line that I did not yet understand. Embarrassment and shame certainly contributed to my silence. One friend has told me she kept quiet because she wanted to protect her parents' innocence.

Over the half-term, someone from my Ashdown dormitory did tell their parents something of what happened during the nights. The morning after the return to school, we were all summoned to Billy Williamson's study. The five of us filed into the little timber-beamed room and the reek of stale tobacco. We eyed the porcelain pot beside the door that contained his canes and a golf club. Even the two bullies seemed small and frightened. Billy was brisk.

'I am disappointed and displeased with you all. As the older boys know, when I am displeased I punish. A boy from this dormitory has, over the half-term, betrayed both the school and his schoolmates. He has spoken to his parents of matters of discipline in Dormitory Five.' He let the weight of that sink in, and then elaborated. I don't know if this time he told one of his favourite classical parables, the story of the Spartan boy who concealed the fox cub in his shirt. (Eventually the animal bit the Spartan mini-soldier to death, but did he complain? No!) Billy certainly would have said: 'Gentlemen do not tell tales.' Tale-telling was actually fine within the school – indeed, the discipline system was built on it. But that was within the club: to the world beyond the gates, all had to appear untroubled. I can't remember how we were punished, but the canes stayed in their pot, this time. He excused us: 'If I hear of anything else of this sort from Dormitory Five, and any

sneaking at all, I shall have no hesitation in beating all of
you.'

And so we learnt the first and perhaps the most important rule.

# 9. No sneaking

Today the 'disclosure' issue is a matter of much debate. Statistics compiled by the NSPCC show that one in three children abused by an adult does not report it, or not until they themselves are adults. As we've seen, there are several reasons why young children don't tell, or speak only partially, or in metaphor. The first brake is shame, and shame comes with sad ease to those who are confused and only half-aware of the rules of sex. It is easy for adults or older children to use those insecurities. The process of 'settling in' to the schools was primarily one of learning the codes and the language of the society. That was how you survived. This process seems, in retrospect, a deliberate part of the construction of the self-preserving club of the elite, and indeed of the growing of that necessary organ, the stiff upper lip.

George Orwell was one of the first to draw wider implications of the warping effect on the adult of the boarding school experience. In a savage essay written in the late 1930s, 'Such, Such Were the Joys', he told of the pressures that enforced silence at his own prep school:

> Against no matter what degree of bullying you had no redress. You could only have defended yourself by sneaking, which, except in a few rigidly defined circumstances, was the unforgivable sin. To write home and

ask your parent to take you away would have been even less thinkable, since to do so would have been to admit yourself unhappy and unpopular, which a boy will never do. Boys are Erewhonians:* they think that misfortune is disgraceful and must be concealed to all cost.

There were some who were brave or angry enough to 'sneak'. As my dormitory found, that rebellious act did not often turn out the way the child hoped. Randolph Churchill, Winston's son, recorded how at Sandroyd he reported some bullies to the headmaster, an act which 'proved no more effective than did the denunciations of a similar nature to the League of Nations'. It could on occasion bring terrible consequences. Here's one of my correspondents, writing about the early 1960s at Temple Grove prep school, when he and two friends went to the headmaster to seek respite from repeated sexual assault:

One morning, I think it was a Monday in the summer term, three of us lined up outside the headmaster's office to complain about the terrible things that had been done to us over the weekend. We came in as a group and described what had happened, actually downplaying the graphic details. The headmaster listened and then sent us outside his office to wait. We were then called in one by one and each beaten to within an inch of our lives for 'telling tales' about members of staff. That of course dealt with once and for all our only 'route of complaint'. It also explains why we never even told our parents for decades. We had been taught the cost of 'telling tales'.

* Referring to the inhabitants of Samuel Butler's imaginary alternative society, described in his novel *Erewhon* (1872).

If the codes did not suppress the children's complaints, many schools, particularly the girls' ones, controlled or even censored letter-writing, just in case some untoward detail should slip out. The same woman who told me about her retreats to the lavatory for privacy, writes in her list of complaints: 'Staff inspecting letters which you sent home. This was a weekly event, after church on a Sunday. Again it seemed such an encroachment upon my liberty, even at such a young age.' At St Aubyn's in Sussex, letter-writing to parents was done communally, and those the teachers judged 'too sad or pathetic' read out to all.

I don't remember being censored at my school, though others have said we were. In one early letter I suggested to my parents that we devise a code system – but that may be just because, like my own children at nine and ten, I liked spies and secret messages. I might not have needed censoring: I think I knew my parents would not want to hear I was unhappy. Our correspondence in my first year was mainly about the new cat, about food I wanted to eat at half-term and my stamp collection. My wife thinks the letters are sad – emotionally constrained, with their dull stories of colds and my weekly class marks. It was not until I was ten or eleven that my letters mentioned bullying. There were incidents with other children, but more often my complaint was the verbal cruelty of the headmaster. There was no mention of canings. My parents cared: often the letters discussed strategies for these problems that they must have suggested. But at eight and nine the letters were short and sunny, though obsessed with the form rankings and with food, or the lack of it.

Some historians base a conviction that children were generally happy at the prep schools on the surviving letters.

This is patently stupid, given the many accounts of censorship. Roald Dahl explained the drill succinctly in his childhood memoir, *Boy*. He boarded from the age of nine, in 1925. 'There was no way, therefore, that we could ever complain to our parents about anything in term-time . . . In fact we often went the other way. In order to please that dangerous headmaster, who was leaning over our shoulders and reading what we had written, we would say splendid things about the school and go on about how lovely the masters were.' Dahl reprints his first letter, which is eerily like mine:

23rd Sept
Dear Mama
I am having a lovely time here. We play football every day here. The beds have no springs. Will you send my stamp album, and quite a lot of stamps. The masters are all very nice . . .

Vyvyen Brendon unearthed some letters that slipped through the censor's grasp. The earliest of all is from young Thomas Macaulay, future politician and historian-poet of the high Victorian age. He wrote desperate letters to his mother from his Cambridgeshire prep school, begging to be allowed to come home. Here he is, aged twelve, at the beginning of the autumn term, 1811:

I cannot bear the thought of remaining so long from home [it would be four months]. I do not know how to comfort myself, or what to do . . . When I am with the rest I am obliged to look pleasant, and to laugh at Wilberforce's [the son of the anti-slavery campaigner] jokes, when I can hardly hide the tears in my eyes. So I

have nothing to do but to sit and cry in my room, and
think of home and wish for the holidays. I am ten times
more uneasy than I was last year. I did not mean to complain, but indeed I cannot help it.

Like many a parent, before and since, Macaulay's father
wrote back telling him to grin and bear it – his pain was a
moral fault and his to bear. 'Pray to God . . . that he would
enable you to give up cheerfully your own selfish prefer-
ences when these stand in the way of duty.'

Peter Scott, the son of the Edwardian explorer, went to
school aged seven in 1918, six years after his father's death
in the Antarctic. The following summer he wrote a letter:

OH MUM DO TAKE ME HOME, HOME, HOME,
SWEET HOME THERE'S NO PLACE LIKE HOME
. . . Get me away from this confounded domatery if you
can. I adore you presious.

Lady Scott relented. She took the little boy out of school
and on a trip to Italy (he was sent back to the school the
next year).

But it is rare to hear of a child taken away from a prep
school because they were unhappy, though sometimes
'nervous illness' did the trick, as with the ten-year-old
Winston Churchill. The mother of Edward Bulwer-Lytton,
the nineteenth-century politician and popular novelist,
did remove him from his school, so shocked was she by her
bullied son's changed appearance. He had only been there
two weeks.

Private school teachers, who know what the life is like,
can be easier on their own unhappy children than their
customers are – it is rare to find any whose children went

to board at eight. John Rae and his wife Daphne spent all their careers teaching at and running schools, including Harrow and Westminster. Three of their six children boarded in the 1970s. When one daughter asked to be released, after only four days, the Raes relented – and did so again when their twin sons, in their fifth term at prep school, ran away saying they had had enough.

Daphne Rae and her husband were lucky to be in a position to hear and react to their children's distress: a lot of parents she met in the schools could not be bothered – 'happy to abrogate their responsibilities'. After twenty-five years dealing with the parents, she seems perplexed at the British upper class's insistence that their children go to board, no matter what. Rae had herself started boarding at four years old. 'Some children are temperamentally incapable of fitting into boarding school life,' she writes; '. . . any attempt to "toughen them up" by forcing them to board can cause utter misery.' Why, she asks, do it at all, unless circumstances at home make it utterly necessary? And why not ask the child, 'often the last person to be consulted'? These were strong views, from the wife of the famous headmaster of Westminster, one of the greatest and most traditional schools. It was said (though denied by John Rae) that her forthright book – which also contained revelations about homosexual bullying and cover-ups at other schools – upset too many. John Rae, though seen as a hugely successful reformer, popular way beyond the school, left Westminster in 1986, aged only fifty-five.

# 10. Cries for help

My own dearest Mother
Thanks so much for your letters & the awfully nice
book. This is an awful change after home so different I
do feel sad & horrible . . . This is an awful hole. I will
never live through this term.
Much love ever
Your very affec loving
Your Hastings\*

Most children whose parents failed, or refused, to hear of
their troubles stopped complaining and accomplished the
settling-in. Many of the stories from ex-boarders looking
back are vague about this transition. 'Eventually things
didn't seem so awful,' or 'I suppose I must have stopped
missing home,' you're told. There's no tipping-point, no
epiphany, but the next event in their narratives is, for contrast, something enjoyable. This blurring and indeed the
surprising absence of a normal trove of memories – most
ex-prep school boarders need to be pushed to come up with
more than half a dozen from the five years they spend there
– are explained by the boarding school psychotherapists
as a blocking process brought on by trauma. This seems

---

\* Letter from Warner Hastings, aged fourteen, to his mother, in
1883. Selina Hastings, *The Red Earl* (Bloomsbury, 2014).

much too pat. But the tailoring of memories to shape a narrative the adult ex-boarder can be at peace with is significant and interesting. There are many examples. I was told by one ex-boarder how he remembered writing to his mother asking if she would take him away – a couple of times in the first term, he thought. Then he settled down. But after she died and he found the letters, there turned out to be dozens of them, sent over a whole year, begging for release. Some children expressed their desires even more dramatically. At my school a boy jumped out of a window deliberately – it was said – in order to get sent home, aged just ten. He was discovered, taken to the doctor, and his broken ankle put in a cast. But his parents didn't find out until he came home for the holidays.

Some historians of the nineteenth-century schools believe that suicide was quite common, though there is no hard evidence. Then and now, schools do their best to keep such things secret, for the sake of the family as well as the institution's reputation. But death in the Victorian schools, as Gathorne-Hardy says, 'was extremely common' – from accidents, exposure and disease, with the youngest and weakest schoolboys succumbing first. Climactic deaths from illness feature in several of the Victorian schooldays novels. Cholera outbreaks regularly closed Rugby when James Fergusson, my ancestor, was there: one killed his housemaster. The death toll in the schools was one of the reasons that the investigative parliamentary commissions were launched in the 1860s.

Sometimes suicides caught the public's attention. The most famous, and heart-rending, was covered by *The Times* in 1877 and provoked public outcry and eventually another governmental inquiry. This was the awful case of William Gibbs, a twelve-year-old scholar at Christ's Hospital. He hanged himself at the school and was declared by the coroner to have done so 'while in a state of temporary insanity'.

It emerged that Gibbs had been happy until bullied by a prefect, and then caned for insolence to a gym teacher. Gibbs ran away. His father forced him to return to the school, where a public flogging – the punishment for running – was in store. He was locked in the infirmary to await this. Two hours later he was found hanged by a cord he had rigged up to a window. Among the correspondence that followed these revelations was testimony from other former 'Bluecoats'. One, a vicar, spelt out in great detail what a flogging for running away meant at Christ's Hospital: thirty strokes with a birch. It was worse than a naval flogging with the cat-o'-nine-tails, he said, explaining how after just one minor punishment he had dug a dozen bits of broken birch rod out of the 'raw meat' that was the back of one 'small and delicate lad', beaten unjustly over the theft of some sugar.

'My own opinion is, sir, that poor little Gibbs has been "done to death" by the bullying and flogging and the fear of more to come . . . ' the letter continues. There was a further outcry when the inquiry decided no individual was to blame for Gibbs's death, but 'shortcomings in the system': it recommended that the school move out of London (which it eventually did). Christ's Hospital still thrives in Horsham, West Sussex, revelling in its ancient costumes and rituals. But there is not a mention of the birch or William Gibbs in the official history.

Gibbs's suicide is one of the very few officially reported. Child development textbooks maintain that suicide attempts by pre-pubertal children are very rare. In fact it seems that, because of the stigma, it is only rare that children's deaths are reported as suicide. Modern research shows that suicide is in fact a leading cause of death for under-fifteen-year-olds. Daphne Rae says 'unnatural death' is more common in schools than people realise, and tells a story of prep school bullying that ended in manslaughter. In my correspondence are a surprising number of stories of attempted suicides, sometimes told as comic and incompetent. But it would be hard to characterise these as mere attention-seeking. There are several attempted self-drownings, often in the school swimming pool; one man told me how, at prep school in the 1940s, he and some friends ate yew tree berries, which they knew were fatal to horses. 'Were you trying to commit suicide?' I asked. 'No,' he said after reflection. 'I think we had just decided we wanted not to be there.' The awful truth is that the bulk of suicide stories I have are of adults who, their friends and relatives believe, never got over what they had suffered at school and killed themselves later. There are at least six such cases from two decades of graduates of my small prep school.

Adults seldom reacted with much sympathy either to the self-harming or to the runaways. Roald Dahl stands for many with his story of having faked appendicitis to get sent home from his loathed prep school. He succeeded, but once there the family doctor saw straight through him. He advised him to go back, with the warning: 'Life is tough, and the sooner you learn how to cope with it the better.'

That was and remains a standard response to the child. Some accounts detail what sounds like unbelievable callousness on the part of parents, but the normal ones are merely lazy: you'll get over it, you're exaggerating, or you're much better off than you might be. Often my correspondents are still indignant, decades later, at being told by parents and teachers what 'lucky' children they were: they might be orphans, or refugees, or poor. One woman, lonely and bullied until she was near-suicidal, says 'I never felt able to tell my parents that I was struggling at school. They had scrimped and saved to send me there and I felt incredibly guilty at that; admitting my unhappiness would seem ungrateful, at best.' As a scholarship girl at Christ's Hospital school, another correspondent was 'constantly reminded of the debt to those who financed us, and therefore obliged to comply gratefully with demands, restrictions, conditions, regardless of their appropriateness . . .'

C. S. Lewis is one of a clutch of twentieth-century ex-boarding school writers who wrote of the power and spirit of children in battles against such tyranny. In his memoir, published in 1955, he writes forgivingly of his father's failure to hear when his sons told him of the cruelties and stupidities of the tiny boarding school in Hertfordshire they went to in 1910. (In the memoir, Lewis calls the school Belsen, after the Nazi concentration camp.) His father heard what he wanted to hear, Lewis decides. Even when he was reading the school's plainly dishonest prospectus, 'he was really composing a school story in his own mind'. But, like many boarders before and after, he lets his father off:

> We did not even try very hard [to tell him the truth about the school]. Like other children, we had no standard of comparison; we supposed the miseries of Belsen to be the common and unavoidable miseries of all schools. Vanity helped tie our tongues. A boy home from school likes to cut a dash . . . He would hate to be thought a coward and a cry-baby, and he cannot paint the true picture of his concentration camp without admitting

himself to have been for the last thirteen weeks a pale, quivering, tear-stained, obsequious slave.

Beyond the fatuities and the wilful deafness, there is in the parents' responses to complaints and cries for help a darker strand. It is impossible not to conclude that the bulk of them knew what sort of unhappiness lay ahead when they sent the children away. C. S. Lewis writes, hopefully, that most parents are like his father, innocently deaf: 'If the parents in each generation always or often knew what really goes on at their sons' schools, the history of education would be very different.'

But how could they not have known? From the early nineteenth century onwards there was little mystery about what happened to children in the public schools. The stories of floggings, deaths, riots, fights, theft and bullying were told in popular novels, from Henry Fielding to Dickens and George Eliot, in newspaper reports, by parliamentary commissions, in the cartoons of artists like Cruikshank and in the pages of *Punch* magazine.

Vyvyen Brendon has many stories of parents hesitating to send their children, put off by tales of swearing and blasphemy, not to mention (as one prospective Eton parent put it) 'impurities, profanities, gluttony and rioting'. Even the deeper secrets – the dark vices mentioned in hushed tones – were pretty well known. There were several well-reported criminal trials of schoolmasters for assault or buggery of their pupils in the eighteenth and nineteenth centuries, and gossip about much more.

The first recorded sexual criminal in the schools was very widely known and written of: Nicholas Udall, a sixteenth-century headmaster of Eton. He was a hard flogger, who gave one of his pupils '53 stripes', when only eleven or twelve years old, for failing a Latin lesson. In 1543 Udall was blackmailed by some of the boys he had sexually abused and then found guilty by the Privy Council of the then new offence of buggery; after an appeal to Henry VIII's court, his death sentence was commuted to one year in prison and he went on to become headmaster of Westminster. The roller coaster of Udall's career was to be a model for others.

# 11. Toughening them up

> Plato taught that the guardians of the State should not
> know their parents; the English did not go as far as
> that, but when they were eight years old the children
> from whom rulers were to be chosen were taken away
> from home for three-quarters of every year, taught not
> to mention their mother or their own Christian names,
> brought up in the traditions of the Sparta which Plato
> admired. And the children grew up to be true guardi-
> ans: no other people in history can equal this record of
> disinterested guardianship.
>
> Philip Mason, *The Men Who Ruled India: The Guardians* (1963)

Many parents believed some unhappiness at boarding
school was inevitable and normal. Judging by the letters
of my ancestors and others, Victorian parents were not less
loving than today's. But 'toughening up' was key to the
production of a fully functional citizen of the ruling class.
This belief echoed religious convictions not yet discard-
ed. Children, born in sin and ignorance, needed to be led
out of their natural wickedness into wisdom and goodness. One of the tools for that job was pain, physical and
mental.*

* Jonathan Gathorne-Hardy in his grand history of the public
schools, published in 1975: 'Behind all forms of education [until
1890] the basic view was the Christian/Pauline one: people, but

It seems clear that the children of the prep schools, although sometimes very young indeed, were not thought deserving of gentler treatment just because they were pre-pubescent. Violent discipline coupled with prescriptive moral instruction was the accepted recipe in the schools for teenagers, and it did very well for six- or eight-year-olds too. 'Lashing', the public school historian Jonathan Gathorne-Hardy writes, was seen by Rugby's Dr Arnold – the most influential public school headmaster of them all – and those who came before him as 'good for the soul'.

If some prep schools were savage and cruel it was because savagery and cruelty were normal at the senior schools: decades of mismanagement at the ancient institutions had let custom become practice. As Cuthbert Worsley, one of the first twentieth-century critics, said, 'The early Public Schools had plainly suffered from gross understaffing, and in the absence of remedying it, it may be said that brutality, fear and force were the only ways of achieving it.' It is hard to see that much had changed before the late twentieth century. Understaffing remained normal, as did violent discipline. Pastoral care and child counselling were not what the normal schoolmaster did, even when I was at boarding school.

Parents believed that the hard regime worked. 'My father's idea was that the more boys roughed it in every way, the stronger and better they grew up,' said the third Marquess of Salisbury, a future prime minister. He was sent to boarding school aged six. 'My existence there was an existence among devils,' he said later. The boys were beaten

particularly children, were innately wicked owing to original sin . . . Children were not naturally good but must be taught to be so and that the method was a superior adult discipline and training.' The thinking, he continues, is 'still very powerful today'.

with shaving straps, woken at 6 a.m. and not fed till 10 a.m. (starvation is often a feature of the Victorian stories, even at the schools of the aristocrats, imposed either because schoolmasters were misers or, it is suggested, because of a belief in the moral benefits of hunger – or both). Salisbury said he 'naturally learnt nothing'. He went on to have just as miserable a time at Eton, where he went in 1849, aged ten – bullied, spat on and beaten up until eventually he had to be removed temporarily from the school.

But though notably modern in many of his attitudes to his own children, Salisbury had them schooled the same way. Some of his sons stayed at home till thirteen, but then all five went to Eton, too. At least two of those did not like their education either – Lord Robert Cecil complained about the 'twelve or fourteen years' wasted on the classics. But they all fulfilled their destinies, rising high in the Church, Army, politics and diplomacy (Lord Robert won the Nobel Peace Prize in 1937), and, of course, sent their children to the same schools.

Charles Darwin exemplifies a very different kind of Victorian parent. The child of a doctor, he had gone to board at Shrewsbury School aged nine in 1818. He had been happy there, not least because he could run to his family home, just a mile away, when he wanted. The classical education he got, though, was 'wretched' and 'stupid', and he disapproved of 'the whole system of breaking through the affections of the family by separating the boys so early in life'. His letters tell that he agonised over whether he should send his adored son Willy away. But, in 1852, aged thirteen, Willy went to Rugby. Darwin's reasoning was not so different from the second Marquess of Salisbury's: 'I dare not run the risk of a youth being exposed to the temptations of the world without having undergone the milder ordeal of a great school.'

The later Victorian parents and indeed the twentieth-century ones were not perhaps sending their children into the bearpits – 'nurseries of all vice' as Henry Fielding put it – that their grand- or great-grandfathers had known. But cruelty, physical and emotional, was an accepted part of the schools' ethos as they began their most successful century, the twentieth.

Again and again stories tell of immense demands made on the emotional resilience of children in the schools, far beyond the need for them to accept the trauma of separation. Sometimes they ended up in boarding school because a parent had died and no one could think of a better way to cope: the tragedy compounded by the fact that often brothers and sisters were thus separated. This happened to Herbert Asquith, son of the Liberal prime minister of the same name. He went to boarding school aged ten, shortly after his mother died in 1891, leaving the budding politician with five children between one and twelve. 'I never met anyone who looked back with enthusiasm to his life at a private school and in this I am no exception,' wrote Asquith junior.

Eddie Izzard, the comedian, and his brother were sent to board in 1968, at seven, shortly after their mother had died. In 2001 he told an interviewer: 'I cried relentlessly for a year . . . My housemaster would help me along with beatings when he could fit them in.' In his 2017 memoir Izzard recounts how, by the age of eleven, he had trained himself not to cry because it did no good. After that, he writes, he became 'emotionally dead . . . emotionally blocked, but tough'.

One of my correspondents told me of being sent to

Britain in 1969, after his parents had died in a plane crash; he was put, aged nine, into a boarding prep school. Soon he was sleepwalking. 'I would be found all over the school at night screaming at walls in a semi-conscious state as I struggled to adjust to my new circumstances.' The solution in the end was to drug him with sleeping pills and put him to sleep in the matron's bed. Often the schools seem not to have acted in any way at all when a child was suffering because of family events. The anthropologist Judith Okeley tells how, aged nine, a matron told her off. 'Your Daddy has died. I know that. But you are to stop crying at once. You know that you are not to make any noise after 7 p.m.' Here is another correspondent, talking of a famous prep school in the 1950s:

> I witnessed the following incident: thirty of us twelve-year-olds went into a big classroom to do a History exam. One of the boys immediately started crying, and cried uncontrollably for the entire forty-minute exam. As we were filing out at the end of the exam, the assistant master who had been invigilating stopped the boy and said, kindly, 'What is the matter? You are obviously very upset about something . . .' The boy replied, and I heard him say the words, 'I've just been told that both my parents have been killed in a car crash.'

# 12. Did the parents know?

The idea of schools as machines for 'toughening-up' did not go unquestioned. In fact, the mid-Victorians often seem more attuned to children's unhappiness, more fearful, and more eager to care for them, than do the parents of a century later. It was an age of increasing sentimentality about children. Charles Kingsley and Charles Dickens novels put orphaned and exploited children into the public gaze; *Nicholas Nickleby* (1838) provides an archetype of grim school and mad, cruel headmaster that is still current. (Try putting Mr Squeers or Dotheboys Hall into a Google News search.)

Lighter fiction told stories of the harsh life in the prep schools, too. *Vice Versa: a Lesson to Fathers* was a comic novel by Thomas Anstey Guthrie, a writer for the humorous magazine *Punch*. It became immensely and enduringly popular after publication in 1882 – it has been adapted for film or TV eight times. It is the story of a pompous, prosperous middle-class father, Paul Bultitude. At the end of the holidays his son is miserable at the prospect of going back to his brutal boarding school and its cane-happy headmaster. Mr Bultitude announces (it was a foolish cliché even then) that schooldays are the best days of one's life. Indeed, he wishes he was going himself. Thanks to a magic stone, that's exactly what happens: son and father swap bodies and places, though not their minds. When Mr Bultitude

returns, battered, having run away from Dr Grimstone and
the intolerable school, he has been awakened to a host of
elemental cruelties and injustices. Meanwhile, the son has
had all kinds of fun, *Trading Places*-style, running his father's City office. It is still very funny.

*Jane Eyre*, published in 1847, is the first literary account
of a girls' boarding school. The ten-year-old Jane is sent by
her hated aunt to Lowood, a school for poor and orphaned
girls. It is as cruel and heartless as Dotheboys Hall: the
girls are cold and hungry, beaten on the neck and cruelly
humiliated. Within a few months there is a typhus outbreak – not uncommon in the mid-nineteenth century,
when the public schools frequently had to close because of
epidemics – and Jane's friend dies in her arms. Thereafter
the school is modernised and improved, and Jane eventually becomes a teacher. Teaching, in schools or rich houses
as a governess, was one of the few jobs available to educated women, and so one of the reasons for the rise of girls'
schools in the nineteenth century.

Just as popular as Brontë and Dickens novels was *Tom
Brown's School Days* (1857), the father and most successful
of the dozens of school-set novels published in the nineteenth century. It's important because a direct line leads
from Tom and his friend Scud to schoolchild heroes like
Kipling's Stalky, Billy Bunter, Molesworth, Jennings and
the girls of St Trinian's and Malory Towers. All their stories, immensely popular way beyond the class that used
boarding schools, share the same core themes – jolly japes
under tyranny, and the invincible power of the tribe. The
literature and cinema of public school chaps in Nazi prisoner of war camps uses the same motifs, and even some of
the same character types. At the end of the millennium,
just when the template might have been abandoned – and

despite a host of parodies in the work of artists from Monty Python to Terry Pratchett – came J. K. Rowling. From the architecture of Hogwarts to the ethos of the child wizards *Harry Potter* owes much to Hughes's Rugby School in the 1830s.

Read now, much of *Tom Brown* is moralising and deeply tedious. For at least a hundred years young readers have been warned to stop reading at the halfway mark. It is also, to the modern mind, pretty good propaganda against boarding school, unlike the works of Enid Blyton and J. K. Rowling, which have between them sent thousands of children off to board. If Dickens's Squeers is the archetypal cruel headmaster, Hughes's Flashman is the entitled upper-class bully by whom all standards are set. The early (and best) chapters contain humiliations and cruelties – bullying, forced fagging, extortion and thrashings – culminating in eleven-year-old Tom's toasting in front of an open fire by Flashman.

But Hughes certainly did not intend *Tom Brown's School Days* as a treatise against Rugby School or boarding. It is a panegyric to his great hero, the reforming headmaster Dr Arnold. And there's no evidence that any Victorian child, or parent, was put off by reading *Tom Brown's School Days* – there's far too much fun in it. Despite the publicised hazards, boarding school then and now was often an easy sell: an awfully big adventure. Dickens's Little Nell dies – poverty is a bad thing – but, bruised, battered and lightly toasted by Flashman, Tom survives to become a God-fearing, upright Victorian gentleman, and a jolly straight bat.

That is why it is the greatest and most influential of all the school novels (a hundred years after publication it still came in the top three of British and Commonwealth boys' lists of their favourite books). It lays out with brilliant effect (albeit at painful length) the key message: hard times make good, Christian adults. *Per ardua ad astra*, is the message. It made it clear that the hazards, however unpleasant, were part of the process and should be welcomed.

Rejecting that was not easy. There are several examples of Victorian middle-class parents criticised by friends and relatives for bringing up children at home too gently. By the end of the nineteenth century, failure to expose a boy to the regime of hard knocks was deemed to risk producing a morally inept adult unable to take his place in the team that ruled society and the Empire. A passage in Plato, where Socrates proposes that children are brought up in ignorance of their parents, was widely quoted. An influential headmaster, Walter F. Bicknell, who was also a parent, wrote in one widely read magazine that to send children away was to save them from the incompetence and moral irresponsibility that characterised modern middle- and upper-class families. 'Frequently all the good which a boy gets is got at school, and most of the evil which he gets is got at home . . .'

It was a common view, echoed in medical journals, in writing by and for women, and of course by the religious. 'The chief thing that is to be desired is to remove the children from the noxious influence of home,' wrote Nathaniel Woodard in 1848. An Anglican priest, he and his supporters, who included the prime minister W. E. Gladstone, raised half a million pounds to found Lancing College and ten more boarding schools, most of which still survive.*

---

* The Woodard Corporation today runs 21 Anglican schools, most of them with full or partial boarding.

The schools were intended overtly to 'get possession of the middle classes', and so make children Christians rather than 'Communists and Red Republicans'. In 1874, despite Canon Woodard's scepticism, a boarding school for girls was started too.

But the most powerful educational instinct in late Victorian Britain was the cult of 'manliness' – induced through sports and hardship and chastity. As the age grew more sexually prudish, parents were worried that adolescent boys should not have sex with the servants. But perhaps more concern was felt over the threat of 'effeminacy'. This was not as simple as an issue of sexuality – after all, most accounts indicated that if you wanted to preserve your boy from perversion, you should keep him close by you – but a notion that too much learning brought about moral and physical weakness. 'A nation of effeminate, enfeebled bookworms scarcely forms the most effective bulwark of a nation's liberties', is a fairly typical educational theorist's remark (from 1872). This author and much of the nation decided that organised sport was the answer to the horror of intellectualism and inadequate manliness. With the Empire in need, not to send the child away to school might be deemed not just irreligious but unpatriotic.

### The Feminine Boy

> If cursed by a son who declined to play cricket
> (Supposing him sound and sufficient in thews,)
> I'd larrup him well with the third of a wicket,
>     Selecting safe parts of his body to bruise.
> In his mind such an urchin King Solomon had
> When he said, Spare the stump, and you bungle the lad!

*For what in the world is the use of a creature*
*All flabbily bent on avoiding the Pitch?*
*Who wanders about, with a sob in each feature,*
*Devising a headache, inventing a stitch?*
*There surely would be a quick end to my joy*
*If possessed of that monster – the feminine boy!*\*

E. L. Browne, headmaster of St Andrew's prep school,
Eastbourne, 1890–1933

Those concerns have abated. But there remain simple justifications for the dispatch of a small child to board that have not changed in 150 years. One is the urge to buy social advantage. The other was illustrated on a 2016 Mumsnet comment thread, which began in reaction to an anguished post about an unhappy and underperforming eight-year-old, recently started at boarding school. The mother lived thousands of miles away. She said the school had complained because he couldn't look after himself adequately or get dressed quick enough – an accusation which left her son 'sobbing uncontrollably' on the phone. Dozens of people on the thread asked, with greater or lesser horror: Why so young? 'The reason we sent him was to attend an English public school when he is older,' answered the mother.

\* The poem, published in the school magazine in 1900, goes on for another five verses, ending with an eyebrow-raising declaration of Browne's 'love' for 'a lad who is eager and chubby'.

# 13. The protective shell

Once the boarding school child has settled in, as they must, a whole set of interesting behaviours begin to emerge. Modern psychology groups them all under 'habituation' or 'normalisation'. Psychotherapists who specialise in 'boarding school syndrome' state that to survive the fracture or loss of normal loving relationships, set processes are seen: grief and mourning lead to the development of strategies for protecting oneself. These may include 'extreme vigilance' and even the 'splitting of the persona' – developing a secret self and a public one.

In a section titled 'The captive child', Joy Schaverien writes of how her patients learned to get by. Some underwent an 'encapsulation of the self' – a common Jungian term. They undergo a psychological 'freezing' which leads to the growth of a protective shell – an 'armoured self'. Despite the mixing of metaphors, this is an analysis that has provable truth behind it: many raw accounts by ex-boarders I have received describe this, or something close to it. (Some of them have narratives that may have been shaped by the analysis – but not all. It is easy to tell, reading the accounts, who has had therapy and who has not.)

The 'shell' is something that some parents notice when the boarder first comes home. It can be shocking. 'Just one term, and he was completely changed, self-centred, uninterested in us or his brothers,' writes one anguished mother. Her son later killed himself. In adulthood the self-protective instinct may lead the ex-boarder to sex addiction or to 'prematurely cut off from intimate relationships', in fear of another abandonment.

Anger is another symptom of the traumatised child. Problems with 'anger management' are high on the list that psychotherapists use for diagnosing boarding school syndrome. There is in many people's accounts of bad times a story of how outraged they were at the injustice: a furious version of the ordinary 'It's not fair' complaint. Anger and hurt suppressed must eventually have an outlet: traumatised children make destructive teenagers and young adults. Here's one man, still burning with rage, fifty years later:

I was a very fussy eater and I think because of my autistic side found certain sensations almost unbearable: fat and gristle, milk, carrots, beetroots . . . Despite learning to sit at the other end of the table so they couldn't see what I had left on my plate, I was constantly mocked and tortured by the masters and mistresses who seemed to enjoy forcing me to eat what I really couldn't eat. The result was I got slower and slower at eating until I more or less stopped.

One lunchtime there was an announcement. It was the headmaster: 'It seems we have amongst us a child whose table manners are so slovenly and revolting that we must resort to extreme measures to teach him a lesson so he may rejoin civilisation again. For that reason, as you may have noticed, there is a table here next to mine, but facing the wall with a mirror, so the pig in question can observe his own revolting face as he mutilates the food in front of him. It is called the Pig's Table, and from now on it will be Watson's place at mealtimes. So, Watson, come and take your place at the Pig's Table.'

I can remember feeling very alone and dejected and also furiously angry as I sat at the Pig Table with my own face staring back out at me. The anger inside grew and grew and I resolved to never eat again even if I died. I don't remember how many meals it took for them to realise this wasn't a battle they were going to win and rather than have a dead child on their hands they relented and let me return to my normal table. But not before there was another announcement expressing the wish that I might have learnt my lesson and that revolting manners would always be punished like this. I developed severe eating dysfunction later on as a teenager, stuffing myself until I could eat no more and my tummy would be distended and painful for hours. I still have to fight not to do that when I eat.

Many ex-boarders, whether treated or not, have come to realise that they were marked by the separation and other traumas. Yet their reactions – their coping strategies, if you like – could differ wildly. If, bereft of Mum and siblings, you reattached your truncated emotional urges to the team or the gang, these could be exciting and fulfilling times. Trauma and happiness did exist side by side. Literature and private accounts are full of intense friendships, deep love and trust between children, born in adversity.

Some ex-boarders will never again have as great a thrill as being promoted to be a prefect, winning a cup, or being a favoured member of a gang of dominant children. Violence helped children bond, too. Many children got enormous pleasure from bullying, and spent large amounts of time and used fantastic inventiveness (there are more than a few accounts of boys using woodwork class to build torture machines 'that would have impressed the Spanish Inquisition') to pursue that hobby. Many schools, and commentators, seem to have viewed bullying as another of the salutary toughening-up sports. There is no question that, until very recently, bullying was tacitly licensed in many schools as a key part of the system of discipline. In later life, it becomes another source of guilt.

Other pleasures come to the adapting, vigilant child. Some of them proved to be the birth of fruitful careers. The cliché of the professional comedian who learnt to entertain by telling jokes to distract the bullies at school is accurate; so is that of the storyteller who learned their craft by entertaining bored dormitories after lights-out. Both these types were present at my prep school: the entertainer as brave as some samizdat writer in a grim dictatorship, because talking after lights-out could mean a caning.

Peter Cook, the comedian and backer of *Private Eye*, devoted his life to savaging pompous and hypocritical authority. Bullied both at prep and public school, not least by Ted Dexter, future England cricketer, Cook told his biographer that most of his humour was autobiographical. Small, lonely and asthmatic, he hated the first two years at St Bede's, Eastbourne, where he went at seven. 'I didn't enjoy getting beaten up, and I disliked being away from home – that part was horrid. But it started a sort of defence mechanism in me, trying to make people laugh so that they wouldn't hit me. I could make fun of other people and therefore make the person who was about to bully me laugh instead.'

Some of the worst affected by the schools become loners. They may withdraw themselves, they may be avoided by others because of the taint of unhappiness or difference. That may be of itself an early rebellion, a purposeful reaction to a system that demands you join the team, or suppress your individuality for the good of the school. Militant refusal to attend games periods was one that came to many of us. I didn't like games, because it was often cold and you got hurt and sometimes humiliated, but on another level I felt I was making a stand, expressing a right as an individual not to subsume myself to the group. Forty-five years later, I met a teacher from my prep school. In the fumbling moments of introduction, I said that I recognised him, chiefly by his blue eyes. He said, 'I recognise yours, too. Sceptical eyes: you were one of those who never really believed in it all.'

Rebellion as a teenager would be much more explosive and exciting – never better exemplified than in the scene in the movie *If* when the rebels of the public school machine-gun visiting dignitaries as they emerge from the chapel. It gave birth to careers in revolutionary culture and politics, to spies, traitors, artists and to great polemicists. But the little boys and girls first grew the seeds of that great, reviving reaction.

The writer Cyril Connolly was at St Cyprian's, the South Coast school that his contemporary George Orwell later described in an essay full of contempt and bottled-up rage. Orwell's recent biographers have made a case that he exaggerated the horrors (despite his own stricture to beware of self-pity when writing of your schooldays). Connolly was contemptuous of St Cyprian's but he adapted enough to have had enormous fun pushing at the rules and codes. He started an underground newspaper, spiced with jokes about St Cyprian's aged teachers and their 'boy-whipper' habits. It has a parody of the pompous essay style required by the English master. Though Connolly was only twelve or thirteen years old, his *St Cyprian's Chronicle* was impressively subversive at times: it carried mock advertising for dusters as anti-beating devices and a promise to write your essay for a fee of two apples. In one column, Connolly promises to give up lying except when wanting to get out of a punishment or to 'damage the character of a friend': the exact reverse of the code.

Some rebellion was done remotely, some was done in secret. But it all could be empowering and restorative, even to those who did not fight back themselves. ('Dignifying,' as one interviewee put it.) One well-known pillar of today's British establishment gave me information about a notorious prep school he attended. He told me about secret acts of vandalism to which his whole school thrilled while the headmaster raged and threatened: 'I honestly believe that the boy who defaced his notices, again and again, did as much to restore our self-respect as a Robin Hood. He was the Scarlet Pimpernel, he was Batman. He still is a hero, in my mind: he risked a lot and he saved us from being ground down to something we might not have recovered from. In a way, that's coloured my life – I am not a fighter, but I like to support those who do fight.'

Secret rebellion was effective, too. Former boarders have told me of the solace they got from intoning their hatred for a cruel teacher or a bully – 'Just repeating forbidden words under my breath – you cunt, you shit, you bastard – that helped me keep my head from going under,' says one. The writer Francis Wheen, who was sexually assaulted by the serial abuser Charles Napier at Copthorne School, got a satisfying revenge by finding the beer and tobacco Napier used to bribe the boys into compliance, and stealing them.

John le Carré (David Cornwell) has spoken and written

movingly of the miseries and, above all, the indignities of his prep school. He was beaten for 'cheek, slackness, filth, lying; the menu was awesome'. He was hit by a teacher, which he blames for his later deafness, and, like George Orwell, punished continually for bed-wetting, which continued until his mid-teens. His biographer Adam Sisman digs into some of the more autobiographical novels (like *A Perfect Spy*) for details of blighted school experience that demonstrably is relevant to a very British scepticism about the establishments, institutions and the humans who flourish within them.

The young Cornwell, at school during the Second World War, called it 'like living in occupied territory'. He started early to rebel, inside his own head: he decided he liked the Germans, 'since everyone hated them so much'. An ex-boarder from a Jesuit prep school talks of developing a sympathy for Russians and Communists, because of endless sermons by the cane-happy priests. Several people talk of simply *not* praying in the school chapel when told to do so by the headmaster, who in the smaller schools usually doubled as chaplain. 'I would kneel down, close my eyes, and sing Beatles songs to myself,' one told me.

Most private rebellions involved a breaking of the rules. Other children lied. The code against lying was perhaps the most strictly applied after the law of not telling tales to outsiders. Several writers have remarked on how odd this was, in retrospect. The seven-year-old Evelyn Waugh's first headmaster was the wonderfully named and preposterous Granville Grenfell: he beat the little boys at a Hampstead prep school 'only for outrageous behaviour: lying and cheating were considered by him and all of us the extremity of wickedness'.

'Laziness, lying, deceit, breaking bounds [running

away], cribbing [cheating], were seen by Arnold and
the headmasters who followed him as *grave sins*,' says
Gathorne-Hardy. In 1832 Arnold beat a boy for lying –
and then apologised to him humbly in front of the whole
school when he found out the child was innocent. In other
schools, lying and stealing was punished with the birch
– which left significant wounds – while ordinary crimes
got the bamboo cane. No one disagreed with that. 'It was
a treat,' said one contemporary writer of Edward Benson,
head of Wellington School, 'to see the zealous satisfaction
with which he chastised a boy caught out in a lie.' After
his schoolmastering career, Benson, a favourite of Queen
Victoria and Prince Albert, became, in 1883, Archbishop
of Canterbury.

Lying and its corrosive, addictive effects are a plot device
in many of the most popular boarding school fictions.
Talbot Baines Reed's *The Fifth Form at St Dominic's*, seri-
alised in the *Boy's Own Paper* 1881–2, remained in print
for most of the next hundred years. Like most from the
time, it is a crude morality tale, yet with enough sporting
heroics for successive generations of boys well beyond its
target audience to enjoy it. The anti-hero is an unpopular
boy, Edward Loman, and the beginning of all that goes
wrong for him is a single lie about the borrowing of a fishing rod. 'He had suddenly made up his mind to tell one
lie, but here they were following one after another, as if
he had told nothing but lies all his life! Alas, there was no
drawing back either!' Next for Loman comes, inexorably, a
succession of greater crimes: billiards playing, gambling,
drinking, debt and theft leading to expulsion and exile to
Australia. The young Jane Eyre is humiliated when her
cruel headmaster stands her on a stool and forbids the rest
of the school to speak to her because her aunt has said she

is a liar. But we know the true liars are the headmaster and the aunt.

Even today, 'lying' is an offence that is taken bizarrely seriously in the schools. The mother of a child newly started in 2014 at one of the grandest public schools told me of his various troubles settling in, and her worries. Early on the school had telephoned to say the boy was in the sanatorium with mild concussion; when she turned up to see him, he told an unlikely story of having fallen down and hit his head on a piece of wood. A few days later his housemaster rang to say that he'd got to the bottom of the story. Her son had actually been punched in the head by another boy, and had made up the piece of wood in order not to get his attacker into trouble. Both were to be punished severely and equally, the housemaster ruled – her son for the lie.

Lying of course comes as easily to children as it does to adults. Clinical studies show that lying is almost universal among children, depending on the circumstances and inducements. Punishments or moralistic warnings – like rehearsing the story of George Washington and the cherry tree – have an effect, but it is only temporary. Modern child development theory asks parents to tolerate and understand lying as a necessary part of the process of building an imagination. It is hypocritical for adults to punish lying harshly, or blindly, given how much of it they do themselves – and, say some, the realisation of adult hypocrisy, though it must come sooner or later, is more likely to make discipline difficult.

But in an attempt to build a self-sustaining team, or a cult – which by the late nineteenth century was the clear and stated purpose of the schools – lying needed to be stamped out. Reliable truth-telling was necessary to the smooth running of the machine, to the fabric of what was inevitably a shaky disciplinary edifice. So the mild and universal sin had to have exaggerated consequences. Lying consigned you to hell, or at least to the headmaster's beating list. Naturally, the lying child could only react with exaggerated resentment when they found out – as they inevitably did – that adults lie too.

# 14. Conforming and rebelling

Other unnatural pressures come to bear on the children, and while they may warp a normal development, they do appear to work to produce the child the schools wanted. The need to conform is the greatest pressure at any school. Even if the schools do not actively work to suppress individuality, as some certainly did, the children will do the job for themselves. All parents of school-age children know of the pressure to wear the right clothes, the basic fear of not fitting in. These worries are compounded when a child has no home life for balance.

A mother told me that she had had to drive to her eight-year-old's boarding school a week after the beginning of his first term with a replacement tuck box (the lockable wooden chest that children brought to contain toys and other personal belongings). He had telephoned, weeping, to say that the tuck box he'd arrived with was 'too posh' – it had leather reinforcements at the corners.

The story was told as comedy, but she clearly wanted me to understand just how sensitive she was to his needs. When she arrived at the school, the headmaster's wife took delivery of the new box. But she rejected the mother's request to spend a moment saying hello to the child: 'not helpful'. Evelyn Waugh tells how he had to write to ask his father to send fewer letters. He loved them, but when the post was handed out in public, the quantity young Waugh received was causing comment.

Many boarders have stories of teddy bears: a memento of happy bedtimes but a dangerous object in a world where sentimentality was suspect. The teddy bears usually ended unhappily, ridiculed, taken hostage, ritually destroyed. The chef Antony Worrall Thompson says that he was first sent to board at a nursery school when he was three. At eight, at a prep school, he watched what can only be called a teddy-bear massacre. 'Once confidence was built, the boys started to turn on their teddies. Arms went missing, ears were cut off, there were bears blocking the loo and one was even ceremoniously burned.' Fred, his bear, missed all this, luckily – 'He would have been very disturbed.'

While physical frailty or incompetence at games might be a dangerous difference, homesickness was so universal that it wasn't usually a cause for exclusion, though it wouldn't do to cry more than a little. But the problem is talked of a lot, in memoirs and by the psychotherapists of boarding school 'survivors'. Joy Schaverien writes with anger at the belittling of what is really, she says, a bereavement: 'The term homesickness doesn't do justice to the depth of the losses to which the boarding school child is subjected . . .'

Homesickness was once considered an infectious disease that could kill. So dangerous to army morale was 'nostalgia' – coined by a Swiss physician from the Greek words for home and for pain – that eighteenth-century generals would discharge or even execute soldiers suffering it before they could infect their comrades. But schools generally seem to have been tolerant of a degree of homesickness – because, like seasickness, it seemed to strike with no regard for how weak or strong its sufferer was. Colin Luke's BBC film contains an interesting session where a kindly female staff member schools the new arrivals in dealing with homesickness. 'It's normal,' she says, 'and you'll get over it.' Kindly meant, but the lesson learned is that the problem and the loss that caused it should be ignored or hidden away. Accepting the emotion, hiding it and developing a mask that protects.

The need to fit sounds relatively undemanding, a normal part of a child's socialisation. But forcing a child to do it at high speed, without any love and little support, was for some the most devastating assault on the sense of self they had to deal with. Bella Bathurst went to board at eleven, because her parents were working in America. She felt from the start she was in the wrong place. She had failed the entrance exam for a better school and strings had to be pulled to get her into this one. She felt stupid and unwanted. 'I was as bad at being young as I was at everything else: unattractive, lumpish, unfunny, neither interesting nor likeable. I was shy, paralytically so. I blushed when anyone spoke to me. The headmistress called me, accurately, "a troglodyte".'

She quickly started to hurt herself. 'I would beat myself with a strap,' she says, 'and soon after that more awful things. Rubbing bleach into cuts was one.' Self-harm in adolescence today is said to be a matter of asserting control or distracting from emotional pain. But Bathurst sees her act as more complex: 'I was punishing myself for not being like everyone else, or not what I was supposed to be. No amount of pummelling or squeezing was going to get me into the box the schools and my parents demanded, so I took on the job for myself. I had been beaten at home for bad school reports, so I thought perhaps it would work.'

The school, naturally, dismissed this as 'attention-seeking'.

Other troubles that needed kindness and understanding might be marked and punished as a failure to conform, by children or teachers. Many correspondents write of the curse of differences or disabilities as mild as a birthmark, a stammer, or dyslexia. Even a regional accent might expose a child to bullying or exclusion. At my prep school the two most-avoided children were one who had a German surname (whose plight figured in my seven-page novel, though I excused the headmaster on the grounds that Nazis had bombed his wife) and another who had a congenital illness which meant he could not always control his bladder. Millham and Lambert quote several children whose worst memories as new arrivals were being singled out by older children for flaws – 'Don't his ears stick out, hasn't he got a funny nose?'

Of course, teasing happens in most communities. But it's hard not to conclude that the revulsion for anything weird or alien was more intense in the closed arena of the boarding school. The snobbery was acute enough for many to remember it: the delineations of caste and wealth so fine that an odd emphasis, a word used wrongly, a parental faux pas like owning the wrong sort of car, could cause a child to be marked as an outsider, for a term or for life. It seems inescapable that the children who learnt these collective habits took them on to use in later life – the finely tuned sense that enables the British to collect themselves in their tribes and classes and exclude those not like them. Simple social snobbery was clearly encouraged at many schools, with headmasters singling out the children of the wealthier and titled parents for special treatment and mocking those who were humbler. At some prep schools, children gathered in gangs according to which London gentlemen's club – themselves ranked by prestige and exclusivity – their father belonged.

Tales of the savagery of schoolchildren's snobbery are rife: there's hardly an account of boarding school life that doesn't include some. Even the upright heroines of Enid Blyton's *Malory Towers* series may join the mockery of a child's common accent or her parents' inferior taste. Snobbery, for child and teacher, was integral to the prep education, believed Orwell. He arrived at Eton 'an odious little snob', as he later put it.

> Looking back, it is astonishing how intimately, intelligently snobbish we all were, how knowledgeable about names and addresses, how swift to detect small differences in accents and manners and the cut of clothes . . .
> 'How much a year has your pater got? What part of London do you live in? Is that Knightsbridge or Kensington? How many bathrooms has your house got? How many servants do your people keep? Have you got a butler? Well, then, have you got a cook? Where do you get your clothes made? How many shows did you go to in the hols? How much money did you bring back with you?' etc. etc.
> I have seen a little new boy, hardly older than eight, desperately lying his way through such a catechism:
> 'Have your people got a car?'
> 'Yes.'
> 'What sort of car?'
> 'Daimler.'
> 'How many horse-power?'
> (Pause, and leap in the dark.) 'Fifteen.'
> 'What kind of lights?'
> The little boy is bewildered.

'What kind of lights? Electric or acetylene?'

(A longer pause, and another leap in the dark.)
'Acetylene.'

'Coo! He says his pater's car's got acetylene lamps.
They went out years ago. It must be as old as the hills.'

'Rot! He's making it up. He hasn't got a car. He's just
a navvy. Your pater's a navvy.'

And so on.

Parents could hardly object to this: it was to iron out
social wrinkles that many of the children were at that
sort of school in the first place. If a drilling in conformity
was what parents paid for, the schools would accomplish
the job, by one means or another. Getting the children to
stamp out deviance from the current middle-class norms
was economically practical, as was getting them to be in
charge of discipline. For many parents, the point of the
schools was class advantage. As one early critic put it:
'Parents themselves could gain social prestige through the
attendance of their sons at famous schools; the sons of *par-
venus* could procure a substitute pedigree . . . There are
rewards, in terms of status, of public school attendance.'

Little has changed. Perceived social advantage will
overwhelm other instincts. In Edinburgh I met a woman
who was removing her fifteen-year-old daughter, happy
and working well at a state school, and sending her to do
A levels at Fettes College, 'so she meets useful people'. I
asked what she meant and she answered impatiently: 'You
know what I mean. The *right* people.'

Children who boarded could be as cruel as the worst of
the adults. They could of course be better than them, too:
extraordinarily kind and empathetic. Many of my correspondents tell stories to illustrate how pupils would step

in to do the pastoral work that the staff could or would not attempt: for them this epitomises the existential perversity of the schools.

One of Joy Schaverien's most harrowing case studies is of a patient she calls 'Theo'. A moment he considers the worst came as he lay in the dormitory listening to the boy in the next bed fighting for breath at the height of an asthma attack. Theo and the other children wanted to go to his aid but they could not, so frightened were they of the rules that forbade getting out of bed once the dormitory lights were off. To be prevented from doing what was clearly right was for Theo 'overwhelming', a soul-shaking injustice, and a moment where he lost hope. Orwell wrote of the earth-shattering effect of the realisation – snivelling on a chair as he waited to be beaten once again for the sin of wetting his bed – 'that I was in a world where it was *not possible* for me to be good'. This, he said, 'was the great, abiding lesson of my boyhood'.

Some children accepted the regime, the rules, the rituals and the humiliations: they made the best of them, grew healthily and, by their own accounts, happily. They had learnt the most important lesson: feelings got you into trouble and were best kept hidden. They went on to secondary schools well prepared for more of the same, with the strains and thrills of adolescence to weather. (By the 1960s, 50 per cent of public school boys, and slightly fewer girls, had already boarded.) Supporters and critics of the system will never agree over whether the happiness was genuine or merely a necessary adaptation without which the child would not cope. The two might turn out to be the same, in effect.

Some did break the code of silence and saw their parents

act. It wasn't impossible. Randolph Churchill, Winston's son, told his sister that a master had taken him to his room at Sandroyd School in Wiltshire and asked the boy to 'manipulate his organ'. A nanny overheard the conversation and informed Churchill. He drove straight to the school. 'I don't think I had ever seen him so angry before or since,' said Randolph. The teacher had already been dismissed.

More often, such 'sneaking' was unthinkable. Quite apart from the humiliation of admitting one had failed to be happy, there was a more awful problem: the prospect of not being believed. One of Vyvyen Brendon's interviewees tells how his headmistress tore up a letter to his parents in which he complained of homesickness. It would be 'kinder and braver' not to send it, she informed him. The boy never did tell his parents how much he disliked the school, or how much he was beaten: 'After all, he thought, if he did tell them and they failed to remove him, how would he know they still loved him?'

I know now that I did tell my mother about the maths teacher who liked to rummage inside our shorts, offering us sweets in return for our silence. But, bizarrely, telling her is a memory that I appear to have deleted. It wasn't until 2013 and the newspaper reports of criminal investigation of abuse allegations at Ashdown House that she reminded me. She said that I had told her Mr Keane was touching me 'in a way I didn't like' and that she had driven to the school to protest. Violet Williamson, the headmaster's wife, had met her, and talked her down. Making a formal complaint would cause unpleasantness, and besides, children made these things up. My mother feels now that she was bullied into silence. (It's clear, from what I now know of others' experiences at the school, that Mrs Williamson must have been well practised in handling such difficult interviews.)

Mr Keane left the school at the end of the summer term. I don't know if my mother's intervention brought about his departure.

Hearing this story many decades later was a revelation. It explained why the headmaster seemed fixated on the idea that I was a 'filthy-minded liar' – an accusation that came up many times. 'Spoof', he called me, for the rest of my time there. But it also contradicted my belief that I had never broken silence to my parents – a narrative I had carried with me through my life. I was left wondering if I had erased the memory of my confession to my mother not because it didn't fit the bigger story of a culture of *omertà* but because of the hurt I might have felt at my parents' apparent failure to act.

There were risks, complex and far-reaching, in speaking up. Michael Bell, one of my correspondents, wrote as he looked back on the breakdown of his marriage:

> My parents didn't want to admit that they had made a mistake in sending me to that school: when I tried to tell them that I was unhappy and a particular master was picking on me, they told me that I was mistaken. So I cancelled out my natural response and tried to see things their way. The result was that I couldn't FEEL for the events of my life, I seemed to be watching myself as a third party, it was a kind of 'made autism' . . .
>
> Now, in the misery of my marriage, this memory came back to me. I saw that this was only the tip of the iceberg, I had been unhappy in many ways at Bootham. I struggled to put my muddled thoughts into words to my parents, but they hindered me, tried to guide my thoughts into other directions, put other words into my mouth: they didn't want to hear that I was unhappy at

school and they should face the difficult decision to take
me away.

And now I understood! My parents had *taught* me *not*
to understand the situation I was in, and not to respond
to it, whatever I thought; it would make no difference.
They put me under great pressure to go along with it
and live that lie. That was what was wrong with me: my
inability to respond to my situation and do anything
about it.

The cult of *omertà* is so powerful that it can force its
adherents to turn the negative into positive – the 'making
of them'. In an ultimate act of normalisation they may
decide that, just to prove how good for them being sent
away from home at eight was, they will do the same to
their own children. I know several men who have done
this, sending their children to the very same school that
was the scene of their miseries – an act either of bravery or
of extreme insensitivity, you think. I do not, though, know
of any ex-boarder mothers that have done the same.

The codes have a power that seems to survive decades
after children have left school. Loyalty to the school and
memory is prized way beyond the reasonable; those who
deny may still be punished for treachery, decades on. When
a celebrity ex-boarder speaks out, as often happens, about
their unhappy schooldays, it is usual for fellow pupils to
follow up with protestations that the account is a sham.
There's often an implication that the complainer's own
weakness was to blame, not the school: they couldn't hack
it. These are all the more sharp if the celebrity is someone
like George Orwell, who is already viewed as a traitor to
the school and indeed the class. More recently, the poet
Andrew Motion and Earl Spencer, Princess Diana's brother,

came under fire after they recalled their unhappy experiences at Maidwell Hall (one of documentary-maker Colin Luke's subject schools, thirty years later). The *Daily Mail* published an article by another ex-Maidwell Hall pupil who described jolly gatherings of old boys, all of whom were able to 'shrug off the slipperings and cold dips, and look back fondly on the adventure we all had there when we were little'. This defensiveness might look attractive – loyal. But it has permitted some brutal and incompetent schoolmasters in the twentieth century to dodge regulation and inspection and collude in the failure to bring criminals and sexual predators to account.

When they are thirteen, the boys and girls take exams and move on to a public school. Even if the entrance exam results were not very good, there would be a school somewhere that would give them a place in return for a sum around, by the end of the twentieth century, the average Briton's annual income. They had learnt some things about life and more about survival inside institutions, though not all of it was on the official curriculum. As one of my correspondents said, 'There's not much I learnt at prep school that didn't come in useful. Though eleven really was too young to know how to give a man a blow-job.'

Perhaps most significant for those who would go on to take positions of power, the schooling had forced the development of two selves – private and true, the real self; and the public, constructed self – the split personae to which psychologists of childhood trauma refer. One self was to harbour personal feelings, one to present to the world and its threats. Evelyn Waugh put it tellingly in the introduction to his boyhood memoir, explaining that his stories would be split between home and school. This was not merely for structural convenience: they were places that had to be separated. 'School . . . was for the following eight years a different world, sometimes agreeable, more often not, inhabited by a different and rather nastier boy who had no share in the real life of the third of the year he spent at home.'

Gathorne-Hardy, quoting research on children brought up communally in the Israeli *kibbutzim* of the 1960s, reckons the prep schools had done something similar, in terms of redirecting a child's urge to bond: 'Separated from their families, children become dependent on each other; a good deal of the love or loyalty they would feel for their fathers and mothers attaches itself to the peer group.' Intentional or not, there could be no better way of forming a self-supporting cadre to go and run a society, or an empire.

The notion that this process might leave scars, or warp the psyche, has been around for a long time. In 1888 the young Rudyard Kipling published 'Baa, Baa Black Sheep', a dark short story which can be seen as a warning to the parents of the British Raj who were in the habit of dispatching children home so they would avoid the killer diseases of the tropics and gain a proper education. It is taken directly from the author's own experience – sent to England and unkind foster parents aged six, hardly seeing his parents for the next five years. When Punch, the little boy of Kipling's story, is reunited with his mother aged eleven, he is delighted and tells his little sister, 'It's all different now, and we are just as much Mother's as if she had never gone.' But the narrator retorts:

Not altogether, O Punch, for when young lips have drunk deep of the bitter waters of Hate, Suspicion, and Despair, all the Love in the world will not wholly take away that knowledge; though it may turn darkened eyes for a while to the light, and teach Faith where no Faith was.

'Boarding school is not right for all children,' say the defenders of the system today. They imply the misfits can be filtered, but that is rarely the case. Once in, it is hard to get out. Those for whom early separation is wrong are not often heard, even in the extremes of grief. They may not, as we've seen, say anything. Here, another graduate of Maidwell Hall sums up the effects of five years of violence, humiliation and anxiety in the late 1960s and early 1970s:

> When I left to go to Harrow I was a complete wreck, although I didn't know it. I was unable to tell anyone when I had a problem. I had an eating disorder. I had panic attacks and I was a bully. I had no knowledge of kindness. It did not exist for me as a reality. I had been systematically and forcefully reduced to brute rage and any chance of a career or relationships or friendships had been completely destroyed. I was so angry with the world that I was uncontrollable. Predictably I had zero respect for anyone in authority and was thrown out of Harrow within two years.

I left Ashdown to go to Eton in July 1974, aged thirteen. My last letter from the school to my parents is not angry but triumphant:

> This time next week I'll no longer be a prep school boy! I'll be a finished product, canned and labelled, but still needing a little processing! See you on Friday – only 120 more hours!

# PART THREE

# Growing up at Public School

# 15. The system enthroned

Wellington taught me no learning, brought me no fame
... But Wellington taught me to smile while I was being
thrashed, though the blood surged like hammer strokes
through my temples; to eat whatever was chucked at me
or go without, to admire without envy Athletes, Caps,
the XI, and even, in a milder way, Prize-winners and
Prefects.

General Sir Ian Hamilton, poet, novelist and commander
of the Mediterranean Expeditionary Force in the disastrous
Gallipoli campaign of 1915

By the early twentieth century the public schools were
part of the furniture of imperial Britain. Even though few
of them were more than fifty or sixty years old, their place
in the nation, its systems and its beliefs, was as established
as the Church of England. It was unthinkable that the elite
or the aspirational middle class might contemplate any
other form of education. The nineteenth century's greatest
prime minister, the Liberal William Gladstone, who had
been at Eton in the 1820s, said in 1890 that 'the public
school system is the greatest thing in England, not even
excepting the House of Lords'. To remove it 'would be like
knocking a front tooth out of our English social life'.

Core to Gladstone's view, shared by almost the whole of
the ruling and middle class, was a conviction that schools

were crucial to the smooth running of the country and the Empire. Eton and the schools upon whose playing fields Waterloo was won – as the Duke of Wellington was supposed to have said* – were now 'mints for the coining of empire builders':† production lines for turning out a standardised Army officer or businessman, administrator or diplomat. More and more women were produced by schools very similar in ethos to the men's, though women's role in society, at least until the First World War, was primarily to support their men and bear children. But all the old boys and girls were stamped deep with concepts of duty and loyalty: a class of clones for the Empire. It all sounds rather un-British.

While a question mark hangs over the degree of conscious organisation that brought the schools to this point, there's no doubting the impact of their systems. The schools had taken much credit for the rise of the British Empire, so it was not hard to construct a mythology of their efficiency. That belief became self-fulfilling. How else would you organise an empire larger than the world had ever seen, with just a handful of prefects to rule 420 million people? A cadre of self-confident, reliable functionaries was crucial.

* The Duke of Wellington (who went on to become prime minister) had attended Eton in the 1780s and sent his sons there. The remark became the greatest advertising slogan in the history of education. But it appears Wellington, watching Etonians playing cricket, said no more than 'There grows the stuff that won Waterloo', a remark one contemporary interpreted as a reference to 'the manly character induced by games and sport'. In his 1856 book on English society, French historian Count Charles de Montalembert improved the Duke's line as *'C'est ici qu' a été gagné la bataille de Waterloo'* – 'It is here that the Battle of Waterloo was won.'
† Edward C. Mack, American historian writing in 1938. He was being ironic.

By 1919 the Colonial Office had stopped advertising for administrators for the imperial possessions: it recruited purely by interviewing candidates suggested by public school masters and tutors at Oxford and Cambridge.

From Canada to South Africa, India and Australia, the idea of the English public school spread, and copycat establishments were built to turn the children of economic migrants and transported convicts into gentlemen and rulers. The magic potion that the schools applied for producing the biddable crew of the ship Britannia can hardly be called education. Most of them were, by the end of the nineteenth century, determinedly anti-intellectual, for reasons chiefly of snobbery – gentlemen should not be taught the skills of tradesmen. Though there were critics of the ethos – not least the great poet of the Empire, Rudyard Kipling – they made little headway. It was generally agreed that the schools' function was to inculcate in pupils the moral codes of nineteenth-century English Christianity, 'manliness', 'decency', and the disciplines of team sport. 'Character', in a word. Knowledge, particularly of a practical nature, was low on the list of priorities.

The construction of a coherent tribe was the true business of the schools; a self-perpetuating, hierarchical system where the means of advancement were bound up with obedience, respect for tradition and one's seniors, and adherence to a collective morality. The historian of empire Kathryn Tidrick sees this as coming directly from the reforms and the writings of the greatest public school master of them all, Arnold of Rugby, who was driven by fear of revolution and the underclass. He introduced a politics of morality as the guiding light of the ruling class: 'Through him the notion of the responsible use of power by a divinely ordained ruling class was introduced directly into the educational system, and boys were exposed systematically and en masse to an idea which only a few of them could have been counted on to pick up informally at home.'

The job was done not by governmental edict or even any particular policy, but by the schools themselves, with the agreement of the class that patronised them. During the whole period of the public school system's emergence, the state stepped in only once – with the Public Schools Act of 1868. This was prompted by the findings of two governmental commissions of inquiry into the 'ancient nine' public schools;* the first was the Clarendon Commission in 1861 (a second in 1868, when the remit included some 780 grammar schools, led to a further act in 1870). They looked at finances – the schoolmasters had for centuries outrageously abused the endowment funds – and at the narrowness of the curriculum. They noted flaws: the excessive number of deaths among pupils, for a start. But more troubling was the fact that children were largely taught classics, and no natural science – physics, chemistry and biology – whatsoever. They questioned Oxford undergraduates who had attended the nine great schools and found they knew very little of geography, history or science, and had 'great deficiencies' even in reading and spelling in English. Education in science was worse than it had been three hundred years earlier, it was said. The schoolmasters were not troubled by these findings. Asked by the Clarendon Commission in 1861 to assess the relative value of learning classical languages, mathematics and modern languages, Charles Goodford of Eton responded,

* Seven boarding schools (Eton, Charterhouse, Harrow, Rugby, Shrewsbury, Westminster and Winchester), and two day schools (St Paul's and Merchant Taylors').

unapologetic, with a formula: '15:13:1'. Science he had no time for at all.

After three years of debate, the 1868 Act that emerged from the commission's report was a gentle thing. The recommendations took the form of a wish list: children should learn classics, mathematics, a modern language, two natural sciences, history, geography, drawing, and music. Religious freedom was suggested, too. But it also insisted that in matters of discipline, hours and staffing 'the Head Master should be as far as possible unfettered'. He was: no effective system of inspection was introduced until 120 years later. Private schools are still treated separately, and more laxly, than state ones.

The schools and their friends had argued the Public Schools Bill into submission – then, as now, there were plenty of old public school boys in Parliament ready to battle for the status quo. They ensured that public schools would remain distinct from state-provided education, and subject to different rules. The Act legitimised the grand theft of ancient buildings and endowments that had been specifically set up to educate the poor, and instead kept for the rich – a process that continued in the modern era, with 'the Eton of Scotland', Fettes College, founded in 1870, a particularly outrageous example.* The legislation left it possible for private individuals to open boarding schools with no regulation or oversight other than that imposed by their customers.

* Sir William Fettes founded the college with a bequest of £14 million (in 2017 money) for the 'maintenance, education and outfit' of orphans and to help people 'who from innocent misfortune during their lives, are unable to give suitable education to their children'. In 2012 only 5 of 750 children enrolled were paying no fees. The school has been severely criticised by the Scottish Charity Regulator.

The only significant changes that emerged from the official inquiries were in the administration of the nine ancient public schools: governors, annual accounts and so on now became the norm. Regularising those aspects boosted consumer confidence: it fuelled the growing boom in the founding of new private schools aping the style and ethos of the 'great' ancient ones – complete with 'bogus traditions and faked-up slang', as A. N. Wilson, a more acid historian of the Victorian age, puts it. In the forty years after the Clarendon Commission's report, the number of recognised public schools went from 9 to 104, or more. By the 1970s there were 200 and today there are 282.*

* 'Public schools' define themselves by their membership of the Headmasters' and Headmistresses' Conference, a self-selecting club of 'leading' private secondary schools (including fifty more overseas). HMC members boasted 86,000 pupils in 1964, and 215,000 in 2015.

# 16. Modernising

The reforms of the 1860s set up an educational apartheid that still exists in Britain today. But they also laid the foundations of what would ultimately be universal education, and, for the first time, protested the terrible state of girls' education. The Clarendon Commission noted that there were only fourteen girls' secondary schools in the whole country, and they had a number of flaws: 'Want of thoroughness and foundation; want of system; slovenliness and showy superficiality; inattention to rudiments; undue time given to accomplishments, and those not taught intelligently or in any scientific manner; want of organisation – these may sufficiently indicate the character of the complaints we have received,' reported the commission.

Soon a movement, a forerunner of suffragettism and feminism, began lobbying for middle-class girls to receive an education along the same lines as their brothers. It had first to win the middle class over to the idea that women should be educated with any equality at all. As late as 1843 the educationalist Mrs Williams Ellis could pronounce: 'The first thing of importance is to be content to be inferior to men – inferior in mental power in the same proportion that you are inferior in bodily strength.' 'Education can be overdone,' wrote Queen Victoria in a letter of advice to her eldest daughter. Those that believed in some education for their daughters paid governesses to work in the home

– there were about 50,000 of them in the mid-century, with Charlotte Brontë, appallingly ill-paid, among them.

Boarding for girls boomed in the twentieth century. In 1910 there were 15 girls' public schools, educating 5,000. In 1944, 10,500 girls boarded at girls' public schools, and another 4,000 at secondary state-supported schools– a fifth of the boy boarder population of 29,000 and 9,000. By the late 1960s, the peak of the boarding school era, there were 140 recognised girls' public schools, more than there were for boys. Almost 50,000 girls were boarding at all types of secondary school, 45 per cent of the boys' total.

The recognised girls' public schools were usually smaller, and catered for more day pupils than did boys' boarding schools. But in most aspects these schools merely aped the male ones, from sporting ideals to the curriculum. 'The girls' schools tended to think that merely by existing at all, they were doing something revolutionary,' writes Gathorne-Hardy. The one thing they did not copy – perhaps because they were too few – was the hierarchies of the late Victorian boys' schools, where some were consciously for the mercantile middle class, others for those with inherited wealth and longer family trees.

The boys' schools ignored their female equivalents. Cambridge University did not allow women to take degrees in the same way as men until 1948. The Headmasters' Conference, the exclusive club of self-selecting elite schools, allowed girls' schools to become members, though it didn't change its name to 'Headmasters' and Headmistresses' Conference' until 1996. With the economic shocks of the 1970s, co-education suddenly became a good thing, offering financially beleaguered schools hope of survival.

When it came to the curriculum, schools and parents largely ignored Parliament's advice to address more subjects. At Eton, ninety years after the Act, my father was spending more than 60 per cent of his school hours on Latin and Greek, and at least another 15 per cent on Christianity. The priorities of the public school masters were clear: Dr Arnold had set them down, and government had no role interfering in them, however much the Empire needed engineers and scientists. A school was in business to produce civilised gentlemen. Over the decades following the Act, many tracts were written by headteachers proffering formulas involving sport, exercise, religion and hard discipline. Hours spent learning Latin and Greek were justified precisely because the boys (and increasingly girls, too) loathed them so much: hateful tedium was good for the spirit. 'The boy who has learnt to work at Latin grammar, which he detests, has learnt an invaluable lesson in citizenship,' pronounced the headmaster of Mill Hill in 1936.

But nowhere was the formula more perfectly summed up than by the rugby-loving, long-distance-running headmaster of Loretto, Hely Hutchinson Almond. His career spanned the period from the Clarendon Commission's report to the beginning of the twentieth century, and he was evangelical in his sport-driven notion of 'Lorettonianism': physical exercise, fresh air and cold baths. He published a book of his favourite sayings from Dr Arnold, and in the *Loretto Register* he itemised in order of importance his agenda for producing a proper boy: 'First – Character. Second – Physique. Third – Intelligence. Fourth – Manners. Fifth – Information.'

The idea that the schools were sceptical of learning – or at least of the sort that required books and teachers – remained current well into the twentieth century. It was key to the criticisms levelled by ex-public school

men and women who made up the left-wing intelligent-
sia. The novelist and publisher Leonard Woolf, Virginia
Woolf's husband, had been at boarding prep school and
then St Paul's at the height of the late nineteenth century's athleticism craze. Bookish and a Jew, he had loathed
the experience. In 1960, he was still grinding the axe. He
would have found many to agree with him:

> The public school was the nursery of British philis-
> tinism. Use of the mind, intellectual curiosity, mental
> originality, interest in 'work', enjoyment of books or
> anything connected with the arts, all such things, if de-
> tected, were violently condemned and persecuted. . . .
> this attitude was not confined to the boys; it was shared
> and encouraged by nearly all the masters. The intellec-
> tual was, as he still is today, disliked and despised.

It's odd that Woolf, as well-read and connected as anyone,
still entertained the idea that the British public school was
for  education. After all, early in *Tom Brown's School Days*,
Squire Brown explained what a parent was after: 'I don't
care a straw for Greek particles or the Digamma – nor does
his mother. What is he sent to school for? Well, partly
because he wanted so to go. If he'll only turn out a brave,
helpful, truth-telling Englishman, and a gentleman, and
a Christian, that's all I want.' The former Rugby schoolmaster Rev. T. L. Papillon wrote a complacent essay on the
schools and citizenship, fifty years later: 'Intellectual interests, we have been assured on competent authority, are of
no account at the most famous of English Public Schools,
which educates a large proportion of our "governing classes".' The schools, to sum Papillon up, provide a ludicrously
inadequate education, but Britain's imperial success shows

that doesn't matter a jot. They turn out jolly useful chaps.

When I was at Eton in the mid 1970s, there was still the sort of suspicion of the 'Tugs' (scholars) that Woolf saw. They were perhaps rather common, and to be friends with one was a statement that you too were a 'swot'. When the High Master of St Paul's tried to make the unsporty George Osborne head boy in 1988, the sports-minded teachers objected so strongly he had to back down: the future Chancellor of the Exchequer was given a lesser post. Will Carling, the England rugby captain from 1988 to 1996, has said that at Sedbergh, where he was in the early 1980s, rugby ruled: 'It was surreal. Everything was still designed to magnify the status of those who eventually represented the first XV.'

A key job of the public schools had always been to deal with the 'rich and thick', as Samuel Beckett, briefly a public school master, put it.* In the late twentieth century, though, the reign of the Bloods came to an end. The dimmest pupils began to be excluded as the more successful schools became far more selective, conscious that published league tables of academic achievements had a direct effect on enrolment. Charles Moore, former editor of the *Daily Telegraph*, wrote that when he was at Eton in the early 1970s it was still full of the unambitious sons of the 'landed gentry': 'Some read only the *Sporting Life*, and that with difficulty.' He concedes that that has changed. Nowadays, to get a child into Eton you need more money – fees are three times what they used to be, in real terms. But the

---

* When he quit his hated post-university job at Campbell College in Northern Ireland, the headmaster protested, 'But, Mr Beckett, don't you realise you're teaching the cream of Ulster?' Beckett replied: 'Yes, rich and thick.'

twelve- or thirteen-year-old boy must be an above average academic performer to get in.

Lord Clarendon's report, published in 1864, contains the first mention of another, more existential problem, one that would drive the schools' twentieth-century critics: the system was inherently unhealthy, self-perpetuating, inward-looking and, as one conservative historian says, 'too incestuous'. Tradition and self-belief hindered reform or even natural development in tune with the changing world. 'It must be disadvantageous . . . [for] any school to be officered exclusively by men brought up within its walls all imbued with its peculiar prejudices and opinions, and without any experience but its own,' Clarendon concluded. When it came to tolerating criminal abuse by the teaching staff, this concern was to prove particularly apt, as the class that used the schools knew all too well. But in part the success of the schools was due to their utter conviction that the work they were doing was exceptional – the same self-confidence that underpinned the Empire.

The government was not to look again at the public schools in the context of wider education and British society until 1942. Then a Board of Education committee – chaired by a Scottish judge, Lord Fleming, and including the headmistress of Roedean and a future headmaster of Eton – put together a radical proposal for the integration of public and state-aided boarding schools, so that all might benefit from the undoubted advantages of boarding. In support, Fleming quotes amazing statistics for the successful entrants to the civil service, the Navy and the diplomatic service in the 1930s and 1940s – all dominated by boarding schools.

Those who objected to the plan often cited the misery

'a poor boy' would suffer if put into public school. One headmaster wrote: 'I cannot see anything but acute unhappiness arising from the well-meaning desire to throw open the Public Schools to all classes. It would entail a complete change of living and habit, and would engender mischievous thought in the victims, to say nothing of the effects on their families. Imagine the Stepney boy during vacation.' The Fleming committee's recommendations were not implemented.

When in the 1960s a Labour government tried to address the disparities, it hit the buffers — literally: an unmoving, conservative, public-school-educated establishment, quite a few of whom were Labour MPs. This despite the findings of the Public Schools Commission under Lord Newsom, published in the 1968 Newsom Report on the future of education. Newsom made the same criticism Clarendon had a century earlier about the self-regarding nature of the schools: 'Seventy per cent of masters at Head Master's Conference schools with boarding pupils had themselves been educated at H.M.C. schools, and not more than one master in five in H.M.C. independent boarding schools had taught in secondary schools, other than H.M.C. They stick in the public schools, as pupil and master, just as the masters in the maintained system stick in those schools; and neither system learns from the other.'

The watered-down reforms of the 1960s left the public schools untouched, while the abolition of pupil selection had the effect of forcing over a hundred ancient state grammar schools to refuse to become 'comprehensives'. Instead, they became fee-paying and private — 'public' schools, in other words. Meanwhile many of the schools took on charitable status, giving them enormous tax advantages — an anachronism that Labour politicians have promised to end, unsuccessfully, since the 1970s. The schools, over the two centuries of their current form, have proven themselves just about immune to politics.

# 17. Sport and God

Life is simply a cricket match, with Temptation as the bowler.

*Baxter's Second Innings* (1892), a bestselling boys' novel by the
Reverend Henry Drummond

'Duty', 'honour', 'chivalry', 'discipline' and 'sportsmanship': these words rang from the pulpits of the public school headteachers, male and female. They resound in the poetry and the novels that their pupils produced. But nothing in the legacy of the schools, or their mythology, is as important in this history as sportsmanship. By the turn of the century, team sport – especially cricket and rugby – had become more than a metaphor for the values and practices a public-school-educated child should espouse. Games were a template for life.

This notion arose quite suddenly. Most of the schools had no playing fields or formally organised games until the 1860s. Yet by the 1890s sport was central to the system. Physical exercise and notions of fair play, discipline and submission of self-interest for the good of the team were what made great communities work – look, the divines in the pulpits said, at Christ and his disciples, or Nelson and his captains.

The diarist Harold Nicolson, writing in 1934 of Wellington College, thought there was more to the cult: it was

anti-learning. He went to the school in 1899, and was unhappy: 'I am certain that had I displayed with ball and bat
the same promise as I displayed in Greek iambics, I should
have been made to feel that with care and application
there was some future available to me . . . ' he complains.
He found his way: he was to become a diplomat, Labour
politician and knight. Nicolson goes on: 'Some boys derived the impression that intellectual prowess was in some
way effeminate, and that it was only by physical prowess
that one could manifest or even subscribe to that air of
"manliness" for which alone we had all, teleologically, been
sent to Berkshire.' The bitterness of the clever, unsporty
child is still keen, decades later.

Certainly the cult of sport rose to dominate most aspects
of life at the schools, not least moral matters. Hence this
in Marlborough School's termly magazine, from around
the time Nicolson was at Wellington: 'A truly chival-
rous football player . . . was never yet guilty of lying, or
deceit, or meanness, whether of word or action.' Quite ordinary sentiments for the time, and they went well with
the new spirit of 'muscular Christianity' – the robust,
manly version of Anglicanism that dominated the schools
from the end of the Victorian era until well into the mid
twentieth century. This could be farcical, as many writers happily noted. 'Three stumps, one wicket,' was how
the cricket-mad, boy-adoring headmaster E. L. Browne
explained the doctrine of the Holy Trinity. 'Christ would
have played hard for His school . . . He might have rowed
for his Varsity, if there'd been a Varsity to row for,' Arthur
Calder-Marshall was told by a senior boy at St Paul's in
the 1920s. Calder-Marshall, who became a novelist and a
Communist, tells us (in his 1934 account) that he soon
gave up religion for mutual masturbation.

Belief in the moral superiority of boy athletes went hand in hand with the interesting and peculiarly British notion that honour was more important than success, playing more important than winning. A mythology of the origins of the British Empire was enlisted to illustrate the paradox that if you didn't care too much about winning, you would probably win. Sir Francis Drake had insisted that his sailors complete a game of bowls before going out from Plymouth to take on the mightier force of the Spanish fleet, boys were told. Insouciance in the face of imminent disaster was an admirable trait, and the fact that such behaviour was incomprehensible to outsiders added to its value.

'We pride ourselves on the foreigners' inability to understand the mad Englishman who finishes his game of bowls within sight of an Armada, or who while his rivals are hurriedly raising earthworks and sinking rifle pits, levels himself a cricket ground,' wrote one headmaster in 1900. Such attitudes, he went on, have 'made England the dominant nation'. Coupled with the belief that public school sportsmen made naturally efficient Army officers, these credos were – in the view of many twentieth-century critics – part of the reason the British Army's officers in the First World War performed so badly and died in such numbers.

It's as if British public schools invented sport in order to have a model and a metaphor for the structures of life. It is true that some of today's most popular team games – rugby, football, hockey – were first formalised at the Victorian schools and universities. But what seems clear is that in the mid-nineteenth century sports were tidied up along with the rest of the ancient practices of the schools – from boys sharing beds to the masters' self-serving use of the endowment funds. Until the early 1840s, fisticuffs, or bare-knuckle boxing, was hugely popular at most schools, with bets laid on the outcome; a favourite game at Marlborough was frog-hunting, with the frogs beaten to death, the highest pile of corpses winning. At Harrow, Eton, Rugby and others there were forms of mass football, not unlike that played on feast days in some towns. In Charterhouse's version a small boy was the ball, until, on Good Friday 1824, the young son of the Earl of Suffolk was 'dragged along the ground for some distance, with a mass of boys upon him, and received injuries from which he died soon after'. By the 1890s unregulated sport was over and gambling stamped out. Rules were agreed, referees, uniforms, pitches and team colours introduced.

These reforms coincided with the rise of a moral panic – in the schools, at least – about homosexuality and masturbation. Rigorous exercise was seen as the prime solution to outbreaks of 'beastliness'. And so morality, religion, health, class consciousness and sport grew together, each thrusting the other on for the glory of the team and the nation, like the hearties of a good scrum. The cult of athleticism that arose bore little relation to athletics in the modern sense, because excellence at individual sports like jumping or running was not the point: it was about the team and the game.

This was misread by some observers. The German journalist Karl Heinz Abshagen spent a decade reporting from Britain in the 1920s and 1930s. He clearly believed the public schools were, wittingly or not, part of a highly successful eugenics programme. In his 1938 book about the British upper class, *König, Lords und Gentlemen*, he describes how the elite sequesters its children from the rest of society for ten years in order to produce a super-Briton of the sort Hitler might well approve. Organised sport and 'superior breeding' had worked in Britain, he reports, having observed 'pronounced racial differences between the upper class and the other categories of the population'. These were not just visible in the amazing submissiveness of the lower orders but also in their size, looks and speech. Only the 'landed nobility, which forms the backbone of society' were able to pronounce the initial letter h – as in house, rather than 'ouse. Even the servants of the great could rarely manage it, however hard they tried. Abshagen goes on:

> The bulk of the population are not tall but of short to medium height, and frequently, where they are sufficiently fed, thick-set. The type of tall sinewy sportsman, the slender, long-legged woman, frequently set before the German public as representative of the people of England, is in reality only to be found in considerable numbers among the upper classes.

This was laughed at when a translation was published in Britain. But one contemporary commentator said, 'It is only fair to Herr Abshagen to add that many of the products of the Public Schools attribute (such is their training) their superior physique and development . . . to "superior breeding", and on the same grounds though with less evidence, their right to privilege. In an only slightly different sense from his, they claim to be a race apart.' The elite whose production was the dream of Plato-worshipping headmasters from Dr Arnold to Gordonstoun's Kurt Hahn was not so very different from the Nazi notion of a ruling master race.

Abshagen may have had his tongue in his cheek. Perhaps he was reporting what he knew Nazi Germany wanted to read. But he is perceptive about the schools themselves, and their purpose. Boarding and team sport, he sees, drills the class in 'comradeship', far more than in a day school. 'The aim of the public schools is not primarily the imparting of knowledge, and certainly not the imparting of practical information that will be of use to them in their future careers, but their training to be members of a clique.' He explains how the middle class can buy — making 'great sacrifices' — their offspring's way into some of the schools, though not the ones of the ruling elite. But even these lesser Englishmen will learn patriotism, team spirit, their duty as leaders and indeed special ways of dressing and talking.

Sport still dominates the schools and their curricula today, to a degree that looks extraordinary to other nations. There's no traditional private school in the land that does not boast on its brochure and website about its sporting facilities and its achievements. Of course, children need exercise and many enjoy it. My own get wonderful pleasure from the tribal thrills of playing for school teams.

This was not my experience. Like many, my sporting career went wrong early: rejected as too small and timid. That hardened into a loathing of both the sports and the system that forced you to do them; a learning experience that had its own positive effects. But — sporty or nerdy, heroic scrum half or reluctant linesman with a novel in your pocket — it's hard to argue with the historian-sociologist John Wakeford's declaration that team sports were and continue to be 'the ritualistic symbolisation of the social values on which . . . the public school system rests'.

They also provide a handy way to illustrate some of the

social gaps in education. In 2014, my sports-mad daughter moved from an urban state primary where there were essentially no games for girls and only break-time kickabouts for boys, to a private primary where there were several hours of organised sports and swimming a week. By the 1990s, independent secondary school children aged eleven were twice as likely to get two hours of 'physical education' a week as their state school peers. Around the same time John Major, a cricket-loving, state-school-educated Conservative prime minister, unveiled a policy document, 'Raising the Game'. It sought to promote sport to address the moral and social problems of the urbanised modern nation – a notion entirely in tune with the late Victorian headmasters' ideas.

But in 2016 the Headmasters' Conference of 'elite' schools was still able to boast: 'Pupils in HMC schools play on average between five and six hours of sports and games a week – double the amount played by pupils in state schools.' Having good sports facilities or a reputation for winning teams continues to be an attraction for parents – hence the modern private schools' massive investment in courts and gyms. But the truth must be that sport and educational achievement are only tenuously linked, if at all: 'more sport for schoolchildren' has long been a policymaker's cure-all, an evasion of more difficult solutions.

The girls' boarding schools eagerly adopted the principle of the moral good to be had through athleticism, as they did most of the core precepts of the boys' schools. Some team sports were not thought appropriate – football and rugby were out, for girls, until recently. But the notion that sport, by making adolescents too exhausted for lower things, was a moral good in itself was just as powerful.

'Run about, girls, *like* boys, and then you won't have to think *of* them' was the ethos at Sherborne in the 1930s, according to the novelist Elizabeth Arnot Robertson. There was cricket in the summer and hockey in the winter, both compulsory. It seems to have worked: 'We were terribly, terribly keen on games. A carefully fostered and almost entirely spurious interest in house matches was our main topic of conversation.' She and several other women note that a sport was used as a metaphor for life at their boarding schools. Prefects would tell girls off for offences against the codes, saying, 'What you've done just isn't cricket', even at institutions where they didn't play the game.

# 18. 'Play the game'

The handlebar-moustached Eustace Hamilton Miles was educated at Marlborough in the 1870s, too late to hunt frogs but at just the right moment to be a philosopher-athlete. He was world champion at real tennis six times between 1898 and 1905, winning at the age of thirty-nine a silver at the 1908 Olympics. When he retired he wrote books on subjects from Greek and Latin syntax to the 'failures of vegetarianism' and, of course, the value of sport. Cricket, he announced in *Let's Play the Game: the Anglo-Saxon Sporting Spirit* (1904), illustrated eleven 'valuable ideas' in life: 'co-operation, division of labour, specialisation, obedience to a single organiser (perhaps with a council to advise him), national character, geography and its influences, arts and artistic anatomy, physiology and hygiene, ethics, and even – if the play can be learnt rightly – general educational methods.' Imagine Wayne Rooney stepping from a boy's bedroom poster and holding forth thus.

Miles's title is a reference to the most famous poem of the era, and its ringing refrain, 'Play up, play up and play the game'. The whole nation, and the ever-swelling list of colonies, knew and subscribed to the values of Sir Henry Newbolt's *Vitaï Lampada*, published in 1892. The poem's references are firstly to cricket at Clifton College, Newbolt's own public school, a new-build consciously aping the 'great' in ethos and architecture. Then we move from the grassy pitch to the bloody desert, and the British Army's disastrous Sudan campaigns of the 1880s and 1890s, in which my great-grandfather fought as a young officer, straight from Eton. This long campaign was, by any measure, a grotesque imperial failure, with parallels to the destruction of Iraq in this century – a pointless and destructive war with a melodramatic climax, the slaughter of General Gordon and thousands of Egyptian troops at Khartoum. But the poem turns all this horror to a pageant of stiff-upper-lip heroism, and thus a triumph.

> There's a breathless hush in the Close to-night –
> Ten to make and the match to win –
> A bumping pitch and a blinding light,
> An hour to play and the last man in.
> And it's not for the sake of a ribboned coat,
> Or the selfish hope of a season's fame,
> But his captain's hand on his shoulder smote –
> 'Play up! play up! and play the game!'

> The sand of the desert is sodden red, –
> Red with the wreck of a square that broke; –
> The Gatling's jammed and the Colonel dead,
> And the regiment blind with dust and smoke.
> The river of death has brimmed his banks,
> And England's far, and Honour a name,
> But the voice of a schoolboy rallies the ranks:
> 'Play up! play up! and play the game!'

> This is the word that year by year,
> While in her place the school is set,
> Every one of her sons must hear,
> And none that hears it dare forget.

*This they all with a joyful mind*
*Bear through life like a torch in flame,*
*And falling fling to the host behind –*
*'Play up! play up! and play the game!'*

Though the sophisticated sneered at this stuff (the first mildly critical novels of public schools, and of imperial bombast, started appearing in the next decade), Newbolt was still reciting it in tours of the colonies until his death in 1938. Like Arthur Hugh Clough's 'Say not the Struggle nought Availeth', published at the dawn of the age of Victorian expansion, 'Play up and play the game' became a text that would define the simple notion that was at the root of British imperial self-belief. According to one of the most famous Harrow headmasters, Henry Montagu Butler, it was all his boys needed to know. On the eve of the First World War, he said: 'Whether it be a matter of cricket . . . or politic or professional engagements, there is hardly any motto which I could more confidently recommend than "Play the game".' It is common in twentieth-century histories to point out that it was with Newbolt's songs on their lips and exploits at cricket on their minds that the troops of the 1914–18 war marched to their slaughter. Naturally, when the war began, Newbolt, now with a knighthood, got a job organising government propaganda.

Did they really confuse trench warfare with school sports? They were certainly a popular metaphor: 'Letter after letter from the front says how glad the writers are not to have let school or house or team down . . . and these themes are echoed again in the school obituaries. To play well for your school meant to die well for your country. Indeed, the first imperative led to the second,' writes Gathorne-Hardy. One of the most famous stories of the war is of men going over the top, out of the trench and on the attack, chasing balls as they went. It happened at least twice, at Loos in 1915 and on the Somme (where a captain punted a rugby ball into No-Man's Land as the assault began) in 1916. Most of the men died, but the balls were saved – they can still be seen, mud-coloured, cracked, in dusty regimental museums.

John Horne and other sociologists of sports history fulminate against the long-surviving spirit of Victorian athleticism on the grounds that it was a Trojan horse for social repression by the upper class: '[The sports] were not conceived as some innocent pastime. They constituted a vehicle for powerful and prestigious social actors, for the transmission of preferred values and for the generation and perpetuation of a culture stressing the moral responsibilities of an elite and the manly virtues . . .'

You could argue with that, particularly over whether school sports were 'conceived' as part of a master plan for sustaining tyranny, or whether the games ethos just emerged because of the coincidence of various pressures on the schools – social, religious and economic. But there is another more pressing argument. It is that the rise of sports as an ethos for life, for ruling, for business and for human relations did far more damage than merely perpetuating the nineteenth-century elite's power. The message of the sports code was that, win or lose, it was the taking part that mattered; an attitude that has inspired both scorn and admiration ever since. It meant that Britons could not be defeated. Its corollary though – and this is clear in a score of favourite stories of British failure, from the Charge of the Light Brigade in the Crimea through to Scott's expedition and all the way to the evacuation from Dunkirk – is that the blood and tears left behind by ill-conceived team jaunts don't figure large in British history's accounting. The costs are insignificant when compared with the glory of the sacrifice and the derring-do. This is a common phenomenon in totalitarian states. But it is a unique and profoundly dangerous ethos for the ruling class of a democracy to have at its heart. Yet it still thrives.

# 19. Bloods and Bolshies

So what to do, if, like Orwell and Nicolson, you were neither keen nor skilled at sport – if you didn't buy into the 'crypto-fascist plan for repressing our sex drive' as a schoolboy character of Julian Barnes's puts it? I didn't and I never made any team, for house or school, but I was forced on to the pitches for my own good, until I was fifteen or so. Here I speak from muddy-kneed, cold, bored experience. You were not just weak and unmanly, lacking in spirit and spunk, but also – God forbid – a coward. This sense of being morally defective stayed with many of us, the unsporty. Others rejected the mania. One of those was George Orwell – who saw plainly the effect of the football cult on those who joined it, and those who did not:

> I loathed the game and since I could see no pleasure or usefulness in it, it was very difficult for me to show courage at it . . . The lovers of football are large, boisterous, knobbly boys who are good at knocking down and trampling on slightly smaller boys. That was the pattern of school life – a continuous triumph of the strong over the weak. Virtue consisted of winning . . .

The conventional view is that Orwell and many others who objected instinctively to teams, hierarchies and the pressure to conform sought intellectual and political

outlets for their hurt and anger: they remained individuals outside the cult. But as a committed games-dodger
myself at both the public schools I went to, I know that
being anti-sports was a cult of its own, a system of beliefs that were the opposite of team spirit and muscular
Christianity. When we stayed behind while the others
trotted off to muddy fields, we read and talked, listened
to music, played, plotted and schemed to cause trouble to
the system. Being anti-sport entailed embracing another
powerful philosophy; resistance to group-think, respect
for the intellect and celebration of non-conformity were
among the ideals. We were the bad-at-games club, and
the twentieth century's tradition of tolerant liberalism is
rooted in it.

While some schools flogged even the most short-sighted
and asthmatic intellectuals on to the rugby pitch, the slightly more broad-minded ones that I went to tolerated and
perhaps tacitly encouraged the rebels who stayed indoors,
and even those who went off to express themselves through
a cigarette behind the bike shed. The binary choice – rebel
or conformist – forced our world view into simple boxes,
too. 'We were book-hungry, sex-hungry, meritocratic, an-
archistic,' writes Julian Barnes of his 1960s schoolboys.
'All political and social systems appeared to us corrupt, yet
we declined to consider an alternative other than hedon-
istic chaos.' In the 1968 film *If*, made by two ex-public
school boys, the rebels' formless, existential disaffection
leads them in the finale to a happy slaughtering of the
headmaster and the prefects with a machine gun from the
chapel roof. Most people who went to public school take
the scene not as metaphor – which is how the critics saw
it – but perfectly feasible.

In fact, few of the sports weeds and prefect-rejects took

up weapons or began revolutions. Instead we became film-makers, journalists, campaigners and centre-left politicians with a sceptical view of regulation, tradition and hierarchy. The establishment accommodated us: the capacity to bend and absorb challenge is of course a reason for its success, and the British, private-school-based establishment is one of the most long-lasting and successful ever. Tolerating disaffection is the best way to disarm it. In the early 1970s, according to John Rae, then head of Westminster, a political poll of senior boys at Eton found that 85 per cent would vote for the Conservatives. The rest were undecided or Communist. Not a single one would vote Labour. Rae felt this was to be expected – and pretty healthy.

More interesting than the rebels, perhaps, are those who did conform and in one way or another enjoyed school. They were the majority, and most were not forced into conformity because they were frightened or emotionally underdeveloped. They simply liked routine, the camaraderie, the sense of a world comprehensibly ordered. For many, school, once understood, was a safe and just place: you don't need modern child psychology to tell how important those are for a child to flourish. Also, the children who had first been sent to board at eight or younger knew the life and how to make the best of it. Most of my correspondents who were unhappy at their prep school were happier at their secondary school.

Prison – the analogy used by boarding school children both happy and sad – is not so unfair. Jails and schools are 'total societies', in the sociologists' phrase: closed institutions generating structures and codes, where one fairly reliable promise is that you will get an easier ride if you don't stick out. It's no wonder that it was a cliché of public school phlegm to say of the Japanese prisoner of war camp or of Wandsworth jail, 'Oh, well, I went to public school, so it wasn't so bad.' When the ex-Conservative MP Jonathan Aitken was about to go to prison for perjury in 1999, he told the *Daily Express*: 'As far as the physical miseries go, I am sure I will cope. I lived at Eton in the 1950s and I know all about life in uncomfortable quarters.' Stephen Fry elaborated on the uses of a boarding school education when he remembered his brief time in prison, for stealing a credit card, shortly after leaving school. (Fry boarded from the age of six, and was twice expelled.) 'I knew how to tease authority enough to be popular with the inmates and tolerated by the screws. I knew how to stay cheerful and think up diversions, scams and pranks. I knew, ironically, given my inability to do so in real boarding schools, how to survive.'

Some socio-anthropologists compare concentration camp or mental hospital systems – particularly the way different groups of inmates tolerate or normalise the regime in order to survive – with that of the boarding school. Equally, there is a school of Freudian post-imperial historians who'll tell you that the sexual and emotional repression of a public school education was a key driver of the imperial instinct; the psychic motor that propelled young ex-public school men (though not the women) to fight, conquer and rule in the warm, erotic East. Horny and confused, but loyal to their class and certain of their right to be prefects, the Flashmans knocked out by the British public schools went off to rule the world. The lesson is that, planned or not, the sausage mill worked rather well.

# 20. Class, race and fitting in

The phrase 'public school sausage mill' dates from the 1930s, if not earlier, picturing a stream of identical boys, their oddities and differences forced out of them with mechanical efficiency. There's truth and untruth there, but more significant than the outward appearance of the product is the idea of conformity to social codes and credos being stamped in by the schools. Race, class and religion are the most obvious of these – and often, in instilling conformity around those, the schools did not succeed.

The most obvious failure is with religion. The traditional schools in the twentieth century were determinedly Christian, whether Catholic or Protestant. But they did not produce a class of devout Christians. Church at school put me and many more off organised religion entirely and left very few fervent observers indeed – religious devotion, like all other enthusiasms, being in bad taste if more than mildly indulged. Noel Annan, the academic and social commentator who became a pillar of the twentieth century's liberal establishment, was at Stowe public school in the 1930s. He wrote in 1990 that the brand of Protestant Christianity taught in the schools set standards of conduct so impossibly high that 'the cult of the gentleman had to be substituted to provide a realisable ideal'. Britain's establishment is now markedly irreligious, compared with, say, that of the United States.

Race and class are more significant. For most of the twentieth century, to be non-white or Jewish at the schools would certainly attract comment and often bullying. The High Tory novelist Anthony Powell wrote, in a reminiscence of Eton in the 1920s, that his house was seen as 'bad' by the school. It had not won any sports trophies for years. Worse, it was looked down upon because 'the non-Aryan [i.e. Jewish] proportion of its membership had seemed to be unnecessarily high'.* Open references to blatant prejudice were unusual. But casual racism that would be unacceptable today was not uncommon in 'polite' society, even among leftish intellectuals like George Orwell before and after the Second World War. The clubs of the middle class, whether Masonic or golf, operated racial bars well into the late twentieth century.

Such racism was built into some schools' admissions systems. Middle-class Jewish children did go to the schools from early in the nineteenth century: the future Conservative prime minister Benjamin Disraeli's two brothers went to Winchester in the 1820s, while he boarded from around the age of eight at a smaller Anglican school. But in the twentieth century, as anti-Semitism became more common, this tolerance changed. India's first prime minister, Jawaharlal Nehru, was at Harrow between 1905 and 1907; in his memoirs he wrote: 'There was always a background of anti-Semitic feeling.' (He does not mention whether the pupils were anti-Indian, too.) Harrow and some other public schools operated a semi-secret quota system on Jewish pupils (a maximum 10 per cent

* Powell's essay goes on to say that 'happily' this was drawing to a close in his time at the school (1919–23), leaving it deliberately vague, you suppose, whether he meant the high proportion of non-Aryans was ending, or the objections to them.

at Harrow in 1945, 15 per cent at St Paul's until the late 1970s) and other non-Christians. So did some of the top American universities and medical schools.

The two boys we were cruellest to at my prep school were unacceptably different: one was foreign and the other disabled. At my first public school, Eton, we bullied a scholarship child whose parents were shopkeepers in Wales, while several boys from prominent and wealthy Jewish families suffered very little or not at all, by their account. In the 1940s, when the publisher Anthony Blond was there, the school had nine Jewish boys including him and his brother. There was 'little in the way of anti-Semitism, except of course in orthodox Christian views of the crucifixion'. Parents and children from several grand schools have told me that anti-Semitic bullying is a problem today: some say that prejudices have been imported with a wave of children from Russia. Eton and Old Etonians like to picture themselves as rather above such vulgar flaws as overt racism – 'So Harrovian!' – but the fact is that it has existed in the school as nastily as everywhere else. Dillibe Onyeama, a Nigerian who in 1965 became the first black person to attend Eton, described his experiences in a sad, thoughtful book whose sensational title caused a stir when it was published in 1972: *Nigger at Eton*.

But class was much more of an issue, then and now. The differences of material status and accent were perhaps the most savagely spotted and commented on, often – as in Orwell's story of the catechism that awaited new children on their parents' wealth and possessions – a reflection of parents' attitudes. This is all easily explained anthropologically, but it could be ludicrously irrational: I have two correspondents who tell how they were rejected on first arrival by their peers at the Scottish public school

Gordonstoun because they had Scottish accents. That was in the 1990s: in the 1960s Prince Charles was cruelly bullied there, not least because he was – incontestably – not too common but too posh. Snobbery was and is another social tool – crude, easy to deride, but crucial to maintain class solidarity. We were taught to distinguish ourselves from the normal. 'Oik' and 'pleb' are both public school coinages, coming respectively from Greek and Latin words meaning commoner.* Andrew Mitchell, the Conservative politician brought down because he allegedly called policemen guarding 10 Downing Street 'fucking plebs', was a pupil at my prep school.

Having the right accent became important a hundred years before Gordonstoun was founded. Educational historians believe that public schools in the late nineteenth century were the main agents in imposing a standard middle-class English way of speaking, and making regional accents something which might be a hindrance to someone attempting to push higher up the ladder. The co-founder of Edinburgh Academy, Henry Cockburn, said in 1844 that the Scottish accent was banished inside its doors 'even in the pronunciation of Greek and Latin', and that the children of wealthy Edinburgh would not understand the dialect verse of Robert Burns.† (In the last four or more generations, none of my Fergusson relations has had a Scottish accent, despite many of them doing time at Scottish schools or universities). Fettes started out with kilts as a school uniform, but soon abandoned them. By

---

* Oik comes from '*perioikos*', around the house, or 'those who live around us'. 'Pleb' is from the Latin '*plebs*', the common people.
† However, my great-grandfather James Renton was educated there fifty years later and spoke with a strong Edinburgh accent to the end of his life.

the mid-century novelists such as Thackeray and Dickens
were lampooning working-class accents and the attempts
to cleanse children of them. One of the reasons Mr Tulli-
ver, owner of the mill in George Eliot's *Mill on the Floss*,
gives for his decision to send young Tom away for 'eddica-
tion' is the practical value of a better voice:

> All the learnin' *my* father ever paid for was a bit o' birch
> at one end and the alphabet at th' other. But I should
> like Tom to be a bit of a scholard, so as he might be up
> to the tricks o' these fellows as talk fine and write with
> a flourish. It 'ud be a help to me wi' these lawsuits, and
> arbitrations, and things.

As the schools matured they developed their own dia-
lects. These were used in initiation tests. Learning the code
words and the school's geography was one of the jobs of
every new boy, with dire trials threatened should you fail
the exam set by the older boys. The information – such as
the colours of different sports teams' caps – was far from
important. The point, as in the learning of Greek verbs,
was the ordeal. (When I arrived at Eton my 'colours test'
was jokey, not too troubling. But these initiations caused
great grief to some newly arrived at other schools, for girls
and boys.) Acquiring your school's slang was another duty.
That had a use beyond school, as a class signifier and a
social filter. I know an Old Etonian who will still add 'er'
or 'ers' to nouns: 'Spot of lunchers, Renters?'

This usage has an ancient history, along with dropping
the final g in gerunds – huntin', shootin' and fishin' – and
the lengthening of 'off': 'I told the orficer where to get orf'.
Both the latter date from upper-class speech in the early
nineteenth century. The compilers of the 1933 Oxford

English Dictionary called the -er suffix 'the Oxford -er', because it appears to have first flourished among students there in the 1870s. Apparently, St Giles was 'St Giler' and the exam in Rudiments of Faith and Religion 'Rudder'. The -er habit spread: it gave the world words like soccer, rugger and header. At Harrow, a waste-paper basket was – apparently – a wagger-pagger-bagger. For those who like to employ them, the joy of such usages today – like the 1930s schoolboy slang of some right-wing journalists – is that they can be used both ironically and to signify shared background at the same time.

Abshagen, the German journalist of the 1930s, wrote: 'Public school English is a language apart, not only in regard to the significance of particular words and phrases but in regard to pronunciation, intonation, and degree of loudness . . . When they are talking informally to one another it is difficult even for a fellow-Englishmen of a different class to follow them.' He might well write the same today, where school jargon is still used by ex-public school boys as a handy code that excludes outsiders. I've met Old Etonians who ask 'Did you go to school?' meaning not 'Did you have an education?', but 'Did you go to Eton?'

# 21. Buying status

If the schools fostered snobbery and exclusivism, it was because parents, then and now, valued these things. The point of spending the money was to ensure that their child got ahead on the class ladder – a matter just as important as the development of their darlings' intellects or moral sensibilities. This was particularly the case with the schools founded later to service the newly rich middle class – which attracted their own snobbish deprecation from the older elite. J. F. Roxburgh, who founded Stowe in 1923, was notorious in his pursuit of titled families to furnish pupils who would then attract the middle class. Though he wanted to abolish both fagging and beating at the new school, he decided that he would have to keep them for fear of being seen as too untraditional. He once congratulated the headmaster of another new establishment, saying that his 'school list would soon resemble an extract of De-brett's', the published register of titled Britons.

Both Brighton College and Cheltenham College banned the children of tradesmen when they first set up shop in the 1840s: quite soon financial difficulties forced them to let the lower orders in. Rossall School and Malvern College removed two of their founding committee members, a hotelier and a factory owner, because, being 'in trade', they were by definition not gentlemen. This sort of attitude may have been more prevalent in the schools that had more to prove. At a grand and established place like Harrow, Dr Vaughan (headmaster from 1845–59) was able to operate without class bars. When one smart mother asked him whether he was particular about the standing of the families whose sons he let in, he responded sharply: 'Dear madam, as long as your son behaves himself and his fees are paid no questions will be asked about his social antecedents.'

But to be commercially successful the schools had to show they were a way of buying membership of an elite which – to outsiders – appeared only accessible through inherited wealth or genealogy. William Sewell, the founder of Radley, one of the mid-nineteenth-century newcomers, expressed this best in a speech to old boys in 1872: 'One of the many great uses of our public schools [is] to confer an aristocracy on boys who do not inherit it.' A classicist, he would have been using 'aristocracy' in the sense of its Ancient Greek root: 'rule by the best'.

Not much has changed. In Edinburgh, where I live, I've met more than one mother and father keen to get their daughters out of a lesser private school and into Fettes or Gordonstoun for the sixth form, not for the education but 'to get a better type of peer group'. Similarly, parents sent their girls to dame schools in Brighton two hundred years ago to prepare them for a better marriage. Many Scottish middle-class parents still send their children to southern boarding schools for the same reasons their ancestors did, readily acknowledging that it's not a better education they are looking for.

At Ashdown and Eton, we were cruel and snobbish and ruthless about anything that seemed to break our complex codes. We learnt the behaviour from our families and our teachers, but most of all from our peers. I am not convinced that we were more exclusive than other adolescents: what was different – and frightening – is that we were guaranteed to have far more power than any other social group. We were aware of our privilege. Dr Arnold's strictures about schools' duty to produce children to civilise the world still echoed in the schools of the late twentieth century. But none of us had the tools to question whether it was right that we should automatically proceed from the mock-Gothic cloisters into the establishment.

Anthony Powell expressed these thoughts in an essay on Eton written for his editor, Graham Greene, at the magazine *Night and Day* when they were both twenty-nine. The piece is lacquered in layers of irony and deprecation: it is very Etonian. Like another friend, Evelyn Waugh, in his accounts of school and Oxford, Powell is naturally avid to tease the *bien-pensant* outsider. Teaching was efficient, he says, and 'the government of the country was somehow made almost a personal matter. It was as if, instead of saying, "If you don't learn to speak French properly, you will never be able to enjoy yourself in Paris," our mentors said: "If you don't learn some sort of civilized behaviour, England will become uninhabitable for everybody."' Of course, Powell goes on, this sort of teaching might well produce a variety of megalomaniacs.

Naturally, the attitudes learned from peers in adolescence tend to stick, especially in a class that even now is inclined to work, marry and socialise among its own members. Anyone who has been to a British university can testify how the public school kids seem to stick together. That looks like arrogance, though it may also be awkwardness. But a case could certainly be made that the conformists who emerged from the system have views that do not shift much during their lives and are essentially conservative.

Often it may seem that no other belief system or notion of how to organise life ever intruded on them after they reached prefecthood. Boris Johnson used both to mock and confirm this by peppering his journalism about Westminster and Brussels with school slang – 'bounders', 'cads' and so on.* School and its structures were a lens with which to view the whole world.

The political trajectory of the public school rebel often veers in their later lives, usually from left to right. Many of them remain torn between loyalty and loathing of the institution – competing pressures that may inform their lives, public and private. Sir Harold Nicolson, diplomat and Labour politician (via a brief 1930s dalliance with Oswald Mosley's Fascists), was one of the revisionist essayists about school Graham Greene published in 1934. His view of his school, Wellington, is the perfect lament of conformism, and much quoted: 'One ceased so completely to be an individual, to have any but a corporate identity, one was just a name, or rather a number, on the list . . .'

But to his well-turned complaints, and those of many others, you find yourself rolling your eyes. Surely, this was the point of the schools. Parents bought these things for their children because they had had them themselves, and they worked. Nicolson bought them, too: his sons, Nigel† and Ben, boarded from eight and were already at Eton when he wrote his essay for Greene. To consider any other option for your offspring would have entailed confronting something quite difficult, which was that your own education had done you no good. It was far easier to conclude that the benefits outweighed the risks – and that

---

* Outdated even in his time; I went to the same schools three years earlier.
† Co-founder of Weidenfeld & Nicolson.

any damage done might have been the fault of your own weakness. In the end, it would be unfair to deny your children the experience just because you harboured doubts – a view I still hear today from people I went to school with who have now dispatched their own offspring to the same.

In his 1934 essay Nicolson makes an extraordinarily honest confession. He expresses something that is widely felt, but never said, by the class that used and uses the schools: they learn to despise those that went elsewhere.

'I am conscious, moreover . . . of a marked distaste for those who have not benefited by a public school education. This distaste is based on no superficial prejudice; it is founded on experience. People who have not endured the restrictive shaping of an English school are apt in after life to be egocentric, formless and inconsiderate. These are irritating faults . . . destructive of the more creative forms of intelligence. Surely I am unfitted to condemn, or even to criticize, a system, the absence of which induces in me movements of such continued distaste?'

In the same vein is the novelist of upper-class debauch, Simon Raven, writing in 1986:

The three paramount qualities of a public school boy, it seemed to me, were loyalty, moderation and fair-mindedness, all of which qualities might be subsumed under the one term, 'decency', and what could be better than that? Of course public school boys included bilkers, shits, tyrants, blackmailers and thieves; but these somehow took on much of the charm and seemliness of the surroundings in which they had been educated . . . The fact that there is a great deal wrong with the public schools, a great deal that is unjust, disgusting, cruel and filthy, does not seem to me to detract

from their charm, and certainly not from the charm
and the peculiarities of those that have attended them
. . . I know [this world], I admire it, I cherish it, I love
it. I wish it well for now and for ever. And for those
who hate it or wish to destroy it (and they are many),
the socialists and the crabs and the spoil-sports and the
do-gooders and the square-toes and the prudes and the
prigs and the egalitarians with their sanctimonious and
drivelling cant – for them I wish drowning in a midden
and a pauper's funeral on a wet Monday in Toxteth.

Crabs? I wondered, after reading that. But the proper public
school boy reaction is that of a Wykehamist (Winchester
pupil) I showed the passage to. 'Oh dear me. But that's a
Carthusian [Charterhouse pupil] for you, I'm afraid.'

# 22. 'Don't let's make a fuss'

Of course, whether you spent Saturday afternoon in your study becoming a Trotskyite and a fan of The Clash, or as a 'blood' thundering the ball gloriously over the try line, much of the experience was psychologically the same. The hormone-heavy culture, the lack of ordinary social contact with other classes or indeed the other sex, the deep-grained beliefs about hiding emotion while smiling at adversity – these all bred extraordinary attitudes. I asked one Old Etonian, the writer John Julius Norwich, for memories that summed up the spirit of the public school. He came back with this:

> A boy committed suicide, and the housemaster summoned the whole house and asked if anybody could suggest a reason. The young David Ormsby-Gore put up his hand and said, 'Could it have been the food, sir?'

There is a perfection in this awful story, as one of its type. Ormsby-Gore (who became, as Lord Harlech, a well-known politician and diplomat) was joking, but the joke is complex: he is mocking a certain sort of British phlegm that denies mental weakness, or at least can't be bothered to explain it. So Ormsby-Gore is mocking himself and his lack of empathy and insight – but lacking such things is not seen as a hindrance. It may well be a positive when faced with life's trials. Humour, at its driest, marches alongside the stiffest of upper lips. The British were swapping dry and dark jokes and anecdotes about the ruling class's absurd imperviousness to emotions or to physical pain more than a hundred years earlier. A favourite tale of pluck and self-control in extremis that most public school boys still remember comes from Waterloo, the bloody, final battle against Napoleon in 1815 where so many myths of English superiority were forged. The Duke of Wellington was riding through the battle with his second-in-command, Henry Paget, Lord Uxbridge. The final volleys of the French artillery barrage were hurtling through the ranks. Uxbridge suddenly turned to Wellington and exclaimed, 'By God, sir, I've lost my leg!' To which Wellington replied, 'By God, sir, so you have!' Uxbridge was taken to a farmhouse where the rest of the leg was amputated, without anaesthetic. Uxbridge, the surgeon said, never even groaned.

This exchange and the attitudes that it embodied and inspired have lived on, in film and story. Monty Python parodied phlegmatic upper-class reactions to instant amputation on the battlefield at least twice, first with the Black Knight in *Monty Python and the Holy Grail* and then again in a sketch on nineteenth-century officers fighting the Zulu Wars in *The Meaning of Life*. ('If you're playing football,' the regimental doctor advises Lieutenant Perkins after a lion has bitten off a leg, 'try and favour the other leg.') It is of course very public school to deprecate tales of heroism, especially one's own. Three of the six Pythons went to boarding prep or public schools, as did their first director.

The most interesting thing about most expressions of stiff-upper-lippery is the self-awareness: a consciousness of the absurdity of it. The Ormsby-Gore story makes ex-public school boys laugh more than other people (and some don't laugh at all) because it is in itself a parody of the trained reaction: it's as much about absurd levels of phlegm as the old high-stakes sport of seeing how far you can go with the housemaster before getting into trouble. Trouble, as we'll see in the next chapter, could often be very painful.

It is at one level a quite private joke, and private jokes are another way of bonding the tribe. Public school boy humour, as practised by adults, from P. G. Wodehouse to Stephen Fry, deserves a category of its own in the taxonomy of comedy. Simon Raven wrote that it was some years after he'd left Charterhouse ('expelled for homosexuality') before he realised that 'what we, as public school or ex-public school men, found moving or amusing, was often to others false, irrelevant or cruel'.

But the rule of not making a fuss was observed just as much as it was privately mocked. Some historians think that the code of suppression of emotion came in quite swiftly in the later nineteenth century, noting that schoolboys and schoolmasters wrote quite openly of feelings of love and of tears at parting and so on until the 1870s. There's lots of meaningful weeping in *Tom Brown's School Days*. But soon tears became shameful; indeed, showing even the mildest emotion was in dubious taste. 'One bottles up that sort of thing, I suppose,' advises a boy in Horace Vachell's Harrow School novel *The Hill* (1905). He's talking about the inadvisability of expressing a feeling – in this case, being 'keen' on cricket. The adult he is talking to nods at this wisdom: 'Ah, if it is the right sort of thing, it's none the worse for being bottled up.'

Long before psychology had made much of a mark on

mainstream culture, commentators on boarding school were well aware of the effects of bottling up. L. P. Hartley, the writer who would celebrate liberated emotions and transgressive love, was at Harrow just after *The Hill* was published. Twenty years later – long before Hartley wrote *The Go-Between*, or came to terms with his homosexuality – he ruminated on his time at the school for Graham Greene's book of memoirs. Hartley wrote of the 'emotional atrophy' that the conflicting codes of behaviour, the 'fierce' struggle for success, coupled with the necessity of appearing unmoved, could produce.

> Every week some valley was exalted, some mountain or hill laid low. It certainly leads in some cases to emotional atrophy. The necessity of disguising what one felt, of keeping the famous stiff upper lip when cursed by a Sixth-former, or wounded by a friend, or hit by a cricket ball, sometimes found its logical outcome: after many repetitions one felt nothing at all . . . The phlegmatic Englishman is often phlegmatic because he has lost the power of expressing emotion. He has repressed his feelings so often there are none left to repress.

The code is principally about the need to appear unmoved. In this society the word 'enthusiast' could be a criticism; of an untoward display of feeling offensive to standards that themselves were described in the mildest way – 'good taste' or 'good manners'. But a second element to this insistence on self-control is important: it is all about surface, about what is on view for strangers or those outside the caste. Like actors staying in character until the curtain goes down, the key thing was that the mystery should be preserved for the unelect. 'Not in front of the servants,' is a rule that applied to all outsiders – foreigners, the lower classes and to children. Hence the British reputation for reserve, though others have called it by many less forgiving names.

The rules for interaction with outsiders were fantastically rigid: it is easy now to forget how limited a 'gentleman' or 'lady' was by the codes that were adhered to just a century ago, particularly those on emotions. The first sentence of a chapter on 'Conversation' in one of the standard books on etiquette tells a gentleman never to talk about religion or politics in general society, for fear of 'irritating differences of opinion that might lead to temper'. 'A man in a passion ceases to be a gentleman' – and of all things, it is being a gentleman that matters most. Similar texts were popular for the production of ladies, from whom self-control and discipline over the emotions was equally required.

Instilling these rules had to begin at school, illustrated with myth. The one of British imperturbability starts quite early. Leafing through the immensely successful Edwardian history book *Our Island Story*, you find little other than tales of pluck and acts of daft and sometimes pointless sacrifice. Plucky women appear in it, too: there is Queen Boadicea, who also played a brave but losing game against an unsportsmanlike foe (the Roman Empire), thereby sacrificing her tribe and her children but retaining her honour. These well-rehearsed tales led in a direct line to Robert the Bruce's fortitude in defeat, Nelson's stubbornness under fire, and of course Scott's suicidal mission in the Antarctic, where he took absurd and ultimately fatal risks not only with his own life but those of his men. Britons, we were taught, were uniquely brave.

But there was more to the indoctrination than just the telling or reinterpreting of the fables. Science came to its aid too. In 1871 Charles Darwin published *The Expression of Emotions in Man and Animals*, a book that for the first time stated the animal and genetic origin of many expressions of emotions. Darwin, a public school boy, found an exception to his general thesis about the universality of emotions across the races: 'Englishmen rarely cry, except under the pressure of the acutest grief; whereas in some parts of the Continent the men shed tears much more readily and freely.' Darwin thought the tearlessness of Britons was a matter of a level of civilisation, rather than genes. In the same section of the book he says 'savages weep copiously from very slight causes', giving examples from Tierra del Fuego and New Zealand. The only thing that he finds universal is that adult men, 'both of civilized and barbarous races', do not weep because of physical pain.

In fact it seems that Englishmen, or those of Darwin's class, stopped weeping over their feelings just about at the time Darwin wrote his book. Harold Nicolson is quite clear – it happened around 1850. Before that politicians, including Pitt, Fox and Wellington, cried. So did Tennyson, the poet laureate, when reading his verse to the public. Then, quite abruptly, it became 'ungentlemanlike' (though Nicolson says he did see Churchill cry, 'quite quietly, but very hard'). Not crying, or not showing any emotion at all, appears to have become a national pastime. During the First World War, patriotic authors would address the evil of sentimentality, the causes and the symptoms of emasculation and degeneracy – though with some of the writing you wonder if it was quite gentlemanly to get so heated on the subject. It is hardly surprising that generations grew up learning that to hide their emotions was not just safe but proper. Thus emotional illiteracy – or suitable reserve, depending on your point of view – remains the first

attribute most nations mention when asked what charac-
terises the British upper classes.

If the British elite abandoned emotions around 1850, it
may be said that around 1970 they started to rediscover
them; or, rather, the bonds that prevented the expression
of feelings began to slip. An elderly relative of mine talked
to me of dealing with death in the family and how it had
changed. She said, of the 1950s, 'In those days, because of
the war it was understood that if you were going to cry, you
went to your room, locked the door, and did it alone.' I've
collected many other stories, mainly of men, for whom the
prospect of public emotion seems to have been terrifying.
There are funerals or memorial services boycotted, elderly
male relatives literally struck dumb by a social situation
that required them to express sentiment or sympathy. For
many, grief was a nuisance and the animal noises that came
with it were best kept private.

A generation later parents started to hug and kiss their
children and the beginnings of child development theory
penetrated middle-class homes. At the end of the 1970s,
early boarding started to decline. But the schools resisted.
As the British middle class slowly embraced more openness about emotion, the schools continued encouraging it
to be locked up. There are ways that this can happen –
one is by medicalising emotional distress, turning it into
something for a doctor's intervention where the rational
approach might be to address the cause.

Parents and indeed teachers have told me of boarding
school children who have tried or succeeded in killing
themselves; they were not bullied, or homesick, or lonely,
but 'clinically depressed'. A doctor said so. Diagnosis of
mental illness exonerates the adults of blame or neglect or

indeed the duty to intervene beyond arranging an appointment. The schools, of course, could not acknowledge that unhappiness was reasonable, serious and avoidable. To do so would threaten their existence.

Normalising misery began at the first parting at prep school, where the young boarders were cajoled or bullied into ignoring homesickness and hiding tears. By the time these children had become near-adults, the lesson had been absorbed, and widened. 'Never show your emotions here,' Royston Lambert and his team were told by many of their boarding school interviewees in the 1960s. A thirteen-year-old advised: 'Try not to speak with a treble voice. Do not cry at all as it is important that you should not seem childish. Never play conkers.' An eighteen-year-old said: 'Never become too intense, it makes you vulnerable. Don't exhibit unbridled enthusiasm – it leaves you wide open to criticism. Be casual, easy going, and don't let them see you're really deep. Above all, keep up a pose.' These, then, were the codes taken by some to the adult world that was ready to receive them, to give them jobs and authority precisely because these things had been learnt.

Lambert emphasises that these strictures against spontaneity and showing emotion were only heard at the smartest schools. 'This norm arises partly from the school's idea of educating a governing elite in which emotional reactions might be out of place, partly from early training in "adult" attributes,' he comments astutely. There is a sharp contrast with the survival codes that were learnt at the state boarding schools Lambert visited. A fifteen-year-old at one of these – usually set up for armed forces children – gives this agenda for novices: 'Be handy with your fists. Have a fight as soon as possible. Regard juniors as scum. Smoke and follow the form leaders.'

E. M. Forster published the first adult novel, *The Longest Journey*, that overtly criticised the rigid systems and proprieties of the traditional schools, in which he had been schooled and had served as a teacher. In a 1920 essay, 'Notes on the English Character', Forster delivers a devastating verdict that still reverberates:

> For it is not that the Englishman can't feel – it is that he is afraid to feel. He has been taught at his public school that feeling is bad form. He must not express great joy or sorrow, or even open his mouth too wide when he talks – his pipe might fall out if he did. He must bottle up his emotions, or let them out only on a very special occasion.

It isn't hard to see where Forster's venom comes from. He had been badly bullied at his prep school and then at Tonbridge School (where he was a day-boy). Bookish, little-loved, homosexual, physically slight, he would hardly have been at home at any traditional school, let alone one that was a factory, famously sports-obsessed, for turning out mid-level colonial administrators. Forster was well aware of all this, and his reaction to it and his fight to stand up for himself and against the damning 'not one of us' verdict of those who knew he couldn't hack it at a public school is one of the moving things about his story. He is a quiet warrior for emotional openness, for honest human relations, and it is that which makes his work survive. In the same essay he delivers perhaps the most damning – and most quoted – of all one-liners on the product of the English public schools: 'They go forth with well-developed bodies, fairly developed minds and undeveloped hearts.'

\*

If the schools were mints for empire-builders, even long after the end of the Empire, I came out of the machine a misshaped coin. In fact, quality control at Eton and then in the Oxford college admissions office spotted my flaws and rejected me, as you would expect of a properly run production line. Surprisingly large numbers of people were expelled from Eton – at least five from my house in the year I was extracted. Three of them were to die young – two by suicide, one from HIV/AIDS as a result of heroin addiction.

In the summer of 1977, I gave up on my Eton career. A whole term of detentions and restrictions loomed ahead, all for various infractions of rules on cigarettes and alcohol. There were O levels to take in a month or so, too. I was just sixteen, obsessed in a platonic way with a beautiful younger boy, and together we decided to go adventuring. We headed for Paris, where we decided we'd begin our new lives as *plongeurs*, dish-washers. We'd read George Orwell, another rebel Etonian (we thought) who had been down and out in that exciting city. When, after a few days on the road, the French police picked us up at Dieppe and returned us to England and our parents, mine asked what had gone wrong. I couldn't tell them. It was all too big to describe, and, besides, I didn't want them to feel bad. They'd done their best. They'd made sacrifices. It had certainly been expensive. How could I tell them that all I really believed as a result of eight years of boarding school was that if adults had rules or advice against doing something, it was almost certainly an excellent idea to go straight out and do it?

We were both dispatched back to the school – a 'last chance'. My housemaster was particularly kind and consoling. 'Are you very much in love?' he asked sweetly. He was homosexual and mildly predatory. I thought, probably unfairly, he was wondering if he might now have a chance with me. But that wasn't why, ten days later, my friend and I took off again. We'd made a plan with some girls from St George's, Ascot, a nearby boarding school (Churchill's old prep school), to meet at night in a barn with drink and cannabis. We had the bicycles and the supplies all ready: when they cancelled on the eve of the adventure the disappointment was too much. We knew a girl with a flat in West London who'd let us sleep on her floor – maybe more – and so we went.

This time, there was no coming back for me. I was the older, and so the ring-leader. The usual negotiation took place; my parents agreed with the school that I would not be formally expelled, I was to leave 'for my own good'. It seemed right – it was something I for once had chosen. I never boarded again: I entered a world that seemed much more real, and more fun. Even then I thought I'd made a lucky escape.

I didn't dislike Eton: after five years in bonds of humiliation at my prep school it had seemed a pleasant place. I had though lost faith in adults and their systems, in religion and discipline, honour and duty, in conventional morality and even in goodness. It was easy to accept the rejection because rejection was something I'd grown used to: I'd already decided I didn't want what the school offered. Now I was ready to go and learn how to be happy. I hope Forster might have seen that my heart was still available for development.

PART FOUR

# The Uses of Violence

# 23. Taking a beating

A small sacrifice for a boy, a great treat for a monk.
Auberon Waugh on beatings at the Catholic school Downside, run by monks. He held the school record for the most
in one term.

Before breakfast, one sunny morning in the spring of 1977,
I am summoned to the headmaster of Eton for a beating.
It feels a bit like a trip to the dentist. Michael McCrum is
a tall and dour man with a heavy black forelock: stern but
reasonable. He and I have already discussed my offence –
repeatedly being caught smoking – and the punishment:
either I am to spend the rest of that term's Saturday after-
noons rebuilding a wall in his garden, or I am to have three
strokes of the cane. The choice was not difficult.

McCrum has taught me Greek: I've come to like the
quiet, wise man who brings Homer's flawed heroes to life.
He is the sort of teacher you want to think well of you.
So my principal feeling as I walk in my tail-suit to the
old building known as Upper School is mild embarrassment. There is a subsidiary worry: I'm waddling rather
than walking through Eton's streets. My friends insisted
on my taking the house flag. We'd lowered it from its pole
and folded it into a neat parcel for me to wear inside my
Y-fronts as buttock armour. Hilarious and defiant though
we all decided this was, I don't relish McCrum spotting

the bulge of it – as surely he will when I bend over. I do not want him to think I am a coward.

I am not worried about being physically hurt. McCrum is a tall man, a rugby player and a former Navy officer who faced Japanese kamikaze attacks. But he has no reputation with the cane. Besides, he is said to be a reluctant corporal punisher. One of his first acts on taking over the school from the celebrated flogger Anthony Chenevix-Trench was to stop boys beating other boys. He also ruled that beatings should be done with a boy's trousers and underwear on.

I know what a real beating is. I was first beaten as a snivelling eight-year-old who had to be dragged into position by a drunk in a rage – the headmaster of my prep school. Those canings, with a whippy dried bamboo rod, left purple welts that lasted for weeks. Williamson had to order some boys not to take part in school sports days, for fear their wounds might be seen by outsiders. Dr Keate, the celebrated nineteenth-century headmaster of Eton who used to occupy McCrum's classroom, was known for savage flogging of dozens (in a few hours) of the bottoms of future eminent Britons. But today, at sixteen, full of hot contempt for adults and authority, the only fear I have is for my pride.

When I arrive in his classroom McCrum is waiting with one of the prefects of Pop, the school's self-electing elite. Both of them are wearing white bow-ties, McCrum his academic gown. I am sent next door into the ancient Upper School to fetch the flogging block. Upper School is an echoey hall where once two hundred Etonians, aged from six to eighteen, slept, fed, fought and were somehow schooled. A 'bearpit', the scene of 'uncommon barbarity', a 'stinking cesspit of the worst immorality' according to accounts from the eighteenth and nineteenth centuries. It was a place that proved the innate wickedness of children. Today it is empty, smelling only of floor polish, like an under-employed church hall.

The flogging block, black with age, is in a corner under a table, like any ordinary piece of superfluous furniture. It is scarred with dead boys' initials, carved in neat serifed script. This relic was immortalised by one of Eton's more famous poets, Algernon Swinburne; today better known for his lifelong taste for flagellation. Here's a typical stanza from the 165-page manuscript of his 'The Flogging-Block':

*How those great big red ridges must smart as they swell!*
*How the Master does like to flog Algernon well!*
*How each cut makes the blood come in thin little streaks*
*From that broad blushing round pair of naked red cheeks.*

In Swinburne's time the whole of Upper School would watch a 'swishing' – it was great entertainment. John Delaware Lewis, writing of the 1840s, said that 'anyone who chose might drop in' to watch; if a member of the cricket Eleven or the rowing Eight was to be swished the crowd might be more than a hundred. They would kneel naked from the waist down, even if, as Lewis says, they were twenty years old. The crimes that earned this have not changed: 'something or other particularly heinous – smoking or drinking, or going to Ascot on the sly'.

The birch-brush rod used until the 1960s could be nearly five feet long, three feet of handle and nearly two of bushy twigs – one of the jobs afterwards for the victim's friends or the doctor was to pluck bits of twig from his wounds before they went septic. The actual strokes 'sounded like the splashings of so many buckets of water',

according to the journalist James Brinsley Richards, who
was at Eton 1857–64. He was incredulous when he first
watched the Reverend Adolphus Carter in action, beating a small, squint-eyed, curly-haired boy called Neville.
Indeed, when Richards had been shown the block and told
what it was for, he'd thought he was 'being hoaxed' by his
friends. When he watched Neville birched six times, Richards 'turned almost faint. I felt as I have never felt but once
since, and that was when seeing a man hanged.' Looking
back in 1883, Richards called the experience 'infinitely
degrading'. Nonetheless, birching was used in schools till
the 1960s and as a judicial punishment for young offenders until the 1980s.

The block is a mini-podium, two steps crudely carpen-
tered of thick oak. It turns out to be as light as an old lady
with brittle bones. I carry it back into the headmaster's
classroom, brushing as rudely as I can past the boy from
Pop, who knows me well. I'm telling him he is a pervert
voyeur and a fascist goon, and he knows I think it. Not so
long ago he would have been more than a witness to this
ritual, acting as one of the two 'holders-down' necessary to
stop boys wriggling away in fear or agony.

I study the cracked ebony gloss of the old wood, wondering if the varnish owes something to long-gone boys'
tears and their blood. I place the block down as instructed
in front of the headmaster's desk. I am asked to remove
my coat and take up the position. The headmaster is holding a piece of bamboo: it's not long or thick, but it is the
whippiness of the stick that counts, I know. I can't see
how whippy this one is. My last headmaster had favourite
canes, and we used to name them. If a cane broke on a boy's
bottom, he was – so the legend went – excused the rest of
the beating.

As I place my knees on the first step of the block, I think that I should be grateful for this moment. Not for the grace of my punisher and the boon that my punishment is, but that I too have a chance to experience a little of this history. I know that my father never knelt here – he was reasonably well behaved, and became Captain of School – but at least one of my uncles did, and some of my older ancestors must have known the steps too. And I am surely the last of the line. What's about to happen could not be more anachronistic. As it turns out, three years later McCrum was to leave Eton to head a Cambridge college. His successor did ban headmaster's beatings at Eton, though a couple of the more traditional bachelor housemasters kept at it for a year or two.

I lean over the upper step of the block, which is taller than the lower, to accommodate a teenager's thighs. Thus my belly is on the step, my bottom in the air and my torso hanging down and forward, where I see a wooden rod, stale and sweat-stained, for me to grip. I wait. At this point, all you can do is listen for the footsteps. The length of the run-up, seasoned flagellees know, is a pretty good indicator of how much it is likely to hurt.

There are many accounts of beatings at Eton and other public schools. There was no doubt that the public was well aware that the practice was often stunningly brutal. In the nineteenth century scandals around boys beaten so severely they needed medical attention regularly surfaced in the newspapers: Harrow, Winchester and Eton all feature in outraged letters to the *Morning Post* and *The Times*.

Edward Lockwood was one of the first pupils of Marlborough College, founded in 1843 for the sons of clergy. The new schools usually aped the traditions of the more ancient ones. But Marlborough appears to have trumped them with the invention of a new kind of beating, in stereo. Here is Lockwood:

> The knoutings which I received from my master's reverend arm, turned my back all the colours of the rainbow; and when I screamed from the fearful torture they produced, the Head Master would send a prefect down to say that if I made such a horrid noise, he also would have a go-in at me, when my master had done his worst. Occasionally two masters would be caning at the same time with the rhythm of blacksmiths hammering on an anvil . . .

A boy was beaten to death at a 'private school of the highest class' in Eastbourne in 1860. After trying to conceal the body, the headmaster was arrested and sentenced to four years' penal servitude. But that was rare. The headmaster of Shrewsbury was castigated in the papers in 1874 for his punishment of a boy who had brought ale back to his study. He got eighty-eight strokes of the birch – 'mere fleabites', wrote a supporter, but a surgeon found the weals still present after ten days. The Shrewsbury governors considered the matter and declared that the punishment was not excessive. But, according to *The Times*, they recommended 'that the future punishments should be more in accordance with public feeling and the practice of other public schools'. That was, presumably, not intended to be facetious, comments the historian Ian Gibson. His history, *The English Vice*, sets out to show that everyone at the boarding schools, young and old, was beaten, a lot, right through to modern times. The effect on the nation's character and, reckons Gibson, its sexuality was explosive and far-reaching.

At Eton a pride arose in the school's reputation as a shrine of excellent and extreme flogging. Outsiders of all sorts enjoyed the tales: King George III's most usual topic of conversation when encountering Etonian boys around Windsor was to ask them for details of their most recent beatings. Georgian London had laughed at the downfall of the eminent veteran of the American War of Independence General Sir Eyre Coote, a former aide-de-camp of the King. Coote had learnt a taste for beating when he was at Eton in the 1770s. A Member of Parliament, a Knight of the Bath and a former Governor of Jamaica, he was found in 1815 to have been hanging around Christ's Hospital School, paying the boys two shillings each if they would agree to flog him* and then let him return the favour.

But to many who suffered them, the Eton beatings were no source of pleasure. There are far more accounts of awful pain and humiliation than there are jokes. The early nineteenth-century headmaster Dr Keate was, by many accounts, a drooling five-foot psychopath with inhuman stamina when it came to flogging. His servant often had to make a dozen birch bundle sticks for a single day's beatings, and – to choose one from many stories of his love of the job – he once encountered a queue of boys outside his study and flogged them all, ignoring their protests that they'd come not for discipline, but for confirmation class.

Keate remains one of the school's best-loved characters, fondly remembered in memoirs, memorials and in the name of a principal street in the Eton village.† Since Eton

* Coote was acquitted of any crime after donating £1,000 to the school. But he was stripped of his rank and honours and lost his parliamentary seat at the next election.
† Dr Keate, who ruled from 1809–34, is a 'figure of fun', according to the college's website.

was the best of the schools, the notion that there could not
be too much flogging spread through the system. When
Anthony Chenevix-Trench was headmaster in the 1960s,
Eton tolerated his excessive beatings with similar wry
amusement. Trench was only moved on (to Fettes College
in Edinburgh) when his heavy drinking and failures as a
manager of the school became too much.

But, on this summer morning, McCrum's stroke is a
disappointment – to me and to the leering ghosts of Algernon Swinburne and Eyre Coote. When the headmaster first
hits my bum with his bamboo I wonder if he's just lining
it up to get his eye in. But no, that's it. The token tap is
his best shot, no heavier than the sword the monarch lays
upon a new knight's shoulder, and the two that follow are
no harder. There's no sting and no need to have desecrated
the house flag at all.

When I stand up, I realise that Mr McCrum is considerably more embarrassed than I. His grave face seems to have
drooped even further. I offer to shake hands. He declines:
that won't be necessary. I waddle off (the flag still in place,
unmentioned), thinking that I've got a story to tell and –
like the journalist Brinsley Richards, when the Reverend
Carter finally got the birch to him in that same room 130
years before – that the beating had really accomplished less
than nothing. 'I rose from my knees completely hardened
as to any sense of shame either in the punishment I had
undergone, or in others of the same kind I might have to
suffer thereafter.'

So what were the beatings for? There is little evidence that
children behaved better for fear of beating, or that schools
that didn't beat saw more trouble, just as children whose
parents don't hit them are no worse behaved. It was widely

accepted by the 1970s that when beating was abolished in a school, bullying and violence between pupils declined. Masters who beat a lot seemed to be no better at keeping order – the noise from Dr Keate's classroom was always said to be deafening. The randomness of the beatings, the injustice of them, seems to have left marks on many. Even in the 1970s at my prep school we were beaten for showing stupidity – failing to do the Latin prose well enough, for instance. There are many awful stories of the punishment and humiliation of children who would now be diagnosed as having 'special educational needs' because of dyslexia or autism. Clearly no one was ever beaten into better spelling. In the accounts sent to me, it is the overt cruelties of the adults that most offend my correspondents as they look back. Making the victim an actor in the ritual was common, as in the duty of carrying out the Eton flogging block. Some headmasters liked to get the children to polish the canes or 'warm them up'. At Temple Grove prep school in the 1960s the child sentenced to a beating was given a knife and the job of choosing and cutting the right cane from a grove of bamboo in the school gardens. 'If it was "too insubstantial" then we received a double beating. So it was a terrible game we played as to what would cause us the least chance of that double beating but also the least pain.'

But the pain and, perhaps more importantly, the humiliation were seen as an important part of a wider notion of good schooling. The pro-school stories are full of boys who find themselves spiritually improved by a thrashing – it is a purification. Lord Lawrence, a Viceroy of India in the 1860s, told with 'grim satisfaction' of the birching at his day school in Bristol, where he was from eight to twelve: 'I was flogged every day of my life at school except one, and then I was flogged twice.' Often boys who were beaten deservedly said they felt love towards their teacher after. In some Victorian accounts, pupil and master hug each other in manly tears after the cane is lowered. 'Then I flung away the cane . . . ' writes the Reverend William Sewell, who was the founding headmaster of Radley, in 1847. 'I think when I made that boy get up from his knees, and he put his arms around my neck, was the most exquisite moment of enjoyment I ever had.'

# 24. Sex and flogging

There are historians who make a case for school flogging becoming the driving force of English upper-class male sexuality. Catering for the tastes or perversions learnt at school was certainly a feature of the late-nineteenth-century sex trade – indeed, the whip remained a symbol of prostitution for another hundred years. The problem that the connection between sexual pleasure and flogging posed for schools was acknowledged quite early. The late-eighteenth-century pioneer of schools for the masses, the Quaker Joseph Lancaster, was removed because of the pleasure he took in whipping his charges. By the early twentieth century, Europe's most famous sexual rebel, the Marquis de Sade, had penetrated the consciousness of the public school men. Memoirs tell of a 'wave of Sadism' and 'orgiastic sadists' among prefects who were allowed to beat at Eton, Marlborough and Winchester. Sophisticated nineteenth-century Europeans like the Goncourt brothers wrote at length on the sexual tastes of dissolute British aristocracy, 'who bring ferocious cruelty to love and whose licentiousness can only be aroused by the woman's sufferings'.

So much – too much – has been written about flagellation and sexuality in British culture. Much of it comes from men whose historical interests are sad – and, now, superfluous – disguises for their sexual ones. But the link between being beaten at school and wanting to beat or be beaten in later life is far from clear psychologically, however much the pornographers wanted it to be. Yet there's no question that flagellation at school had a lasting resonance for the secret sexuality of the British male. Pornographers are market-driven, after all. The literary historian Deborah Lutz estimates that 50 per cent of Victorian porn was flagellant.

Confessional novels of schoolboy flagellation and sadism were still being published until the 1970s: they were the main business of the Fortune Press, publisher also (in the 1940s) of Philip Larkin, Dylan Thomas and Roy Fuller. When not publishing the brightest young poets, Fortune was rolling out dozens of titles like *Diary of a Teen*, *Boys in Ruin* and *Chastisement across the Ages*. But porn is not about the reflection of reality: Ian Gibson makes the good point that a huge amount of Victorian crypto-porn (which appeared in the letters, columns and adverts of respectable periodicals) was centred around the physical 'disciplining' of young women at schools, even though that appears to have been very rare.

But there are enough stories to show there was quite frequently a sexual interest on the part of the men and women who disciplined. Just as some schools – like Crookham Court – were deliberately taken over and run by paedophiles for their purposes, for some teachers a primary attraction of the job was the sexual pleasure they could derive from administering physical discipline. 'They might as well have had me educated at a brothel for flagellants,' said the poet Stephen Spender of his prep school.

The artist Roger Fry was beaten by the headmaster under whom Winston Churchill suffered; Fry was convinced that the Reverend Henry Sneyd-Kynnersley got sexual thrills from the elaborate ritual beatings that were sometimes so violent that Sneyd-Kynnersley and others in the room were splashed with blood and, on one occasion, excrement.

Older children are usually alert to the faintest whisper of sex and they often noticed the strange behaviour of the floggers: the stirring in the teacher's trousers, the heavy breathing and a red, excited face. I could retell a hundred stories from my own research and correspondence: here is one that's less ordinary.

At one eminent Yorkshire prep school in the 1970s the twelve- and thirteen-year-olds in their final term were summoned one evening to the headmaster's study for a goodbye ceremony. After pouring them all sherry and delivering the usual sentimental summings-up, the man, relaxed in his dressing gown, acknowledged that he had been pretty handy with the cane during the previous five years. This wasn't an apology – indeed, he said the boys had benefited from every stroke – but the preamble to a time-honoured ritual. After he had extracted a promise from them to keep what was about to happen a secret, the headmaster stood up, handed the nearest boy a cane, and dropped the dressing gown. Underneath he was naked. 'Now, boys,' he said, 'it's your turn. You may get your own back.'

Did some see a beating as a sacrament, a gift from the wise parent-figure to the deserving child? Clearly this chimed with Christian belief about exculpatory suffering. Much quoted by the Victorians is a line derived from the Book of Proverbs: 'Chasten thy son while there is still hope, and let not thy soul spare for his crying.' That, with 'Spare the rod and spoil the child', is used still by some Christians to justify corporal punishment. It is pithy, but not accurate. The Bible is tougher: 'He that spareth his rod hateth his son.' Modern translations of Proverbs 13:24 make explicit the connection between inflicting pain and love: 'Whoever refuses to spank his son hates him, but whoever loves his son disciplines him from early on.' It is clear that many used these texts to justify sadism. But there were also decent men like Michael McCrum, 'conscientious floggers, conscientiously whipping virtue in and vice out', as one early public school teacher-turned-critic put it, no matter how unpleasant the task.

It isn't surprising that there are many stories of children permanently parted from religion by the hypocrisies of headmasters who wielded a cane just as avidly as they thumped a bible. Whatever Proverbs might advise, it did not seem as though the New Testament was on their side. Roald Dahl was one of these born-again sceptics. At Repton School in the 1930s, he watched Geoffrey Fisher, who was to become Archbishop of Canterbury, in action.

> If this person, I kept telling myself, was one of God's chosen salesmen on earth, then there must be something very wrong about the whole business . . . I would sit in the dim light of the school chapel and listen to him preaching about the Lamb of God and about Mercy and Forgiveness and my young mind would become totally confused. I knew very well that only the night before this preacher had shown neither Forgiveness nor Mercy in flogging some small boy who had broken the rules.

Like so many, Dahl toned down his descriptions of the bullying and beating at Repton for the published version of his memoir of his schooldays; though the stories are pretty savage, there are notes of comedy. But an early draft, discovered by his biographer Donald Sturrock, delves deeper into the psychology of the beaten, the Repton adolescents whose 'lives were quite literally ruled by fear of the cane'. Talking of how his classmates gathered round to inspect the stripes on his bottom and dispassionately analyse how efficient the beating had been, Dahl wrote:

> It is clear to me now that these boys had developed this curiously detached attitude towards these vile tortures in order to preserve their sanity. It was an essential defensive mechanism. Had they crowded round and commiserated and tried to comfort me, I think we would all have broken down.

Beatings, even mass ones, continued to be held in public right up to the end of the beating era in the 1980s. It is certainly the case that many beating teachers believed that the drama should have an audience, whether of other boys waiting their turn, or of the entire school. There are historians who see the public beating as a great bonding rite of the public school experience, a service of sacrifice, which induced in the spectators the orgiastic fervour of the crowd at the Circus Maximus or a Tyburn hanging. Many nineteenth- and eighteenth-century accounts talk of the air of festivity and intense excitement among the boys as the moment approached.

Despite the occasional mutter of public disquiet, floggings were, for much of the twentieth century, a hallowed element of public school life. This culture, both its myths and realities, was enjoyed way beyond the school boundaries and indeed Britain's. 'Swishings' provided pivotal moments in the plots of the school novels and illustrated comics that the public – of all classes – consumed in enormous quantities for the first half of the century. They were part of the drama and the fun of school, and an easy way of sorting heroes from villains: the cads and cowards dodged their beatings or blubbed; good chaps took it with a smile and a joke afterwards. Flogging the children of the upper class was an accepted pastime in the Britain of *Carry On* films and warm beer. In the 1950s BBC radio ran a comedy series about a school 'for the sons of Gentlefolk' and its rascally, flogging headmaster, played by Jimmy Edwards. It was titled *Whack-O!* So popular was this show, it was revived for TV in the 1970s.

Clearly corporal punishment was as integral a part of the full public school experience as boarding and sport. Flogging survived longer than the Empire and the death penalty; it outlasted compulsory Greek and Latin, top hats, boaters, fagging and mass football. Even towards the end of the great liberalising decade of the 1960s, with corporal punishment for adults finally abolished in 1967, all but 2 of the 134 major private schools that were members of the Headmasters' Conference still beat their children. In 60 per cent of them, pupils were allowed to beat each other. Williamson, the headmaster of my prep school, was faced with a problem in 1975 when the first girl – Boris Johnson's sister, Rachel – was admitted. He was informed by his deputy that he wouldn't be able to beat her. The old man decided to retire.

'Angela' is the daughter of a headmaster who presided at a well-known boarding school on the South Coast and then one in the Midlands during the 1960s and the 1970s. The arrival of boys for discipline by her father is one of her earliest memories. He would take them into his study,

close the door, and then administer the beating. 'To us he
would say he loathed doing it, but the parents wanted it. I
remember him telling how a well-known medical consultant thanked him for beating his son: "It was the making of
him." Parenting and discipline was sub-contracted out to
my father. I don't think the consultant would have hurt his
own son, but he was very pleased that someone else would.'

One of the housemasters at the school beat savagely,
with evident enjoyment – it was well known, and the boys
would tell Angela – 'but it was impossible for my father
to interfere. The man was long-standing and he would
have been supported by other teachers and some of the
governors. There were teachers, and parents, for whom
punishment and humiliation were intrinsic to the package
the school was offering.'

Angela felt that her father was torn. 'It was the early
1970s, I think he had a strong sense that beating was
out-of-date, and he hoped it was unnecessary. Co-ed would
be the next thing, and he would have welcomed it.' But
he and his employers saw the school as a bulwark against
the frightening social changes of the time. 'The discipline
issues were about long hair, earrings, dope, "not being able
to tell the difference between a boy and a girl" – these were
the signifiers of a collapse of the moral order. The school
needed to hold the line. That was what was being asked of
it by the teachers, the government and by parents.'

# 25. The backlash

Throughout the history of school beating there is much – written by adults – to say that the boys welcomed being beaten: it hurt but it was good for you. This principle was stamped in from the beginning, with the stories the class was brought up on. The self-sacrificing bravery of the warrior children of ancient Sparta is core to the mythology: 'Once a year all the boys were brought to the Temple of Diana, where their courage was further tried by a severe flogging; and those who stood this whipping without a tear or moan were duly praised. The little Spartan boys were so eager to be thought brave, that some let themselves be flogged to death rather than complain,' goes a standard late Victorian account for children. As Darwin's principles of evolution entered popular consciousness, the harshness of the school regimes – from flogging to fagging and poor food – began to gain spurious scientific justification, to go alongside the Biblical one: the words 'survival of the fittest' begin to appear more and more in educational tracts. Besides, as Orwell points out, even the children believed flogging worked, and not just in improving their morals:

> There was a boy named Beacham, with no brains to speak of, but evidently in acute need of a scholarship. Sambo was flogging him towards the goal as one might do with a foundered horse. He went up for a scholarship

at Uppingham, came back with a consciousness of having done badly, and a day or two later received a severe beating for idleness. 'I wish I'd had that caning before I went up for the exam,' he said sadly — a remark which I felt to be contemptible, but which I perfectly well understood.

Some pupils' enthusiasm for beating may have come from fear of the alternatives. The choice Michael McCrum offered me was pretty common: long and tedious labour or a short sharp shock. The unsaid aspect of that dilemma was that to refuse the beating would be to risk public accusations of cowardice. In some 'progressive' schools for the upper class, beating was abandoned quite early, usually on grounds of its barbarism but also because as a disciplinary tool it didn't actually work. But to the pupils, and in girls' schools, the alternative could be equally hateful. George Howson, also known as 'Howson of Holt', was famous in the early twentieth century for turning the Norfolk town's ancient grammar school, Gresham's, into a thriving and thrillingly modern public school. It still exists.

To the school he brought notions of moulding boys into citizens of an 'ideal society'. The regime was unusual for the time: science was on the curriculum, and corporal punishment out. The latter was replaced with an 'honour system', which required the boys to report on each other if they saw any rule being broken. For the poets W. H. Auden and Stephen Spender, two years apart at the school, each child became a paranoid policeman. Spender thought Howson a tyrant and his discipline system like that of 'a Fascist state'; Auden wrote of it in 1934: 'I believe no more potent engine was ever devised for turning boys into neurotic innocents' – and attributed his opposition to fascism to the fact of having lived under it at Gresham's.

Both were badly bullied and felt the school had damaged them, though they might quite easily have gone to schools that enrolled the children in hateful self-policing systems *and* beat them. Nevertheless, Howson and his modern methods were hugely influential. He died in 1919 'from grief' – according to the school's website – at the loss of 110 Gresham's old boys during the First World War. It is interesting that, of the pupils who survived the trenches, so many – not just the famous poets – went on to unorthodox careers in the arts. Most were left-leaning and some homosexual. One, there just after Howson's death, was Donald Maclean, diplomat and Soviet spy.

# 26. Punishment in girls' schools

The statistics on corporal punishment above are all for boys' schools. There are no figures and indeed no debate on corporal punishment in girls' boarding schools because few people – starting with the government inquiries of the 1860s – seem to have believed such a thing happened. But there was birching in the day schools for girls, and in the fictional boarding establishments of both Dickens and Charlotte Brontë. Many women at private boarding schools in the later twentieth century tell stories of beatings, both with straps and rods to the hand and on the bottom with a slipper. One of my female correspondents attended a colonial prep school from the age of seven, where beatings with a stick for such sins as laughing in class went hand in hand with sexual abuse by the headmaster's son. Complex punishments without direct violence are more common in the accounts women have sent to me – a girl made to drink salt water, or being forced to contemplate her own vomit in the dining hall. Public humiliation is a common factor in the discipline systems for boys and girls.

Ysenda Maxtone Graham, who has collected and published women's reminiscences of boarding school from the Second World War on, says that vicious beating, especially in convents, was not unusual, though being locked in an unused room was more common. Verbal cruelty, 'something frustrated, angry women can do so viciously', was

what really cut her correspondents. Still, she told me that
when three girls ran away from her prep school in the
1970s, they were caned. Their parents had been offered a
choice of that or expulsion.

It is clear too that quite commonly the adults used the
beatings or the threat of them in emotional abuse. Often
the women, like the men, talk of being informed, hours
or days ahead, that a physical punishment had been decided on – and then enduring the dread of waiting for it to
happen. Honour systems like the one that so disgusted the
future poets and artists of Gresham's School were normal
in girls' schools. There too, the moral dilemmas were con-
founding and the atmosphere of suspicion deadening to the
adolescent spirit. Here is the novelist Elizabeth Arnot Robertson on Sherborne Girls' school during the First World
War, in an essay titled 'Potting Shed of the English Rose':

> Everything affected one's 'honour', the hardest worked
> word in our narrow world. And if one broke a rule one
> was expected to confess it to a prefect and have a nice
> spiritual wallow together . . . This system produced
> the most thorough-going prigs imaginable. At my
> first smaller, healthy minded school we all smuggled in
> sweets whenever we could: at Sherborne when I man-
> aged to bring some back one term everyone refused
> them smugly because they were against the rules, and I
> was forced to give them up to authority.

Robertson's essay – more wry than angry – pictures a totalitarian system that brutally imposed Stiff Upper Lippery
(her phrase), ignorance and fear of men and sex. It was licensed bullying: it had no physical side, but it was more
painful, perhaps. Those who baulked at the regime were

cast out, socially, and so became very unhappy. Twenty years on, Robertson's regular, most awful nightmare is a simple and familiar one:

> I am going back to Sherborne, starting all over again, and there is no chance of escape. Inside I am exactly what I am to-day, married, and an author and so on, but I cannot convince anyone of this because I cannot remember the names of my books, everyone assures me that there is no such man as my husband, and outwardly I am exactly what I was at fifteen.

This notion that the moral strictures and the systems to enforce them that the schools imposed were unhealthy, a perversion of the natural development of children, was much discussed in the 1930s, when Robertson wrote her essay for Graham Greene's collection. The contention that school warped children is perhaps the most serious intellectual challenge to the private schools until the Second World War, when the system began to come under serious attack as fount and perpetuator of social and educational inequality. It was not just left-leaning novelists who spotted a problem.

Discipline systems based on fear are 'disastrous', wrote a public school housemaster – electing to remain anonymous – in 1938: 'They make boys secretive and cunning [or] . . . build up a sense of guilt out of proportion to the offence.' They should be compared to Fascism: 'Not unnaturally one result of this schooling has been to perpetuate in adult life that human beings can be made better by being afraid . . . At the present moment in Europe an attempt is being made to frighten people into being better people, and that is simply another outbreak of the Public School philosophy.'

# 27. Resisting reform

It was a [twentieth-century] public school invention, that the masters, too, should come to put a moral value on the flogging itself, and should therefore be serving a double purpose in their whipping – expiating the offence and at the same time giving an exercise in physical courage . . . The point was that the beating was a good thing in itself, because it taught the boy to take it.

Ex-public school pupil and teacher T. C. Worsley in his 1940 book assaulting the system, *Barbarians and Philistines: the Democracy and Public Schools*

The fact that the public schools believed they had to beat to do their job properly – and the job was producing the best education known to humanity – must explain why so many attempts to stop it came to nothing. Nearly everyone in the profession (and many ex-pupils) believed in it. In 1952 a government survey of teachers from state schools found 77.8 per cent strongly in favour of corporal punishment and only 5.6 per cent in favour of abolition.

When he had settled into his public school in the Midlands in the early 1970s, Angela's headmaster father declared he wanted to abolish beating. He faced a rebellion:

Partly from the housemasters, who saw it as a central

tool to what they did and how they kept control. Partly
from the governors, who felt really strongly that what
was being offered was harsh discipline and that was in
itself character-building. Particularly from those with a
military background, who thought that physical punishment was central to the package of making a man a
man. And partly from parents, who on social occasions
would come up to my dad and say they were appalled
that beating was being phased out. There was very
strong and overt pressure. He dropped the plan, for a
couple of years.

The resistance to change is all the more extraordinary
in light of what had been going on elsewhere. In much of
Europe (but not the United States), corporal punishment
of children had stopped in schools in the nineteenth and
early twentieth century.* In 1669 the English parliament
was presented with a 'Children's Petition' against the 'intolerable grievance our youth lie under in the accustomed
severities of the school-discipline'. But that cry went un-
answered for more than three centuries. Even when the
'great' public schools were beginning to abandon corporal punishment in the 1980s, their product was insisting
in Parliament and the letters columns of *The Times* how
vital to British life and prosperity beating children was.
Still, the practice was ending, for younger children at least.
In 1994, in a piece titled 'Where to send your children
to school if you want them beaten', a Sunday newspaper

* Poland abolished the beating of children in schools two hundred
years ago; controls or bans came in in Holland in 1850, 1887 in
France, 1890 in Finland, 1917 in Russia, 1935 in Norway, 1928 in
Sweden, and 1968 in Denmark. Sweden made corporal punishment
in the home illegal in 1979.

could only find four independent prep schools willing to admit they still used corporal punishment.

Yet physical assault for disciplinary purposes as a punishment wasn't illegal in the private schools of Scotland or Northern Ireland until the early 2000s, a couple of years after England and Wales, and almost twenty years after it was outlawed in state schools (after a ruling in a European court). Even then the matter was not settled. In 2001 forty Christian schools challenged the law, arguing (unsuccessfully) in the High Court that there was a 'God-given right' to chastise. In 2011, a survey for the *Times Educational Supplement* found that 49 per cent of parents believed schools should be allowed to smack or cane. We have long been a society that is extraordinarily violent to children.

Yet there is ample research to show that children who are punished physically are more likely to suffer depression and other disorders in later life. A 2016 meta-analysis by psychologists at the University of Michigan looked at seventy-five studies conducted over fifty years, involving 161,000 children, to see what happened to spanked – but not otherwise abused – children. It decided that 99 per cent of the statistically significant results from the research 'indicated an association between spanking and a detrimental child outcome'. Those outcomes were: 'low moral internalization, aggression, antisocial behavior, externalizing behavior problems, internalizing behavior problems, mental-health problems, negative parent–child relationships, impaired cognitive ability, low self-esteem, and risk of physical abuse from parents'. It is hard to see why those problems should not occur in children beaten at school.

For a hundred years or more, long before scientific meta-analyses of spanking data, boarding school teachers and ex-pupils had spoken out against a 'savagery' that tended to make boys uncooperative and rebellious. When Daphne Rae, a magistrate and veteran of twenty-five years in boarding schools that beat children, wrote in 1983 that she was convinced 'violence breeds violence' and 'that corporal punishment inspired bullying', she was laughed at by the schools' establishment, and, naturally, its product.

But what she said was obvious. Harrow – considered the most brutal of the 'great' schools (in the first half of the twentieth century at least) – was notorious for formalised bullying and indeed for suicides. It also had the most baroque system of punishment by older boys on younger. The novelist L. P. Hartley, there from 1910, remembered some of the listed reasons for which he might get a 'whopping' from a sixth-former: 'leaning too far out of the window on a Sunday, letting a Sixth Former's fire go out when "on boy" [fagging], walking in the middle of the High Street when not a "blood" [senior boy] . . .' Wearing coloured socks, a grey waistcoat or the wrong collar were also beating offences. Like me, when he was whopped he took precautions – like wearing three pairs of trousers. By contrast, Hartley remembered his housemaster and teachers as wise, kindly and enlightened, not least, you imagine, because they had given the job of violent discipline to the boys.

Royston Lambert's work shows that schools where beating was permitted tended to be the ones where bullying was worst – and the more beating, the more bullying, especially if older children were allowed to beat the younger. Lambert also uncovers some nasty quasi-formal physical punishments dealt out by prefects to younger boys: whipping with a piece of rope dipped in brine at one school, fixed numbers of punches to the face for different crimes, and a Russian roulette game called pinfinger, which involved stabbing at the fingers with a geometry compass.

Some of the disciplinary punishments inflicted at girls' schools by the pupils sound even more cruel. My correspondent Alison Collett, at Red Maids' School, tells of being 'sent to Coventry' (ignored and ostracised) for *one and a half years* by her class because she refused to obey the older girls.

In the bulk of the schools, bullying seems to have been licensed; a part of the system of discipline that, if teachers were in short supply, could operate cheaply and automatically. If the beaten schoolboys were savage to each other, they were often far crueller to outsiders – whether 'oiks' from town, or other schools. Those who get a taste for bullying tend to go on doing it in adult life: Daphne Rae tells a story of a prefect who bullied at one of the schools her husband ran later being accused of the ill-treatment of prisoners of war. It was no surprise then, continues the argument, that a properly barbarised public school boy after school appeared to show little empathy or compassion for anyone else – whether it was unruly natives in the colonies, or the classes beneath him. This connection, often made by left-wing critics of the public schools, appears early in the twentieth century, first from George Bernard Shaw.

The playwright was an immensely influential figure in progressive thinking in the late nineteenth and early twentieth century. The beatings he received at school left a wound that festered productively, as they did for so many politicised writers of the time. Shaw's experience provided gritty insight into group psychology and what would soon be called 'normalisation'. In the preface to his play *Misalliance* (1914), he wrote: 'We are tainted with flagellomania from our childhood. When will we realise that the fact that we can become accustomed to anything, however disgusting at first, makes it necessary for us to examine carefully everything we have become accustomed to?'

The most important point – and the most challenging, even today – is that parents knew. If they had not been through it themselves, there was more than enough evidence, from their own children, from literature, from gossip, of the physical and emotional violence that was universal in the schools, especially the boarding ones. Summing up, the historian of Victorian education John Honey says this:

> So far from being a deterrent to parents, the aspects of cruelty, humiliation, fagging, and exposure to disease and privation which we have been examining fulfilled important functions in terms of a toughened end-product able to 'stand on his own two feet', to 'take hard knocks without flinching', served to prepare pupils for new roles in adult life, for which family life was an inappropriate preparation . . . The contempt for 'coddling' was afterwards held to justify primitive buildings, defective drains, public floggings and the tolerance of a measure of serious bullying, though of course no Lancing or Hurstpierpoint prospectus ever advertised these methods, or, explicitly, the end they served.

With the exception of the drains and the diseases, not much changed in the schools for most of the twentieth century. There was no demand for it to do so.

# PART FIVE

## Sex and Some Love

# 28. The war on lust

Public schools are the very seats and nurseries of vice. It
may be unavoidable, or it may not; but the fact is indis-
putable. None can pass through a large school without
being pretty intimately acquainted with vice;* and few,
alas!, very few, without tasting of that poisoned bowl.

Dr Thomas Arnold, headmaster of Rugby 1828–42, in a
sermon

The only thing that kept me going was love. I never
dared touch anyone. I thought I would have gone to
gaol – and hell.

John Betjeman

It is no surprise that sex was always pretty popular among
adolescents in the boarding schools. What seems significant, in a story of how the schools shaped the psychology
of their product, are the efforts to control or suppress the
children's sexuality. There was hardly a matter concerning
the genitals, from masturbation to menstruation, where
the traditional boarding schools did not utterly fail in

* The mid-Victorians used 'vice' or 'evil' for sins from rebelliousness
to gambling. 'Immorality' could mean masturbation, or more. In
1896 Winston Churchill successfully sued for libel over an allegation that he had committed 'acts of gross immorality of the Oscar
Wilde type' while a cadet at Sandhurst.

their job as educators. Instead they fostered in their charges ignorance, prejudice, fear and guilt – and some of those, quite deliberately. The history of sex education in British schools is a story of stupid mistakes and ideologically driven failures, right up to the present day. (Though now falling, Britain still has the highest teen pregnancy rates in Western Europe.) But in the closed and over-heated world of the single-sex boarding school, with amateurs, moral crusaders and the sexually confused often in charge of policing children's sexual lives and knowledge, some very strange things happened indeed.

Many have theorised – and fantasised – on the effect on the British ruling class of these strange and sometimes dangerous practices. A cast of entertaining sexual stereotypes have emerged from Victorian education: the flagellomaniac, the hairbrush-wielding lesbian sports mistress, the predatory male teacher, the asexual gynophobic upper-class Englishman, the painfully confused wedding-night virgins. The most famous of the latter was John Ruskin, nineteenth-century art critic and aesthete, who, discovering on his wedding night that his wife, unlike classical statues of women, had pubic hair, was so shocked that he fainted. (The story may well not be true, but it was widely enjoyed.) Effie Ruskin was only nineteen: she divorced him six years later on the grounds that the marriage was never consummated. Clichés these sexual types may be, but all are born of the truth that sex was one of the things the schools handled with perverse incompetence.

In the late nineteenth century, just as the schools regularised methods of discipline, a great moral panic overtook the headmasters. Gathorne-Hardy writes that fear of sex swept 'the public schools like a medieval plague, raging unchecked in the dormitories, changing rooms and studies, now torturing, now delighting, dictating the contents of sermons, the forms of social life, the minutiae of discipline, influencing the curriculum, the sport, even the very architecture . . .'

Many histories contend that the rise of official school sports in the late nineteenth century was driven by the belief that exercise would distract from homosexual activities. Card's history of Eton states: 'Theatricals were stopped, games took on an increasing importance . . . [the headmaster, Edmond Warre] had already used his influence to promote rowing, and to prevent punting and excursions up backwaters because of the moral hazards he suspected.' Dr Warre had been a boy at Eton, so he may have known a thing or two. But did sex really alter school architecture? I think Gathorne-Hardy is referring to the habit in the late nineteenth century of dividing the boys' dormitories into cubicles, so these could be locked from outside at lights out. That wasn't always judged sufficient to stop the most lustful. At Wellington, the headmaster, Edward Benson, had the cubicles topped with tangles of wire. Benson had worked at Rugby before taking command of the new school in 1857, so you have to suppose he had experience of the animal lusts of adolescents. (None of Benson's six children ever married.)

Schools were still altering their furniture to control the children's lusts well into the modern era – removing the doors from toilets, for example, or building whole rooms with rows of them unshielded from each other. When he designed the chapel (opened in 1929) at Stowe School, J. F. Roxburghe, the first headmaster, told the architect that seats in the choir shouldn't face each other, exchanging 'ravenous glances'. Christopher Hitchens writes about having to defecate and shower communally in the 1960s at the Leys School, not that this put boys off their vigorous mutual masturbation sessions. The vigilance and prudery often came with odd rules denying normal privacy, like the widespread insistence well into the modern era that children should swim naked. There was an important rationale behind this, as John Rae found out when he was a master at Harrow in the 1960s.

Rae tried to end nude bathing at the school's outdoor pool, partly so women could use it. The boys were pleased by the move but many teachers lodged passionate objections on moral grounds. The school's chaplain told Rae, by way of evidence: 'I find that little boys are more erotic with costumes than in the nude.' (A contrast to the worries of the late-nineteenth-century clergyman-headmaster of Rugby who designed a new form of elasticated rugby short to keep boys' knees hidden* in the turmoil of the scrum.)

Even at the high tide of Victorian panic about beastliness in the dormitories, there were people ready to mock the scare-mongers: it is a stiff-upper-lip trait to tell people to calm down and stop making a fuss. In 1881, the headmaster of Clifton College, the Reverend J. M. Wilson, gave a much-reported speech titled 'Morality and the Public School', that kicked off the nation's first ever debate about sex education.

Wilson starts with a dire warning: 'It must, I believe, be admitted as a fact that immorality, used in a special sense, which I need not define, has been of late increasing among the upper classes in England, and specially in the great cities.' This, along with the shocking outbreak

---

* This was John Percival, who had made his name at Clifton College and then became headmaster of Rugby in 1887 and later Bishop of Hereford. He did, however, appoint the first woman teacher at any boys' public school: Marie Bethell Beauclerc.

of 'voluptuousness' afflicting the nation, had begun in the great public schools, he was sure, often among boys at the age of eleven or less, though it was likely that the same problem could be found in 'the schools of the Middle Class'.

Wilson's prose is ponderous – but the message is panic-struck. He offered 'remedies' to his fellow schoolmasters for dealing with this nation-threatening immorality: exercise 'to the point of exhaustion', occupations to fill dangerous spare time, and 'mechanical arrangements'. These may have been dormitory cubicles or perhaps the metal chastity devices then available. There was also religion, that proven anti-aphrodisiac. His speech was given to the Education Society and later published as a pamphlet. It was widely reported. There were fulminations about 'vicious habits' and 'monastic evils' in the *Journal of Education*. It applauded Wilson for attempting to 'lay bare the cancer of upper-class education'.

Into the seething letters column of the *Journal* stepped 'Olim Etoniensis', an Old Etonian. He pooh-poohed all the fuss. It wasn't that there was no immorality, he said – there was lots. But its effects were 'ludicrously misrepresented', as he could show from the long list of his own immoral contemporaries. If the Reverend Wilson & co. were right, then:

Why, of course I should have to point to physical wrecks, men who have dragged hitherto a miserable existence, preys (not martyrs) to consumption and atrophy and insanity; or else outcasts from all good society. Now what do I find? That those very boys have become Cabinet Ministers, statesmen, officers, clergymen, country gentlemen, etc; that they are nearly all of them fathers of thriving families, respected and prosperous . . . The moral to be pointed is that happily an evil so difficult to cure is not so disastrous in its results. How many boys, or rather men, can Mr Wilson point to who owe their ruin to the immorality which he talks of?

Olim Etoniensis was not alone. There are plenty like him in the Victorian periodicals, most often leaping with worrying enthusiasm to the defence of school flogging. But for the next three or four decades, the moralists were firmly in charge, battling beastliness with trusted tools: sermon, Bible, cane, hard physical exercise and, occasionally, patented chastity gadgets made of tin and leather.

# 29. The sinful child

Beautiful: beautiful outside but corrupt within, like the boys.

The headmaster of Marlborough College contemplates the autumn foliage, 1920

Schoolmasters and mistresses clearly had very little trust in children when it came to 'immorality'. Some decided the best approach was complete denial. Many women's memoirs talk of headmistresses going to extraordinary lengths to hide and conquer sex. 'Our Headmistress encouraged the belief that sex was filthy, and the very thought or mention of it degrading . . . Marriage was for the lower orders and the stupid.' In her collection of women's boarding school stories, Ysenda Maxtone Graham tells of headmistresses snipping out suggestive words from programme titles in the *Radio Times*, and glueing together pages in books that had anything rude on them: 'Girls would hold them up to the light trying to glean a single exciting word.'

At the smart convent school St Mary's, Ascot, Chaucer's earthy proto-feminist the Wife of Bath and her Tale were banned, even though it was on the O-level syllabus. In some of the convent schools, well into the twentieth century, girls were not allowed to see their own bodies, bathing instead in calico tent-tunics with their arms inside and their heads poking out. The novelist Antonia White

wrote that at her convent school, she was once gently informed that she should not sleep curled up. 'Suppose, my
child, you died in the night,' the nun said. 'Would that
be a becoming posture in which to meet our dear Lord?'*
Antonia should sleep on her back, straight-legged, hands
crossed on her chest. The calico tents, writes White, were
tied around the neck and hung to the feet. 'They made
washing difficult,' she says. So White just lay and enjoyed
the hot water, 'with my cloak swelling round me like an
inflated balloon until the bell rang'. At other religiously
minded girls' schools, baths were taken in swimming costumes, 'in order not to offend the angels'.

Many Victorians believed that women had very little
to do with sex, anyway: 'The majority of women (happily
for them) are not very much troubled with sexual feeling
of any kind,' wrote a mid-century reproduction specialist, Dr William Acton. The headmistresses, almost always
unmarried, took that notion as their code well into the
twentieth century. Most of the accounts of girls' boarding
schools before the 1970s tell of boys and fertility being
seen largely as threats. When a hint of sex did break out,
the girls' schools reacted with extreme severity. Virginity was prized, at least by parents, until quite late in the
twentieth century, and as in so many patriarchal cultures,
chastity had to be closely guarded. While boys sometimes
got away unpunished, there are many stories of girls being
expelled for acts with boys far short of intercourse. At Wycombe Abbey School in the early 1980s, two girls were

* Lippington was the fictional name of the school in White's first
novel *Frost in May*. She later said that correspondents who had read
the book made her realise nothing had changed there, whether they
were writing in the 1880s or 1920s. The school is now called Wold-
ingham.

forced to leave for having flashed their legs at boys who were standing outside the school walls. Roedean School put up wooden hoardings when it was realised that passengers on the top deck of buses passing the school on the coast road might be able to glimpse the games pitches.

In the 1950s and 1960s complete sexual segregation was demanded by some schools outside their boundaries. In Sherborne and Cheltenham, where there were both girls' and boys' boarding schools, the boys had designated streets and so did the girls according to a colour-coded map. Breaking the rule might mean expulsion. At one provincial public school boys were told that they might consort with girls from the town's grammar school, but not those from the secondary modern.

By the 1980s, when Bella Bathurst was at school, the sexual liberation of the times had just produced more confusion. 'The English Language teacher liked to tell us that the happiest day of her life was the day of her divorce, the English Lit. teacher would point to Angel Clare's cigar in *Tess of the D'Urbervilles* and remind us of its penetrating implications. [A male staff member] liked to chase eleven-year-olds into the bushes for a bit of extra-curricular friskiness and the biology teacher would cover any topic except reproduction.'

The fear of women seems to have been just as strong in the boys' schools as the fear of sexualised boys. The headmaster of Harrow issued instructions in the 1960s to shopkeepers in the town about the need to keep 'young girls' from working behind the counter when the boys might come on to their premises. One argument against co-education advanced by a housemaster in the 1970s at Marlborough was that the arrival of a few girls in 1969 had so stimulated the boys that homosexuality increased.

John Rae, who tells this story, writes of the 'negative, even hostile' attitude to women in the traditional boys' schools. When he arrived to become headmaster at Taunton School in 1966, his wife came with him to the school chapel service on their first Sunday. Chaplain, masters and boys were all taken aback at this intrusion – 'One might have been introducing a strip tease dancer to the Athenaeum.' It was nearly a year before any boy spoke to Daphne Rae. Not much had changed in the course of the century: 'The opposite sex is despised and hated, treated as something obscene,' wrote Robert Graves of Charterhouse, where he went in 1909. The misogyny that is taken as a defining characteristic of the twentieth-century British upper-class male was born in the schools.

Comical though much of this seems now, some of the attitudes of the adults – whether inspired by prejudice or mere ignorance – caused anguish, especially to children already lonely or unhappy. Many grew up not just in fear and ignorance of the other sex, but also of their own bodies. Many women who were at boarding school as late as the 1970s and 1980s tell stories of humiliation around menstruation. Some just had not been informed of the practicalities of their fertility; for others, shame and stigma had been attached to anything connected with sexuality. There are numerous stories of convent schools where nuns refused to explain things like sanitary protection or persecuted girls over their choice of bras. In other schools custom rendered menstruation utterly unmentionable, even between friends. Another 1970s Wycombe Abbey girl remembers being forced, when her first period came, to carry a bloodied sheet through the corridors by an angry teacher.

# 30. 'Most vicious beastliness'

In extreme cases the outward signs of debasement are only too obvious. The frame is stunted and weak, the muscles undeveloped, the eye is sunken and heavy, the complexion is sallow, pasty, or covered with spots of acne, the hands are damp and cold, and the skin moist. The boy shuns the society of others, creeps about alone, joins with repugnance in the amusements of his schoolfellows. He cannot look any one in the face, and becomes careless in dress and uncleanly in person. His intellect has become sluggish and enfeebled, and if his evil habits are persisted in, he may end in becoming a drivelling idiot or a peevish valetudinarian. Such boys are to be seen in all the stages of degeneration, but what we have described is but the result towards which they all are tending.

Dr William Acton, 1857

The extraordinary catalogue of rules and sermons ('If you touch it, it will fall off,' was the unusually succinct advice of one Edwardian headmaster) condemning masturbation was being used to scare children well into the 1970s. But in the nineteenth and early twentieth century, schools would expel masturbators, fearing they would infect others: 'indecency' was a virus. Masturbation was widely said to lead not just to stupidity but homosexuality and murder; it is hardly surprising that there were suicides from guilt and shame about the act. Elsewhere, education about masturbation led to quite unintended results. The novelist Arthur Calder-Marshall remembered how, in the 1920s, his religiously minded school, St Paul's, used to take boys on prayer retreats in the holidays. There the older ones were tasked with warning the youngest about the risks of masturbation. The teenage instructors used to compete to get the prettiest youngster as their pupil. Adults or older schoolboys teaching the younger to masturbate is quite common in accounts I've been given.

Even today, shame persists; I have spoken to men who talk of enduring decades of worry about masturbation and its damaging effects, all instilled at school in the 1950s and 1960s. As contemporary American evangelical propaganda shows, the twin threats of hell and insanity for the masturbator have had powerful effects on adolescent minds. Even as medical opinion moved on from the William Acton view, the British schools took their time catching up, as they have with most advances in the science of child development. Edwardian boys were still being informed that 'one ounce of semen is worth forty ounces of blood'. Cuthbert Worsley's housemaster at Marlborough, where he went in 1920 aged thirteen, was less frightening: he told young Cuthbert not to worry, should he find 'white matter exuding from your private parts . . . It's only a sort of disease like measles'.

In the public schools, children were still being frightened about masturbation well into modern times. As late as the 1950s, both boys and girls had pockets sewn up, and hairbrushes with long handles were indeed banned in some girls' boarding schools. At one convent school in the 1970s, girls were instructed to sleep with their hands outside the bed-covers. David Hare, a gap-year teacher at Cranleigh School in 1965, heard the Christian, rugby-playing headmaster address the boys about the twin evils of masturbation and borrowing bicycles without permission. A much-reprinted Penguin book of the 1960s and 1970s, J. A. Hadfield's *Childhood and Adolescence*, wags a finger against 'self-love', proposing that girls who 'over-stimulate' themselves will be frigid in marriage. Even today, adolescents who are Catholics or Orthodox Jews have to confess the 'sin' of masturbation.

I was a thirteen-year-old in 1974, but I don't recall anyone warning against masturbation. The act was normally private but hardly shameful among my friends. It was not, as far as I know, a shared competitive sport as it was at Christopher Hitchens' school and many others. Some accounts talk of being taught to masturbate so early at their prep schools that it became a 'comfort blanket', a 'solace', an emotional crutch that remained necessary for years; still others of it being an act that stated freedom and individuality in a world that demanded conformity.

# 31. The facts of life

Mr Waterfield used to give all leaving boys what was called a pijaw. It was a brave but incredible attempt at sex education, to prepare the young boy for going out into the world. He always asked the same questions so everyone was prepared. His first question was usually: 'Do things happen at night?' We weren't entirely sure what he meant, but knew that the answer he wanted was 'No'. So this is what we all said . . . and went on to the next question: 'Do you know where babies come from?'

'No, sir,' I said, looking innocent. (I was.)

'Well,' he said, 'you know that hole that women have in front?'

Remembering seeing my sister's navel in the bath at home, I replied, 'Yes, sir.'

'Well, that's where they come from. Goodbye. Thanks for what you've done for us and good luck at Eton.'

Brian Johnston, cricket commentator, remembering his prep
school, Temple Grove

Most sexual education classes throughout the twentieth century were inept. One Cheltenham Ladies' College pupil remembers a slide lecture given by a medical doctor, brought into the school to educate the over-fourteen-year-olds. 'It showed a picture of two frogs in a tank of water. One of them jumped on top of the other. The doctor banged the screen with his stick and said: "There you are! That's it!" . . . Until I got to Oxford I didn't know the facts of life. When a man unbuttoned his trousers I was absolutely appalled.'

This is far from uncommon. The novelist Theodora Benson wrote of girls in their late teens at her boarding school asking each other how babies came. 'I had a sort of hazy idea but was not very sure of my ground, so I benevolently answered that I should only embarrass us both by telling her.' Much of girls' sex education until late in the twentieth century seems to have revolved around disease and pregnancy, the risks of both exaggerated (and the precautions largely ignored) in order to underline the message that virginity should be preserved. Even that could be obscured in metaphor. 'I want you to think about what it's like when you go into a bookshop,' a teacher-nun told her class at St Mary's, Ascot, in the 1970s. 'You buy a really *nice* new book, with a cloth binding and crisp new pages, and you open it and read it with great pleasure. Now, I'd like you to think how preferable that book is to a nasty old dog-eared paper-back that has been read lots of times before.' Benson insists that she and all her peers turned out 'completely normal': but she is in a minority. Many of the women of her era say that it took many years, and more than one marriage, to be at peace with their sexuality. 'Overstrained honour' was the cause of much suffering, Benson admits.

It was, as so often, what was not said that we needed to hear. I, like Brian Johnston, emerged scoffing from the sex talk given us at thirteen by my prep school headmaster, having learnt nothing new except that he had clearly developed some awful problem as a result of 'not having "gone" when my body sent the urgent message that I should' at Lord's while watching the cricket. Had his bladder actually burst, we wondered to ourselves? At thirteen in the mid 1970s we thought we knew all there was to be known about sex. We'd been fully briefed in dormitory talk and many of us had experimented on each other. But the list of things we needed to know about – and didn't – was long: sexual diseases, different sexual orientations, and most mysterious of all, women and how they functioned. There are many stories of children left blinded by euphemism. 'If a man takes a man into the corner of a room and talks to a man, a man shouldn't listen,' was the solemn advice given by a master to a young pupil at Marlborough in the 1930s.

The most glaring mistake in this tragi-comedy was that we were never told what should have been said first, and loudest: if someone older or stronger than you tries to make you do something you think may be wrong, or you don't like, then you can speak up about it without fear. Even today, NSPCC studies show that most children who are being subjected to sexual abuse do not report it until adulthood, if at all – and this in an age when educators are offered 'safeguarding' courses focusing on how to help children to 'disclose'. Unlike my day, when Billy Williamson, the headmaster who taught us about sex, had already made it very clear that disclosing anything about his staff's behaviour would get us, not them, punished.

Not all the traditional schools avoided talking about illicit sex. Alisdare Hickson, chronicler of public school sex anecdotes in *The Poisoned Bowl*, has a story of three sex talks given at one school. One warned the new intake of thirteen-year-olds to 'avoid older boys'; one cautioned sixteen-year-olds 'to avoid younger boys'; and one advised school-leavers 'to stay away from Piccadilly Circus'. Sex education was not compulsory in any schools in Britain until 1993, though by then it was common, even if only the strictly biological issues were discussed. The Conservative government passed a law in 1988 that effectively prohibited any free discussion of sexual orientation in local authority-run schools. There doesn't seem to have been any education about contraception in any of the schools, state or private, until the panic over HIV/AIDS in the mid 1980s.

The public schools created an unnatural environment for adolescents to mature in. It wasn't just the lack of the other gender – the case in most schools until the 1980s. Many of the children arriving at them had been separated from their families for eight months or more of the year since the age of eight, and had gone through the painful psychological processes resulting from the break with their families. While some, as we've seen, had been successfully hardened, others were full of fear and confusion as they arrived in a larger, even less safe world. Conventional psychology says that all of them, the tough and the fractured, would be lacking in self-belief and emotionally needy. 'All insecure children have compromised self-esteem; it is hard to feel loveable if you did not feel unconditionally loved by your parents.'

The luckiest of us translated those flaws and needs into friendship and love. There's no way of telling whether children separated early from parental love and tenderness form more passionate relationships with their peers. The only literature is around those who suffered early sexual abuse along with broken attachment – one of the after-effects of that sort of trauma is often a chapter of sexual promiscuity, as the victim tries out their own sexual power or their attractiveness.

What is clear is that, as with most growing teenagers, there was passion as much as there was lust. There are moving accounts of loving, platonic friendships between schoolboys, playing and poeticising together, in the nineteenth century. Later, when the laws on homosexuality were reorganised and notions of 'unmanliness' came into the dialogue of the public schools, all that changed: but before the 1880s adolescent boys had no fear of using the word 'love' about each other, or indeed their teachers. The fear was all about the opposite sex.

These sorts of relationships have been described evocatively in the context of the girls' schools, most of which tolerated love between younger and older girls in the form of 'pashes' and 'crushes'. Organising these might be tricky: 'Darling Angela, will you be my VBF, Pat says she won't be my VBF any more, only my BF. I MUST have a VBF so PLEASE be mine, love and kisses', runs a line from a schoolgirl's note. Women who were at the schools generally remember the courtships and the dramas with a smile, while agreeing that they were all about power. The younger girl was usually a devoted acolyte, choosing a good-looking prefect or 'a sporty girl with long legs' to adore, and then performing small tasks and giving presents in a ritual that sounds as much like worship as love. But there's little in the accounts to say these relationships caused any lasting hurt, or ever went beyond hugs and hand-holding. 'They would offer to empty your waste-paper basket, or they'd give you a note saying, "You looked so wonderful in chapel today." It was part of the whole language of how the school worked,' remembers one of Ysenda Maxtone Graham's interviewees. These rituals hardly existed in day schools.

They may seem charming now, but they were, surely, another symptom of a grave failure on the schools' part. Bathurst told me: 'Don't underestimate how obsessed we all were with sex, and how ashamed we were of being virgins. We were all longing for experience, and because we were so naïve about the opposite sex, a lot of us got ourselves into really stupid and dangerous situations – rape, in other words.'

For the adolescent boys, emotional relationships were certainly intrinsic to the working of the school. Ours were often less innocent than the girls' platonic courtship rituals. Many thirteen-year-olds tell of being thrust into a cattle-market system that immediately made judgements about them and their looks. In some schools the roles of 'bitch', 'lusher', 'catamite', 'cherub', 'stigg', 'T-boy' or 'tart' were in the ancient fabric of hierarchy and ritual; servants, decorative items or sex objects to serve the purposes of the 'bloods', 'Gods' and prefects, whom one day they would replace. That last fact must have been the only consolation when you were a small boy at the bottom of the system. Such structures hadn't changed much when I was at Eton, judging by the eighteenth- and nineteenth-century accounts of the school, though there might have been less coercion. John Addington Symonds, the poet and first historian of homosexuality, was at Harrow in the 1850s. Then, night-time in the dormitories and studies was 'incredibly obscene'. This is from a suppressed section of his memoirs:

Every boy of good looks had a female name, and was recognised as either a public prostitute or as some big fellow's 'bitch'. Bitch was the word in common usage to indicate a boy who yielded his person to another . . . One

could not avoid seeing acts of onanism, mutual masturbation and the sport of boys in bed together. There was
no refinement, no sentiment, no passion, nothing but
animal lust in these occurrences. They filled me with
disgust and loathing.

As his biographers have pointed out, Symonds' feelings
were in fact more complex, and he fell in love with several
boys. Though he was to marry and have children, his diaries make it clear he was largely homosexual. At Harrow
he claims to have successfully rejected the advances of the
'beasts' and remained 'clean'. But he was to help get Harrow's most famous headmaster, Dr Vaughan, sacked for
having a relationship with a pupil. Prostitution, casual
or organised, within the schools remained an issue into
modern times, and was often the subject of scandal. It was
still customary for a senior to use a pretty young boy as a
bed-warmer at one of the 'most important public schools'
at the end of the nineteenth century, or so claimed the then
headmaster of Rugby.

For adults, another literature of the schools was emerging – and one of the things it was most interested in was
sex. Alec Waugh's novel *Loom of Youth* (1917) was a scandalous and ground-breaking text; not the first to talk
openly of love\* between schoolboys, but certainly the most
overt. Waugh, Evelyn's older brother, wrote it when he
was eighteen, just after he'd been forced out of Sherborne

---

\* Love and lust at school make their first appearance in the novel
*Eric, or Little by Little* (1858) by the Harrovian Dean Farrar. This
was mocked, then and for ever after, not least for its hysterical warnings against immorality, especially masturbation. The latter led to
'polluted affections and an early grave', though an innocent reader
would have trouble working out what the fatal crime actually was.

School (amid a homosexual scandal). It was published the following year when he was serving as a machine-gunner in Flanders. It caused as much stir, and sales, as *Tom Brown's School Days* did in its time. It seems very light now, but it did open the public's eyes to everyday features of school life that schoolmasters and old boys 'preferred to keep hidden' – as Cuthbert Worsley, a near-contemporary, put it – 'homosexuality, bad language and games-mania . . .' By March 1918 Waugh was a hero and a prisoner of war. Nonetheless he was expelled from the Old Shiburnian Society by unanimous vote.

It seems improbable that parents – the fathers, at least – did not know what was commonplace. Squire Brown did, in a novel that out-sold Dickens's. He warns young Tom, just off to Rugby: 'If schools are what they were in my time, you'll see a great many cruel, blackguard things done and hear a great deal of foul talk.' The schools being founded at around the same time were taking action. At Radley, the founding headmaster, Reverend William Sewell, wrote that he had had enough of the notion 'that a schoolboy must needs go through a career of carelessness, irreligion, acquaintance – familiarity, rather – with sin and defilement in order to [enable] the formation of a manly character'. He ordered that all school doors be locked at night and ground-floor windows have iron bars installed; no one was allowed to leave the school bounds alone. Visiting sports teams from other schools were vetted for moral risks. Sewell warned the boarders:

Constantly we shall be visiting the dormitory, coming upon you suddenly – (until we feel you have strength enough to resist the temptation of being left alone) coming among you at all hours, myself, the fellows, the

prefects and if we should find it necessary even our con-
fidential servants.

This severe regime didn't last. By the 1940s at Radley,
'romantic, homosexual hero worship' and a tradition of
appreciation of good-looking younger boys – known as
stiggs* – appears to have been quite normal. Several old
boys told Alisdare Hickson jolly stories of this for his com-
pilation of anecdotes about sex at public schools. At the
height of one widely known affair between two boys,
the hymn at morning chapel was 'New every morning is the
love – our waking and uprising prove'. Having sung
the line, the 'entire school collapsed in giggles'.

Well into the 1950s and 1960s some of the girls' schools
frowned on the passionate, non-sexual friendships that
were formed between younger and older girls, and there
are stories of cruel interventions to prevent them – which
tended to make the romances all the more tragic and obsessive. At some schools the rule against fraternisation
was put in place and enforced by the children themselves:
it is still there in some of the schools that Royston Lambert visited in the mid 1960s, and there are taboos to this
day in schools where there's a climate of suspicion about
homosexuality.

In most of the single-sex schools amorous relationships between pupils were quite ordinary. By the 1920s
and 1930s writers who liked to mock Victorian morality, such as the Waugh brothers, Alec and Evelyn, Cyril
Connolly, W. H. Auden and Graham Greene, talked of

* The same word was in use at Repton College, accounting for the
name of the silent, helmeted driver in the BBC's *Top Gear*. Jeremy Clarkson, its most famous presenter, and his producer went to
Repton.

extra-curricular lust with enthusiasm. Connolly in his memoir *Enemies of Promise* (1938) was effusive about his love life at Eton. Romantic affairs in his group of aesthetes were the only thing about the place he enjoyed, so much so that until he was thirty-seven he believed he was homo-sexual. (Yet, by the time he left school, he had not had sex or even masturbated.)

Other writers, from E. M. Forster in his secret novel *Maurice* to Julian Mitchell in the 1980s play and film *Another Country*, made schoolboy love affairs the basis of romantic rebellions against harsh, straight, author-itarianism. These followed a tradition that began in the nineteenth century with Alfred Tennyson, writing of pas-sionate, platonic love affairs that were prosecuted with beautiful boys at school, the message often being that as adults they would never love so fully and purely. (Though when re-encountered in later life, the object of their teen adoration turns out to be awfully dull.) Summing up this period, Gathorne-Hardy attempts statistics: 25 per cent of the boys had 'lust affairs', 90 per cent had 'romantic passions'.

In a 1934 essay, the twenty-nine-year-old Graham Greene – son of a headmaster – summed up what certainly was becoming the prevailing notion among the intellec-tual left, at least: 'It is a curious system, but one common to all public schools, which prevents a normal sexual rela-tionship but punishes harshly any temporary substitute. It is the method of the State which offers no other means than theft to an unemployed man to feed his family, and then punishes him when he steals.'

At the same time, something of a revolution of tolerance was happening, albeit at the pace of a timid and conserv-ative snail. Cuthbert Worsley was probably reflecting a dominant view from within the institutions when he blithely announced in his 1945 tirade against private education *Barbarians and Philistines: Democracy and the Public Schools* that 'the majority of adolescents somewhere between the ages of 10 and 15 tend to be homosexual'. Given that Worsley was homosexual and had been both teacher and pupil in boarding schools, there's no reason to doubt him. But the prevailing view became that there was little danger of the 'queer' habit sticking, which was an excuse in itself. Why, in that case, was it seen as such a sin? wondered C.S. Lewis in his 1955 memoir of Malvern College, where he had been forty years earlier. 'There is very little evidence that it [leads to 'permanent perversion']. The Bloods would have preferred girls to boys if they could have come by them . . .'

In modern times, and certainly at my schools, it was certainly insulting to call someone 'gay' or 'queer', but few of us believed our affairs and experiments with our friends would dictate a lifetime's sexuality. If that sounds confused, we were also in the late 1970s embracing the politics of punk and the notion of homosexuality as an exciting rebel culture, way beyond the bisexual posing of glam rock: we all sang along to the Tom Robinson Band's anthem '(Sing If You're) Glad to be Gay', and then to Boy George. Attitudes were changing fast in the girls' schools too. My first serious rival in love, at seventeen, was the head-girl of a famous boarding school with whom I competed for the my first serious girlfriend. At that establishment it was quite fashionable, I understood, for the senior girls to have sex with younger ones: it made me very anxious. It wasn't really true, but as a sixth-former I told everyone I was proud and bisexual.

*

By the mid 1960s, adolescent children in the boarding schools felt able to inform the government-sponsored soci- ologist Royston Lambert and his team about their sex lives. (He says in the book that resulted, *The Hothouse Society*, that he and his researchers didn't ask for information about sex, 'but it sought us out in abundance'. In some of the sixty-six boarding schools they visited, 90 per cent of the answers to the questionnaires they distributed addressed sex. This led Lambert to a surprised conclusion: 'Sex is a major element of their personal and social existence.') The story his lengthy chapter on sex tells was shocking to the researchers and to Lambert's readers (the book was also very popular, for a dense work of socio-anthropology, re- printing several times). 'Large numbers of boys' among his interviewees (who totalled over 13,000) said that boarding 'stimulates pupils' homosexual instincts', and that many acted on those feelings. Some posed as homosexual because that was the cool thing to do: 'If you want to be in with the crowd, grab a junior quick, and use him supposedly as your "bum-boy",' said one sixteen-year-old. Other boys resented the fact that this had been forced on them: 'We get too fond of each other. We start thinking *only* of boys,' said two from a state boarding school. 'You have to exert strong will-power not to be a practising queer here,' said a seventeen-year-old public school boy. Others were blasé: 'I don't worry about homosexuality, I just enjoy it,' said a sixteen-year-old.

In some of these 1960s schools the sexual stereotypes – 'lushes' and 'tarts' – and the ritual of forced or bought sexual service by the younger for the older were still operating, just as they had in the nineteenth-century in- stitutions. 'If you've got a pretty face, watch it: there'll be a queue in no time,' said one subject. In one school, sexual affairs were not condemned – showing emotion was a worse crime. At another, love affairs 'bring prestige'. But there was still worry: 'Some fear discovery, others are preoccupied with the moral implications of their attachments or battle with feelings of guilt.' Lambert's sample did not look at any single-sex girls' schools: the 15 co-ed ones he did examine produced nothing so revelatory from the girls, who were policed much more fiercely than the boys.

And so, it became official knowledge – Lambert's study, the only one of its kind ever done, was funded by the Department of Education and Science – that teenagers were very interested in sex. 'To adolescents . . . the development, control and fulfilment of their sexual energies is a matter of overriding importance and a subject which pervades the talk, the imagery and the activity of the communal underlife.' But even if that was no surprise, what might have got official minds worrying was the copious evidence that single-sex boarding was often traumatic, psychologically and sexually.

How such trauma was dealt with varied from teenager to teenager. In his memoir *Hitch-22*, Christopher Hitchens – at boarding school in the late fifties and early sixties – describes his schoolmates enthusiastically masturbating each other (without ever making eye contact). But he adds that 90 per cent of these boys 'would have punched you in the throat if you had suggested there was anything homosexual (or "queer") about what they were doing . . . The unstated excuse was that this is what one did until the so-far unattainable girls became available.'

Hitchens enjoyed the 'monastic sex drama' at the Leys School, did not lack for partners and, like many of us, he fell in love, too. Deprived of obvious love objects, schooled in Victorian romantic verse, he says, he was vulnerable to the 'fantasy of the "romantic" idyll'. A boy called Guy was his willing partner. When Guy and Chris were exposed by an envious 'thick-necked sportocrat' they were forbidden ever to speak to each other again. It was a properly romantic penalty for love; it might have been imposed on Lancelot and Guinevere. 'At the time, I vaguely but quite worriedly thought that this might have the effect of killing me,' writes Hitchens.

# 33. Liberation

Many of us who lived through the schools in the late twentieth century can tell similar stories to Hitchens', and, like him, smile at them. But in my correspondence and interviews I have accounts from men who were much more troubled by these liaisons. There are those who believe they were 'turned gay' by experiences at school, sometimes unwanted. A few others talk of life-long suspicion and fear of homosexuals as a result of school problems – 'They are paedophiles, it's the same thing,' one man said to me. These though are largely the older men; the younger ones usually seem able to separate their consensual sexual experiences from those that were forced on them.

Sexual bullying was as common as bullying itself, and fagging systems could be part of it. At Eton, it was considered proper to select the prettiest boy you could as a fag (though that didn't necessarily mean you then had sex with them); and at Stowe and others there were systems whereby sexual favours were traded. 'They never happened with violence,' said Peregrine Worsthorne, the journalist and newspaper editor. He boasted that he had been 'seduced' in the school art-room by a younger boy, George Melly, later a famous jazz singer. 'A lot of buggery went on,' Worsthorne told the *Guardian*, 'and things in that area – but I don't think there was ever anything that brutal.'

Worsthorne's tone is the habitual one: wry amusement

at boyhood peccadilloes. When he first arrived at Stowe the boys tried to drown him in a bath. He continued sleeping with his male friends into his twenties. But while Stowe may not have been brutal, other places were. George Monbiot's account of his prep school in the 1970s is not unusual. 'New boys were routinely groped and occasionally sodomised by the prefects. Sexual assault was and possibly still is a feature of prep school life as innate as fried bread and British bulldogs.'

There are many reports of rapes of boys by other pupils in my correspondence and from my interviewees. This should not be surprising, given that nearly one in ten rapes or attempted rapes investigated by the police now is of men. More accounts of boarding school rape emerge now in published memoirs, as the stigma of being victim to something that might once have been seen as the ultimate in unmanliness lessens. Robert Montagu has told of rapes at Eton in the 1960s, and having to intervene to stop a victim killing himself. The disc jockey John Peel wrote in his autobiography how older study monitors (prefects) at Shrewsbury School swapped the younger boys amongst each other when he was there in the mid-fifties. The account is characteristically calm, but Peel's fury seeps through:

> They were not, generally speaking, interested in penetration, but more, as we have seen, in what we have come to know as relief – massage or even, in the absence of the below-stairs staff or hunting dogs they possibly slept with at home, warmth. Having experienced few physical expressions of affection at home – something that would have been true, I imagine, of almost every boy in the house – I was rather flattered by these

attentions and was aware, too, that the only people to
whom I could turn for help were, by and large, the very
people who yearned to cuddle me.

One of these prefects eventually enticed Peel, aged thirteen
or fourteen, to a public lavatory in Shrewsbury cemetery,
and raped him. 'Oddly enough, much as I hated the experience, I think I had become so accustomed to systematic
sexual abuse that I wasn't especially traumatised by the experience,' he writes. It was not until thirty years later when
he and his wife happened to drive through Shrewsbury and
past the lavatory, that he spoke to her of it.

The other detail that emerges from the accounts is this:
while not all schools saw sexual activity, there seems to
have been more between the boys at schools where there
were sexual predators among the teachers. Many people
who report sexual abuse by adults at their school go on
to mention what they now see as astonishing levels of
sexual activity generally among pupils. But then I've had
accounts of largely happy schools with no record of abuse
where the children were very active by the age of twelve or
so. 'We were amazingly sexualised,' says one correspondent
of his famous co-ed boarding prep school in the late 1970s.
The darkness of film nights at the school allowed 'heavy
petting' sessions between girls and boys that the teachers
did nothing to prevent. This perhaps says more about that
period than it does about pre-teen sexuality; I doubt such
a thing would be nodded at in today's more nervous and
sensitive schools.

There were still outbreaks of moral outrage and extraordinary purges, even as society began to relax a little about
sex. Harrow regularly expelled boys en masse in the 1920s
and 1930s for homosexual offences; at Eton in the 1930s

two hundred boys were found to be members of a 'mutual masturbation club': their parents were summoned, and the son of a peer was expelled for sodomy. In 1892 Brighton College closed an entire boarding house and expelled eleven boys in an attempt to root out the homosexual virus. But, slowly, as the twentieth century wore on, the moral panic subsided.

In the ups and downs of my school career, I went to both Eton and Brighton College; male pupils certainly did have sex with each other, though the fact was not openly discussed. I don't think that – unless bullying was involved, or the age gap was significant – either school would have reacted with anything as harsh as expulsion, if the authorities had found out. Schools acknowledged what seemed, at least in the boarding single-sex schools, an anthropological truth about adolescents kept in confinement. A famous story of one charismatic 1930s headmaster has a parent asking him what he's 'done' about homosexuality among his charges: 'Well, I haven't made it compulsory yet, if that's what you mean,' he replied. By the 1960s, when Francis Wheen was at Harrow, a master was well known for his stated view of where the limits lay: 'I don't mind mutual masturbation, but I draw the line at buggery.' John Rae, headmaster of Westminster in the 1970s and 1980s, remembered a Harrow housemaster referring to one of his younger charges as 'the school tart'. The majority of the teachers then and now had been through the same system. What they knew to be normal would only seem strange or wrong to an outsider.

Rae was the first headmaster of any of the 'great' public schools to write openly about sexual matters, and he did it while still in the driving seat. His target, in a polemical book published in 1980, was the old guard still insisting

on the virtues of single-sex education. Rae had been educated at boarding school, and he had taught at Harrow and
other traditional boarding schools before taking over at
one of the oldest and most hidebound. He was certain that
homosexual relationships 'flourished', and that exploitation including prostitution happened too. He was just as
definite about the damage he had seen in the old mono-sex
schools, where the adolescent sex drive was 'turned in on
itself' and any emotion that was tender or affectionate for-
cibly suppressed:

> It would be ludicrous to suggest that *all* public school
> boys grew up emotionally crippled; but in the old-style
> boarding school there was a risk of this happening . . .
> In that tight little world of taboos and almost total lack
> of privacy, survival depended on being able to hide your
> emotions. As a result some – perhaps many – boys found
> that as adults they were incapable of giving themselves
> freely in love. The risk was too great. Their emotions
> were like the inmates of a concentration camp: they had
> been confined harshly for so long that when the chance
> came to go free, they hardly dared do so. This rather
> than homosexuality or pseudo-homosexuality was the
> likely psychological aftermath of the single-sex board-
> ing school.

Rae's feelings were widely shared, including by Michael McCrum, the modernising head of Eton in place
from 1969. But it was a slow road. It wasn't until 1971
that the first traditional private secondary boarding school
(as opposed to the rare progressive ones like Bedales and
Dartington), Oakham School, went fully co-educational.
In 1979 only 26 of the 210 self-chosen 'elite' schools

of the Headmasters' Conference were co-ed. Eton only
had a couple of girls in the mid-seventies, the children
of teachers, though McCrum and the more enlightened
staff he recruited did encourage dances and debates with
the girls of neighbouring schools. At Wycombe Abbey
in the 1980s, all the sixth-form girls were members of
the Scottish Dancing Society: 'so we could get to snog
Etonians'.

But this was no real solution: these encounters didn't
begin to civilise us, even if that were possible. One girl
remembers the inter-school dances as 'cattle markets . . .
pandemonium': 'I seem to remember the ultimate goal
was to get off with as many boys as possible in the short-
est possible time.' The boys had similar aims: 'How many
did you finger?' we would ask. We were well-schooled in
competitiveness.

Co-education was a politicised issue, where liberal re-
formers warred with conservatives. The first of the grand
schools to admit any girls was Marlborough, in 1969: the
then headmaster said later that he had done it as part of a
campaign of 'jettisoning most of the remaining barbarities
and authorities which were thought (and still are in some
quarters) to be central to the public school ethos'. The
girls, he thought, would 'consolidate the liberal position'
against a 'fascist backlash'.

At one of my schools, Brighton College, in the late seventies there were a few girls in the sixth form who boarded:
their lives were not easy under the gaze of hundreds of
hyper-critical, sexually competitive boys. Many women
have terrible stories of the early days of co-education at the
grand old boys' schools. But today a minority of schools
are still single-sex, mainly because of the belief that adolescents perform better academically when separated. But

some of the older ideas still persist. The outgoing head of Eton, Tony Little, made a speech in 2015 saying that 'in a single-sex environment, you can allow innocence to last a little longer'. Many an ex-boarder will have smiled over that.

It's easy to laugh at the anachronisms now. But the confusions, the prejudice and the lack of help with adolescent difficulties caused vast anguish to some people, and to those with whom they lived subsequently. My correspondence is full of tales of sexual shame and confusion, sometimes life-long, all of which might have been avoided. When these culpable failures on the part of the schools were accompanied by invasions of sexual privacy, the effects could devastate, especially when the child was already schooled in hiding his or her emotions. Here's one of my correspondents, telling the story of what happened after he had had to fight to get away from a teacher who was trying to fondle him.

When my father came to take me out for the weekend I told him the story in the car. His initial response was, 'Well, I can see that it's upset you . . .' which sounded to me as though there was no real reason for me to be upset. He did speak to the headmaster about it, and the headmaster interviewed me. He took the view that I was probably telling lies with malicious intent but I must have convinced him because the teacher was relieved of his assistant housemaster duties so he would no longer patrol the dormitories at night. However he kept his job, teaching English to second-stream students.

I don't think I was the only boy that this teacher approached but for some reason I became known as the one the teacher tried it on with, and that may be why several older boys made approaches to me in the succeeding years. I had reported the abuse to the authorities (my father and the headmaster) because I knew in my heart that what had happened was wrong, but the response I got felt like sweeping it under the carpet rather than dealing with it to make clear that such behaviour is wrong and will not be tolerated. As a result I was no longer quite as sure of my moral compass, and I was not always able to say no with the conviction that was needed.

I left school without having come to terms with my sexuality and the social group I fell into, based around church, was entirely intolerant of homosexuality. I was delighted to have found friends and enthusiastically joined in, unknowingly banging nails into my coffin in the process. At the age of thirty I got married and am still with my wife twenty-eight years later, although after a breakdown nine years ago I finally worked out that I'm gay. I blame Boarding School for screwing me up so that I didn't know myself and made life choices that I would make differently if I had the chance to go back and make them again.

There were many endings to the narratives of sex at the schools. Some ex-public school adults can now see their illicit school relationships as unharmful or healthy, even if the need for them was born of unhappiness and lack of emotional fulfilment. Even Peregrine Worsthorne, who railed against 'queers' in his newspaper columns, was able in his eighties to remember his school and Army love affairs happily – 'I might well have been gay, but there was such pressure to be non-gay', he said in 2011.

C. S. Lewis writes with poignant compassion of the love

affairs that went on at his cruel and hidebound public school, Malvern College (which he called Wyvern), where the rituals of power and hierarchy seemed the only frame on which young lives might grow. 'Spiritually speaking, the deadliest thing was that school life was a life almost wholly dominated by the social struggle; to get on, to arrive, or having reached the top, to remain there . . . And that is why,' he concludes with wonderful aplomb, 'I cannot give pederasty [he means love between older and younger boys] anything like a first place among the evils at the Coll . . . Cruelty is surely more evil than Lust.' He goes on:

> If those of us who have known a school like Wyvern dared to speak the truth, we should have to say that pederasty, however great an evil in itself, was, in that time and place, the only foothold or cranny left for certain good things.
>
> It was the only counterpoise to the social struggle; the one oasis (though green only with weeds and moist only with foetid water) in the burning desert of competitive ambition. It softs the picture. A perversion was the only chink left through which something spontaneous and uncalculating could creep in. Plato was right after all. Eros, turned upside down, blackened, distorted, and filthy, still bore traces of his divinity.

Clearly there was no emotional crippling – as John Rae put it – for C. S. Lewis or for tens of thousands of others who emerged from the schools enriched by the sexual and romantic relationships they'd had. By the seventies a dawn was at last breaking in Britain: the long night of sexual ignorance and barbarism that had affected the schools for a hundred years or more was coming to an end. Guilt ebbed away, and what had seemed perverse or shameful became for many of us the stuff of wry reminiscence; and the relationships, loving and lustful, we were forced into in that strange environment just part of the complex story of growing up. But what remains is a legacy in the schools and the class that used them of misogyny and sexual prejudice. That's anthropologically interesting. But what's still pressingly important is the continuing failure to properly inform children of their rights, encouraging them to speak out, and warning them of how easily those that would exploit them can use their best instincts — of loyalty, of bravery — to procure their silence. Joan Smith, co-chair of the Mayor of London's Violence Against Women and Girls panel, wrote in March 2016:

> Children cannot possibly be expected to anticipate [sexually predatory] behaviour from someone in a position of trust. That is why they need to be told about warning signs, making sure they know what to look for and who to tell if they are worried by someone's behaviour. The obvious place for that to happen is in schools but a vociferous lobby exists, dedicated to opposing every attempt to introduce compulsory sex and relationships education on the ground that it would unnecessarily 'sexualise' kids. The truth is the opposite: denying children knowledge about the world puts them at risk from paedophiles who may inflict lifelong damage.

It is a paradox that dates back to the Victorian sexual confusions. By denying children's normal sexuality, the schools and the class they educate put children at risk of worse problems, including aggressive adult sexual predation. Yet, that same month that Smith wrote, the then

Education Secretary Nicky Morgan once again rejected a call, backed by police and a hundred organisations, to make such education obligatory. It is hard not to connect such obtuseness with the fact of her political colour: the Conservative Party must take some responsibility for what went wrong in the private schools, since for decades it rejected regulation and inspection of them. The reason for that was deep in the principle of stiff upper lip and not making a fuss. 'It never did me any harm' has succoured and supported child abusers for all that time, as the next chapter will try to show.

# PART SIX

# Captain Grimes and
# Captain Hook

# 34. 'Unfortunate predilections'

Some liked little boys too little, and some too much.

Evelyn Waugh, *A Little Learning* (1964)

Sit a group of ex-boarding pupils, men or women, down to talk of the teachers who made their lives difficult and the jokes will start. Dry, dark, competitive – but often terribly funny. One of the ways we were all schooled to deal with tribulation and suffering was with humour, though the jokes will often confuse and offend outsiders. 'You deal with the serious things in life by not taking them too seriously,' I've heard an ex-public school boy say to his girlfriend. 'Abuse is not a joke,' she replied. But the rest of us were enjoying the banter. We were taking turns to chip in with our own experiences, absurd, outrageous, hilarious. Then another grown-up public school boy capped all the stories with a wry account of his experience, aged thirteen, of multiple rape. That ended the conversation, not for embarrassment, but because his contribution couldn't be beaten.

So it is no surprise that the first sexually-abusing teacher to appear in English literature is also one of the great comic figures of fiction. Captain Grimes of Evelyn Waugh's *Decline and Fall*, published in 1928, is a happy-go-lucky, one-legged conman. He turns up to fill a staff vacancy in the failing Welsh prep school where disgrace has stranded Waugh's hero, Paul Pennyfeather. Grimes has only a walk-on in Waugh's semi-autobiographical novel, which was published when the writer was twenty-five. But his carefree criminality endeared him to generations of readers: he plays a note in tune with the anti-bourgeois song that was first heard among the social uncertainties of the 1920s, and which has resounded for those questioning received morality ever since.

Grimes must have reminded many people educated in mid-century Britain of a certain type of male teacher, often damaged in one war or the other. Unpredictable, fascinating, terrifying, their careers were often abruptly curtailed with no explanation. They wafted sulphur round the dull classroom. When I read *Decline and Fall* as a teenager, Grimes's face was that of the young and unpredictable Irishman with a scary maimed finger who taught science at my school. Mr Keane used to throw children down the stairs during his frequent rages and, if you were unlucky enough to find yourself alone with him, he would offer sweets in return for a fumble down your shorts. He too left in a hurry. One of my correspondents writes:

> The masters at my secondary school in Surrey were mainly just returned from WWII, bringing with them a violent, sadistic streak (that, perhaps, was there before the war), one making us 'parade' relentlessly. But it was their need to not only use corporal punishment on students, but to humiliate them in the process. And, of course, in modern parlance, we 'sucked it up', never complaining, never showing 'weakness'. And why not? There would be little sympathy at home if one were to reveal the extent of the abuse.

In the novel Waugh only hints at what crimes Grimes committed before his arrival at the spectacularly awful Llanabba Castle school, or what hastened his departure. The headmaster refuses to say. As much as Waugh liked to shock, he could not have published such detail in the 1920s, though that in itself told a lot to his more sophisticated readers.

Captain Grimes's original – a man called Richard or 'Dick' Young – worked with Waugh in 1925 as a schoolmaster at Arnold House, the prep school on which *Decline and Fall*'s Llanabba Castle was modelled. His colleague, Waugh told a friend in a letter, was 'monotonously pederastic and talks only of the beauty of sleeping boys'. But they became drinking buddies in the pubs near the school. The acquaintance continued after Waugh had left the school. 'Young of Denbighshire came down and was rather a bore,' wrote Waugh in his diary in April 1926; 'drunk all the time. He seduced a garage boy in the hedge.'

In his partial autobiography, *A Little Learning*, Waugh is frank about Young (whom he still calls Grimes). He says he was puzzled by his colleague, initially. Why would a man with private means choose to exile himself at a failing school in the gloomy wilds of Wales?

His weakness (or strength) was soon revealed. After a week or two a whole holiday was ordained in honour of [the headmaster's] birthday. It was no holiday for the assistant masters. The whole school was packed into charabancs in the early morning and driven to the slopes of Snowdon, where games were played and a picnic luncheon devoured . . . When it was all over and the boys in bed we sat in the common-room deploring the miseries of the day. Grimes alone sat with the complacent smile of an Etruscan funerary effigy.

'I confess *I* enjoyed myself greatly,' he said as we groused.

We regarded him incredulously. 'Enjoyed yourself? What did you find to enjoy?'

'Knox minor,' Grimes said with radiant simplicity. 'I felt the games a little too boisterous, so I took Knox minor away behind some rocks. I removed his boot and stocking, opened my trousers, put his dear little foot there and experienced a most satisfying emission.'

Dubious though this anecdote seems, it was Young's 'shining candour' that fascinated Waugh as much as his escapades. There is admiration for the amorality, his su-perhuman untouchability, in all Waugh's writings about the teacher:

> . . . Expelled from Wellington, sent down from Oxford, and forced to resign his commission in the army. He had left four schools precipitately, three in the middle of the term through his being taken in sodomy and one through his being drunk six nights in succession. And yet he goes on getting better and better jobs without difficulty.

Waugh certainly had, or had had, homosexual leanings, but it is Young's exuberant certainties, his obsessive pleasure-seeking – and the private income – that he envies. It's not hard to see why. Waugh's writing, private and public, is suffused with a cynicism and contempt for conventional morality that's familiar from other writing by the more self-aware ex-boarders of the time. His elder brother, Alec, had written that famously scandalous novel about love between boys at his school, Sherborne.* Waugh knew how wide yawned the gap between the terrible strictures against 'immorality' in the schools and the reality in most of them.

In today's psychotherapeutic jargon, we all had to 'normalise' that contradiction. You did that by accepting it, or following the problem's logic and questioning all adult strictures about morality and social regulation. In Waugh's case and that of many others, the problem of reconciling a love of traditional English culture and the hypocrisy and self-delusion of those greatest exponents of it was two-edged; an engine for their art, but also a source of depression and anger. Waugh's progression from punk novelist, rebel voice for a class and a generation, to curmudgeonly country gentleman, Catholic and Conservative is well charted. It reflects the experience of many others who found the hypocrisy too awful to be able to make peace with the society.

In Waugh's view, Young's activities were nothing that deserved reproach. Far from it: he was admirable. Young 'was a man without deceit'. Honesty, especially with your friends, is a cardinal virtue for many writers from the public schools – sometimes it seems like the only one. As we've seen, the chief moral message of the schools – and it seems to have been hugely pervasive – was against lying. And that is one that even a rebel might agree with.

Grimes's predilection was entirely forgivable, even laudable, for Waugh, who had a taste for behaviour that flouted social conventions. Most to the point, Grimes/Young had not committed the greater sin of being dull (except, on

* Both Alec Waugh's *The Loom of Youth* (1917) and Evelyn Waugh's *A Little Learning* (1964) were banned by their respective public schools, thus ensuring healthy sales.

occasion, when he was too drunk or talked too much of little boys for Waugh's taste). He may be – he is – a child-molester, but he is also one of Waugh's greatest comic characters. The lesson is important: it is small-minded and awfully bourgeois to support society's plainly hypocritical rules about sex – and that air of jaded knowingness about such matters is something Britain's upper class have liked to affect ever since. Who could behave differently when pondering the hazards their children might face at school?

Waugh says elsewhere in *A Little Learning* that 'pederasty' was normal in the schools. 'Assistant masters came and went at Heath Mount . . . According to their tastes they mildly mauled us in the English scholastic way, fondling us in a manner just short of indecency, smacking us and pulling us and pulling our hair in a manner just short of cruelty.' The accepted limits implied by 'just short of' have now shifted, but he is right that such behaviours were more normal than not. I had a teacher at Eton whom I liked well enough: when we were thirteen, but not older, he would idly run his hands up and down our thighs while we stood at his desk to have work corrected. (This was not uncommon – many accounts feature similar 'gentle molestation', as one correspondent puts it.) It was unpleasant, but more embarrassing for him, I thought, than me: trying to excuse Mr Payne, who was also my housemaster, I used to think to myself this was exactly how he caressed his golden Labrador. Today of course he might have been arrested.

Dick Young was never arrested, as far as I can make out, even though he had sex with boys in many places – a railway station waiting room, for example – much less safe than boarding schools. Unlike in the novel, he continued as a schoolmaster until 1928 – three years after Waugh and he were at Llanabba together. Young became a solicitor. He published his own novel *The Preparatory School Murder* in 1934. It contains a revenge: there's a Waugh-like character whose turn it is to be the pederast. Young died in poverty in 1971.

As was the custom, Evelyn Waugh sent his own son to a boarding prep school, the Catholic All Hallows; the boy went just two months after he had reached his sixth birthday. A Grimes awaited him. In his memoir, Auberon Waugh tells of the pipe-smoking proprietor-headmaster, F. H. R. Dix. He was war-damaged and in his way just as strange as Captain Grimes, though considerably more violent. Dix liked to look at the little boys naked, en masse, and when not beating them in his frequent rages was apt to pull out tufts of their hair. 'Even now,' Waugh wrote, aged fifty-one, 'I cannot smell pipe-smoke without feeling a strong urge to run away.' Others recall Dix as cruel and sadistic. But he is still celebrated today as a great schoolmaster: the Catholic public school Downside has an annual scholarship named in his honour.

Auberon Waugh wrote in the *Spectator* in 1977 about the peculiar relationship between the class that used the boarding schools and sexual predators who worked in them:

Members of the upper and upper middle classes (we, gentle readers, the Beautiful People) have always got rid of our children by sending them to boarding schools. We have usually known that a small but significant proportion of the teaching staff of these establishments is paedophile. Such stirrings of guilt as we might have felt at this inhuman treatment were subdued by the reflection that the education was better and we were making enormous financial sacrifices to send our children off in this way.

Those parents who were prepared to face up to the matter – I am amazed by the number of my contemporaries who assure me that homosexuality has now disappeared from the nation's preparatory and public schools – accept that there must be some consolation in the miserable life of those who choose to look after children.

Which may explain the fairly tolerant attitude towards these unfortunate people which has grown up in our bourgeois society. It does not extend to child rapists or violators of pre-pubertal girls, but if the boys end up buggered that is accepted as a small price to pay for the opportunity to develop their whole characters etc. which separation from parents must bring.

Auberon liked to tease as much as did his father. But he did not send his children to board.

# 35. The first confession

Richard Meinertzhagen, soldier, spy, scientist, sportsman and ornithologist, is the very stuff of British boys' fiction. Aristocratic, brave and cunning, he made a late-imperial superhero so perfect he might be a parody. He was – to choose just one from a host of escapades and adventures – the inventor of the 'Haversack Ruse', the deliberate loss of secret battle plans to fool the enemy into posting its forces in the wrong place. He had wit and sangfroid, important in a fully rounded, stiff-upper-lipped *Boy's Own* hero. 'Why waste a good meal?' said Meinertzhagen, as he polished off the Christmas dinner of a German officer whom he had just killed at the table. This was in Tanganyika in 1916. Two years later, he was in Russia attempting the rescue of one of the Tsar's daughters from the Bolsheviks. Meinertzhagen survived many manly scrapes and some humiliations: he was Bond and Bulldog Drummond with a touch of something seedier, too.

Since his death, Meinertzhagen (CBE, DSO) has been the subject of hero-worship and a savage revisionist biography. He has been accused of fraud and the murder of his heiress second wife. But no one has questioned his story of the abuse he suffered at his preparatory school, or questioned the extraordinary psychological insights he drew from it. If it didn't happen, you have to ask, why would this proud man bother to invent it?

Meinertzhagen published his memoir, *Diary of a Black Sheep*, in 1964, when he was eighty-six years old. It was, he claimed, based on the seventy volumes of diaries that he kept, starting at the age of six, in 1884. It is a loosely structured collection of anecdotes, war stories and accounts of everything from encounters with poachers and insincere women to his meetings with Oscar Wilde and Cecil Rhodes. Among all this you find a short account, leaning heavily on the diaries, of his time at the Sussex school Fonthill.

In May 1889, Meinertzhagen's parents removed him from Aysgarth, a boarding school in Yorkshire, and sent him to one in southern England for his precarious health. They chose Fonthill, near East Grinstead in Sussex. It was run by two brothers, Walter and Ashton Radcliffe, whose father had started it. Shortly after the eleven-year-old arrived, he complained to his mother that he was frightened of the 'cruel' Walter Radcliffe, who 'makes me stand in front of him as I go to bed', and had threatened him with a beating. 'Please don't tell Dan [his older brother] and please may I come home at once?' his letter, preserved with his mother's papers, concludes.

Georgina Meinertzhagen was one of a famous set of sisters, the Potters, who made their lives busy with good works and socialist politics. She wrote back telling him that masters did not punish little boys without good reason, and 'whatever punishment would be to my own good'. Richard, like so many little boys before and after him, felt desperate. 'If I could not appeal to my mother with any success, to whom then could I turn?'

But things soon got 'one hundred times worse':

Walter was in the habit of visiting my room after I had retired to bed. [Richard had been moved from a dormitory to a single room, without explanation]. I regarded the man with a feeling of loathing and revolt. Bolting my door was no protection, for on the next day the bolt was removed. I did not understand the full import of his behaviour for many years. I sought refuge in prayer, but that was of no avail for I would be jerked to my feet. Soon after I was bullied in the classroom when Walter would demand an answer to some grammatical conundrum which he must have known I could not answer. A stick was sent for and I was beaten, not once but several times with real hard welts. This was a new terror but it continued throughout the term, beatings taking place three or four times a week. At times I was so bruised and bleeding I could not play games or sleep at night. I was completely cowed, shamed, terrified and distraught with fear.

At the end of June, Richard Meinertzhagen appeals again.

My darling mother,
Walter is a devil and is very cruel and he beats me many times a week because he says I am obstinate. I am so frightened I cannot answer sometimes and I think I shall kill him because I hate him so. Do please take me away because last time I was beaten there was lots of blood and I have never done anything wrong here, it is all because he hates me so. Please come down and talk to Walter. Oh do please help me.

He does not tell her about the visits to his room at night – the 'other treatment that shamed me into silence' – just as he doesn't enlarge on that to us, seventy-five years later.

Similarly, many people in my correspondence seem to have been able to tell their parents about beatings and bullying, but not the more shameful event of being sexually assaulted. The latter might be because of a sense of complicity, all too common, or threats from the abuser. But the fear of not being believed is a powerful deterrent too.

Nothing penetrates Mrs Meinertzhagen's conviction that her son's suffering was for his good. You wonder if it might have made any difference if she had found out about Walter's sexual assaults. Even when Dan, Richard's elder brother, intervenes, on seeing the injuries that the eleven-year-old brought home at the summer holidays, she does nothing. Meinertzhagen's hurt and fury is palpable.

> If one of my boys [he had a daughter and two sons] had returned from school with his back and buttocks black and blue from bruises and his vest stuck to his back with congealed blood I should have been furious and distressed . . . I certainly would never have allowed my boy to return to further sadistic cruelty. I should also have given my boy as much devotion and sympathy as I could, in an effort to heal the injury to his soul and his character. My mother, on seeing my weals, told me I must have behaved very badly.

Meinertzhagen resented her all his life: not for sending him away, but for failing to believe him. You can't help but think – and child psychotherapists know the mechanism – that he was using the beatings as a flag for the thing he couldn't talk about, the sexual abuse. But Georgina Meinertzhagen rejected the cry for help. Richard's reaction was extreme:

At that moment something broke within me. Even now I can feel the pain of that moment when something seemed to leave me, something good; and something evil entered my soul. Was it God who forsook me, and the devil who took his place? But whatever left me has never returned, neither have I been able to cast out the evil which entered into me at that moment.

Like many another child, the realisation of the failure of the adult system of justice results in a dramatic decision, essentially to reject the entire structure of belief. These feelings caused me, at Eton aged fourteen, to declare (with high self-regard) that I was not going to be confirmed as a Christian, since some of the Christian adults I had met had been brutes and hypocrites. These acts of rebellion and rejection are pleasurable, and many ex-boarders talk vividly of such feelings.

But to decide you are evil? That is not uncommon, either. A man who wrote to me about his bad experiences – chiefly unjust beatings – at my own school, twenty years earlier, says that the anger about them made him 'demonically focused – aka successful', attributing a lucrative career to his realisation that rules were of no use to him. He adds: 'If the child is broken or weak he will perish.' The psychoanalyst Francis Grier talks of the phenomenon of patients who, as children, decided they were evil to explain why they were sent to board. 'At that age it is easier for you to think you are bad than to think that your parents are.'

These realisations form habits, modes of survival, that may shape a life. They did Meinertzhagen's. But the decision to overturn or reject the natural order does not necessarily cure the trauma, or soothe the child's hurt. Another result of these traumas for many children – it is told again and again in my correspondence – can be the quite conscious forming of two selves as a device for protection, a notion understood by the psychiatry of personality disorder. I have several correspondents who have acquired this diagnosis and now use it as part of the narrative of their lives and their ups and downs – and ascribe it to others.

Similar is the phenomenon psychiatry calls dissociation: ex-boarders also talk of their 'inner world becoming detached from the day-to-day world', or 'going through life as an observer, distant, detached'. So it is fascinating to read Richard Meinertzhagen, writing in his diary long before the era of cognitive behaviour therapy on the NHS. On 8 November 1889, back at Fonthill and into his abuser's clutches, 'Walter has started again, the beast.'

> There are two MEs, the outward and visible one, gloomy, argumentative, intolerant and suspicious. The other ME is right inside me fighting against all these things, longing for a little encouragement and appreciation, hoping that some day and somewhere I shall find love and peace.

The formation of 'two MEs' allows one persona to do things the other does not approve of. Four weeks later, he was contemplating killing Walter. Then he sank into depression: 'The end of term is near but I feel I don't care if I go home or not. I feel so unattractive, such a wanderer and outcast and only half alive. I believe there is good in me somewhere but it is all trampled down and crushed.'

Meinertzhagen remained at Fonthill till his time was up, in July 1891. He was 'intensely unhappy' for all of it. But he did learn to fight back against Walter, once hitting him on the head with a stick and then running away from the school, in the hope he would be expelled. He does not muse much on the long-term effects of Fonthill. He reveals that he was sexually prudish and inexperienced for many years, without making any connection. But he does say:

> Even now [three years before his death in 1967] I feel a comparative stranger with many members of my family. The intimacy of childhood can never be perpetuated in manhood unless it has remained unbroken . . . My false dreams of universal love were dashed to the ground at Fonthill.

Meinertzhagen went on to Harrow, where he was a little younger than Winston Churchill, 'a lonely boy', with whom he fought. He soon joined the Army. Some eminent people were entranced by him: the First World War prime minister Lloyd George wrote that Meinertzhagen struck him as one of 'the ablest and most successful brains' he had met in any army. Lloyd George added, 'That was quite sufficient to make him suspect and to hinder his promotion to the highest ranks of the profession.' Others admired him less. Some who were not seduced would perhaps nod at the notion that evil had found a place in Meinertzhagen's soul. He and his troops carried out massacres in East Africa and, since his death, Meinertzhagen has been accused of at least two cold-blooded murders.*

* In his book *The Meinertzhagen Mystery – the Life and Legend of a Colossal Fraud*, the thriller and cowboy novelist Brian Garfield paints a picture of an entrancing fabulist, utterly immoral, so addicted to falsehood that he will invent everything from his meetings with Hitler to thousands of records of bird spotting.

One of Meinertzhagen's detractors was another loner hero of the late Empire, T. E. Lawrence. That warrior called the other 'savage'. In *Seven Pillars of Wisdom*, Lawrence wrote of Meinertzhagen's 'hot immoral hatred of the enemy' (in this case of the Ottoman Turks during the Palestine campaign of 1917):

> Meinertzhagen knew no half measures. He was logical, an idealist of the deepest, and so possessed by his convictions that he was willing to harness evil to the chariot of good . . . He was a strategist, a geographer, and a silent laughing masterful man; who took as blithe a pleasure in deceiving his enemy (or his friend) by some unscrupulous jest, as in spattering the brains of a cornered mob of Germans one by one with his African knob-kerri. His instincts were abetted by an immensely powerful body and a savage brain which chose the best way to its purpose, unhampered by doubt or habit.

What happened to Richard Meinertzhagen? What psychological motor drove this man, so rich in empathy and insight, yet undeniably sociopathic too? He was a collection of paradoxes: moral and amoral, loving and hate-filled, callous and gentle, self-deprecating and self-aggrandising. He was haunted by the notion of evil, and his capacity to do it. That is not uncommon, but what is remarkable is the level of self-awareness.

The answer to the Meinertzhagen conundrum lies, you have to assume, in the dual self he constructed at the age of eleven. It enabled him to be both the sadist and murderer his enemies saw, and the sensitive moral man who appears in the diaries and other accounts. The one certain thing is that at the beginning and end of Meinertzhagen's eighty-year-long psychodrama, his tribulations and his undeniable achievements, stands another two-faced man: Walter, the headmaster of Fonthill School.

# 36. Different times

Some schools were quite relaxed about children sleeping with teachers. At Dartington Hall, set up as progressive and co-educational in 1926, such things occurred long before the Swinging Sixties. William Curry, who had also taught at Bedales, a school unfairly notorious for sexual licence throughout the twentieth century, was headmaster of Dartington from 1930 to 1957. In 1936 a director of the school's parent company wrote furiously to Curry asking if the school actively encouraged sexual intercourse between staff and pupils. Did Curry himself do so?

Curry's reply cannot have satisfied the man. 'Most English girls, brought up in the English climate, do not want complete sexual relations while they are of school age.' Dartington was partly run by the 'Group' of older pupils. In the 1950s, a meeting of these considered the case of a girl pupil who 'had an affair' with a male teacher and, though generally disapproving of sex, gave approval to this liaison because 'it would be good for her to have a physical relation with someone she loved'.

'Jane' was at the school in the early 1970s. Royston Lambert, the pioneering sociologist and investigator of children's feelings about their schools, was headmaster. She remembers him well and very fondly: a rare adult who was really interested in what she and other children felt, in solving their problems and getting the best for her. 'Jane' had a sexual relationship with a different senior teacher. It did her no harm, she now says, though she was only fourteen. 'It was not coercive, and went on for a while – it ended when he turned his attentions to another of my friends.' She believes other teachers must have known about this teacher's affairs, though she has no proof that they did. Sex and illegal drug-taking were very common at the school, and not much policed. Lambert survived only three years as headmaster, though it appears he fell out with the school board over matters of business strategy, not moral policy.

A few years earlier, Lambert was taking testimony from private and public secondary school pupils, providing us with the closest thing to hard data that exists on the extent of adult predation in the boarding schools. This is far from conclusive, but certainly disturbing. Here's a twelve-year-old, answering the question, 'What problems does life hold for you at school?':

What I do not like is my Housemaster, Mr Tompkins. He is very dirty in his mind and it affects his actions. He looks at you in the toilet and in the bath. When he canes somebody he hits you anywhere, on the arm, legs, back anywhere. He has had a warning from the head-master about being sexy. Nobody likes him.

There's more like that. At another school, a housemaster is accused of trying to 'bum' a pupil, and 'get the Corps members to take off their uniforms'. In one school three children warn Lambert's researchers about certain members of staff – 'keep your legs crossed'. This sort of thing might be maliciously invented, but Lambert took it seriously: 'In these schools the constant reiteration of this sort of comment and other supporting evidence forced one to accept them as plausible.'

But Lambert did not dig further. In fact, he suppressed this information. 'These are only a fraction of their comments and by no means the most sensational – many more disturbing expressions are withheld in our research files.' Professional qualms appear to have stopped him from reporting any of the allegations. As the writer and psychotherapist Nick Duffell has commented, it is extraordinary that Lambert does nothing, given the danger these children were in. 'Perhaps the fact that the language was jokey and crude led him to imagine these things childish pranks,' writes Duffell:

> But this is a problem that those who work with child sexual abuse will recognise. The language with which children describe such situations, whether they involve sexual harassment, propositioning, or sexual acts, is invariably childish and often regresses since it involves things which children do not know how to talk about, and certainly not to adults.

In an odd phrase, Lambert dismisses the reports of sexual activity between teachers and children as 'widespread in only four out of the sixty-six schools' at which he collected testimony. But as Duffell points out, these are multiple disclosures – three-quarters of the children brought the subject up – from 6 per cent of the sample schools. If that ratio was spread through the school population, that would involve more than one child in every class. Given the pressures on children not to 'disclose', it is hard to avoid the conclusion that sexual abuse by adults in schools is and always has been underestimated, perhaps grossly so.

Official inquiries into child abuse in the American Catholic Church in the twentieth century have come up with similar percentages: around one in sixteen, 6.5 per cent, of Catholic priests were accused of molesting children, with the allegations peaking in the 1970s.

It is even rarer to find accounts of predatory adults from the prep boarding schools. But that is not because abuse was not happening there. Rather it may be because no researchers have ever systematically asked the question. Vyvyen Brendon, who trawled published material and interviewed ninety former prep school pupils, male and female, for her book, writes: 'Generally sex does not loom very large in memoirs of prep school life and still less is it the subject matter of letters home. Indeed, it is probably safe to assume that most of these pre-pubertal boys were . . . innocent.' Her conclusion does not follow: the censorship of letters home would certainly rule out any confessions, and few of her correspondents are the sort to publish stories of pre-teen sexual experiences in memoirs.

Brendon writes that she never asked about paedophiles in the schools, nonetheless she received several stories similar to the Caldicott one (that is, of schools with groups of adult abusers) – 'painfully enthusiastic paederasts' in one of her interviewees' accounts. Generally, modern historians of the schools seem to have been successfully misled by a class that was not just notoriously circumspect about sexual matters but also trained to keep silent about shameful scandal, especially when the revelations might damage its power. The most recent history – by David Turner, a former *Financial Times* education correspondent – only considers predatory teachers in any depth at all in looking at a couple of famous examples from Eton in the mid-nineteenth century. Turner dismisses every account or allegation since then in less than a paragraph, concluding that 'a tiny minority' of public school teachers sexually abuse their pupils.

Statistics are never going to be available. The eight hundred or so first-hand accounts of boarding school, 'prep' and 'public', sent to me are almost entirely unhappy stories. But it is interesting that more than half of these mention some form of physical or sexual assault (often both) by an adult that would have constituted a crime at the time (I am not counting caning, which was still legal in private schools in England until 1998). With women correspondents, more of the accounts are of psychological and emotional abuse, but there are stories of sexual assault by adults among those too.

Before the end of the twentieth century, a combination of the codes of secrecy and normal prudishness about sexual matters (and the habitual destruction of private diaries) may account for many of the accounts of 'romantic attachments' between children and teachers not being explained as the physical relationships that they were. Gathorne-Hardy writes that the Victorian headmasters and headmistresses, more often than not unmarried, simply 'did not talk about sex'.

That is not entirely true. But the language must have been difficult for the adolescents to decode: clearly 'vice' could mean anything from masturbation to a failure to get out of bed on time. A century later, little had changed. Auberon Waugh reports the interrogations at his prep school after 'an epidemic of pseudo-buggery' in the dormitory. This was translated by the deputy headmaster as 'vulgarity'. 'Were you vulgar with Crichton-Stuart?' he asked. 'Were you vulgar with Niven?'

Waugh may have been teasing the readers of the *Spectator* – who knew him best as a satirist – when he suggested that the upper class knew their children were quite likely to be in the care of paedophiles. But it's hard not to conclude he was right. My research and that of journalists such as *The Times*'s Andrew Norfolk indicates that, within living memory, at least a quarter of British boarding schools have had credible allegations of sexual abuse by adults – at least of abuse and neglect in which adults appear to have been criminally negligent.

But that may still be to understate the size of the problem. At the few schools where we or the authorities have been able to dig deeply, what was reported as a single or a few cases of criminal assault has always turned out to be more than that. At Gordonstoun, Aberlour House, Allen House, Crookham Court, Caldicott, St Paul's and its junior school Colet Court and a host of others, the case that comes forward turns out to be a flag for others. Lone sexual offenders in the schools were rare: groups offending, often over long periods, are far more common. With that in mind, I looked at the hints in the history of the schools in a different light.

# 37. Traditions of tolerance

Most historians tend to excuse the senior teachers in the most famous scandals – Charles Vaughan of Harrow, William Johnson Cory and Oscar Browning of Eton, Anthony Chenevix-Trench of Bradfield, Eton and Fettes – because, though their behaviour with their pupils certainly led to their dismissal, the fact that sexual acts were not alleged or detailed allows the teachers to be given the benefit of the doubt. Others, like Jonathan Gathorne-Hardy, tend to see sex behind every anecdote.

But the first-hand accounts sent to me indicate that many teachers who could behave in a 'romantic' but platonic way with several pupils would often be having a sexual relationship with another child. The romance was 'grooming' and a way of testing if a sexual advance was possible. It fits a pattern of behaviour among preferential paedophiles that professionals in sex offender treatment are all too familiar with. One serial offender, convicted several times, talked to me of his young, prep-school-age conquests entirely in terms of teenage romanticism; a 'fanciable' boy might 'be keen' on him, or vice versa, a friendship would evolve and eventually, after much flirtation and testing of the water, a sexual element to the relationship would begin.

Tim Card, the long-serving Eton housemaster who published a ground-breaking history of the school in 1994 (unlike almost all accounts, it dares to look at the institution's darker moments), examines the Victorian-era scandals of teacher-pupil relationships. He advances compelling evidence that there was a physical element to the relationships that caused scandals at Eton in the late nineteenth century. He says, without reference, that 'sexual passion' was afflicting William Johnson, a celebrated poet and a revered teacher there of three future prime ministers including one of my great-great-uncles, Arthur Balfour. Johnson's twenty-six-year career ended very abruptly. Like many bachelor teachers of the time, he was at Eton as child and adult, with only a short break to go to Cambridge.

Both Johnson and Oscar Browning – another well-known teacher who was forced to leave in 1875 – took notably good-looking boys as favourites. Johnson liked to arrange 'tableaux' in his rooms, with piles of his boys in each other's arms, and watch as they petted and kissed. Both teachers flourished in their careers until they made mistakes that the authorities could not ignore – though in both cases their arrogance precipitated the fall. Was this normal? It is hard to say. Etonians who were not invited to these parties certainly thought something was amiss. One, Abbot Sir David Hunter-Blair, wrote in his memoirs, published in 1939, of the 'great and vital' difference between the modern Eton and that of 1870. 'The masters – housemasters and form masters – are human beings today. In my day they were not: they were (almost without exception) *freaks* . . . [His housemaster], as a master responsible for the moral, religious, and intellectual well-being of generations of boys, at the most critical period of their lives, was a hopeless and deplorable failure.'

Johnson had an adored coterie of beautiful adolescents, often excellent sportsmen. He sent them letters so emotional no one today could excuse them in a teacher. 'I long

to dream of Elliot, I adore him more every week,' he wrote
to Reginald Brett, who was fifteen. (Francis Elliott, then
seventeen, was cox of the Eton rowing eight and the son
of an aristocratic British ambassador. He was to become
an eminent diplomat himself.) Four years later, in 1871, a
revealing letter from Johnson to another boy he fancied fell
into the Eton headmaster's hands. That led to his downfall.
It may be that a parent insisted on Johnson's removal; other
historians have claimed he fell victim to a power struggle
in the school. That seems more likely, because, as has been
pointed out, if Johnson had not actually sexually assaulted
a boy, why – given the attitudes of the times – sack him?

It was a different age. Card, another bachelor devoted
to Eton as man and boy, pupil and housemaster, called the
story 'a case-study of the many schoolmasters who have
been great teachers because they have been romantically
drawn to their pupils'. Card is forgiving: 'it is possible to
rationalise [Johnson's] behaviour by reference to the Platonic conception of the younger boy learning wisdom and
good behaviour from the reciprocated love of the older boy
or man . . . How are we to weigh the possible emotional
damage against the encouragement to achievement?'

It is a fair question and many have considered it, both
as pupils and teachers. That good teachers might well be
drawn to the children emotionally or sexually was a popular strand of thinking. In 2016 Colm Tóibín revealed that
Padraig Pearse, one of the heroes of Irish independence ex-
ecuted after the Easter 1916 rising, was both a much-loved
teacher and a sexual predator at the school he set up and
ran in Dublin. David Hare remembers in his memoir Mr
G, a charismatic French teacher who was wild, unpredictable, easy to imitate: 'everything schoolboys most enjoy'.
It was 1958, and Mr G was exotic in staid Bexhill-on-Sea

and at its smartest private school, Harewood Preparatory. One day the young Hare found the word '*mignon*' (sweetie) written in red ink beside the mark, nine out of ten, on his French essay.

A platonic affair began between the eleven-year-old Hare and the teacher, in his twenties. Mr G demanded passionate hugs ('Even then I felt a flood of relief when I realised these needs were not going to be overtly sexual'), but in return – the bit Hare liked – there was a programme of cultural education, with trips to the cinema and theatre. Mr G opened Hare's eyes, he writes, to all that was most interesting to him, then and now. You wonder, though, how platonic the connection might have been had the boy and the man been confined to a boarding school.

The relationship went on until Hare's mother put a stop to a proposed car trip to see the film *Our Man in Havana*. 'Mr G has been kind enough,' she announced. The affair was over. But nearly sixty years later, Hare was still ruminating in interview about the long-lasting emotions these events inspired, the 'very powerful sense of guilt' that even a sexless relationship with someone in power can create in children: 'the sense that you're always in the wrong, and you can never, ever be in the right. And that feeling really drove my life for so long'. From this and other encounters Hare writes (in his memoir):

Many of the teachers at all my schools had chosen their profession for a reason. They wanted to pass the whole day in the company of young boys . . . To call such tortured and impossibly unhappy souls paedophiles is to make them sound predatory. At the time, they just felt like landmines you must step around.

Ruminating on the sexuality and the platonic boy-love of J. F. Roxburgh, his teacher at Lancing College (which Hare was to attend, forty years later), Evelyn Waugh says 'most good schoolmasters – and I suppose, schoolmistresses also – are homosexual by definition – how else could they endure their work?' This is a remark intended to tease, coming from someone who liked, for humour, to tell people how much he loathed children. But it does also sound a note that was familiar to every questioning pedagogue of the Victorian age and after: the issue of 'Greek love' – the phrase, he notes, could be used freely 'by innocent scholars and clergymen until Oscar Wilde's trial'.

# 38. Out as a paedophile

While Captain Grimes is the first schoolmaster paedophile to appear in English fiction, Cuthbert (or T. C.) Worsley is the first to out himself in autobiography. A near-contemporary of Waugh's, Worsley had his own long argument with restrictive sexual convention. That too started as a child at boarding school and continued when he became a schoolmaster at Wellington College and then Gordonstoun. But in Worsley's case that debate came to a remarkable conclusion in 1967 when he published a memoir, *Flannelled Fool*. It is a historic text in the history of British homosexuality (and a hugely entertaining read): the first autobiography – as one critic, Sheridan Morley, happily remarked – in which a man who was a member of both the MCC and the Garrick Club* came out.

Morley took a copy of the newly published *Flannelled Fool* to Noël Coward, hoping to persuade the actor to come out for the biography on which Morley was working. 'Not at all,' retorted Coward to the suggestion. 'You forget that the great British public would not care if Cuthbert Worsley had slept with mice. My old ladies do care about me and I am not about to lose their favour, dear boy, not

* The MCC is the ancient and grand Marylebone Cricket Club; the Garrick, London's almost-as-exclusive artists', actors' and writers' club. Founded in 1831, it does not allow women to be members.

even for the sake of the truth, which has always been very over-rated in my view, as indeed has sex itself.'

Coward was probably right about the wider impact of Worsley's revelation. But in London literary and artistic circles, still adjusting to the decriminalisation of homosexual acts between adults that same year, his frankness was shocking. Sophisticated London knew that Worsley, who was the *New Statesman*'s literary editor and then the *Financial Times*'s theatre critic, was homosexual, but it also knew of his past as a revolutionary socialist writer and activist (he had served in the Spanish Civil War). That – and his reputation on the cricket field – conflicted with the old stereotypes of homosexuality; Worsley's CV and his self-outing chimed better with the fresher notion of gay liberation as a political movement. Also, Cuthbert Worsley was an early and fierce critic of the private education system that had schooled and employed him.

*Flannelled Fool* is a wry and breezy account of an extended adolescence spent in England's most gilded and privileged places – the corridors of ancient schools, the colleges of Cambridge and on a series of lush cricket fields. But these are arenas not just of Englishness at its best, but also of a society riddled with hypocrisy, confusion and lust. Marlborough College, where he was from thirteen to eighteen, was 'rife with homo-erotic passion' – including among 'most' of the masters.

This, Worsley explains, was often sublimated into hero-worship of the school's sporting stars, just as sport itself was a sublimation of sexual activity. 'I was hiding my repression of sexual potency . . . The generalised homo-eroticism which I discovered in the rituals of the playing fields satisfied my inclinations enough to keep them "pure". And though the moralists may think this was an estimable outcome, I have good reason not to agree with them.' Worsley was sexually indoctrinated at thirteen by a group of older boys – they used to sodomise him with a cane. But he secretly enjoyed it, enough to feel enormous shame when some of the boys were expelled after he had told a teacher not about the cane, but that they used bad language.

Whatever you think of his self-analysis, there's no doubt that Worsley's confusion was later to get him into great trouble. Guilt is at the root of his complaint about the boarding school system, which he was to take forward – after two decades of comical worrying – in anti-private school polemics for left-wing publishers in the 1940s.

Worsley was to see a lot more of the system before he – by his own analysis – managed at last to grow up. It was not until he was in his mid twenties that he managed a satisfactory sex act, with a German man he met on holiday in Munich. But by then, the 1930s, Worsley was a senior master at a public school even more traditional and re-pressed than his own had been: Wellington College.

At Wellington, Worsley lurched unhappily through a series of passionate relationships with the boys, narrowly avoiding the terrifying – on all sorts of grounds – trap of sexual intercourse. He was a terrible, sweaty mess of un-fulfilled lust and moral confusion. Often the boys initiated the affairs, but they would have been expelled and Wors-ley sacked, if not jailed, should they have been found out. Later, he acknowledged his hypocrisy: 'I had worked up a fine moral indignation about [another teacher's] attitude to sex, without perceiving that the reasons for my own permissiveness might reasonably be suspect.'

Boys flirted and arrived semi-naked in his room to offer themselves to him (in later life, one asked Worsley why he hadn't accepted). One particularly affectionate child, whom he believed had orgiastic sex with other boys at the school, Worsley actually took on trips to Paris and Wales during the holidays. But the boy rejected Worsley when he hinted at his physical interest – 'He simply didn't fancy me.'

As part of his campaign for reform at the school, Worsley arranged for an eminent 'sexologist', a Dr Jameson, to come and lecture older pupils. (This caused outrage among the staff, most of all because the expert was a woman.) After the lecture, Worsley sought a private audience, in which he gingerly confessed 'to being over-fond of one of the boys'.

'You mean you're in love with him?'

I still hadn't put it to myself in those terms, but faced with the question I supposed I was. Yes, that must be it.

'Well then,' she went on with her brash and straight-forward questioning, 'how far has it got?'

It had 'got' no distance at all, though this sounded, in front of so formidably progressive a woman, a feeble confession to have to make.

'You mean,' she went on disbelievingly, 'you haven't had his organ in your hand?'

Ugh! Ugh! Ugh! I was nearly sick at her progressive feet. Such a proceeding hadn't even entered my fantasies, much less had I contemplated it in real life. I was much too amazed by this totally unfamiliar suggestion to register even the repugnance which was to follow later.

'No, indeed not.'

'Oh, bad luck,' she said encouragingly. 'Bad luck. Never mind, that will be the next step, won't it?' And she briskly rounded off the interview.

*

Worsley's story is a unique account of the attitudes of the time. Our age is more permissive but that applies only for sex between adults. The rules, both legal and social, around the age of consent and the duties of an adult in a position of care over a child were much looser in the 1930s – as Worsley's scary 'progressive' sexologist shows. Within living memory, the age of consent* in Britain had been only twelve, as it still was in British-ruled India and other sub-tropical colonies (where, it was believed, girls 'ripened' earlier).

The age of consent became sixteen in the UK in 1885. But it was not until women's rights were an issue on the political and intellectual agenda in the late 1960s that children's rights became a talking point. Then, perhaps, attitudes against sex with children hardened, as the campaign to suppress the Paedophile Information Exchange, which had several teachers in its membership, in the 1980s shows. Even then, society had a long way to go in recognising the nature and the extent of sexual abuse of children. In a 2013 essay the psychoanalyst and veteran child abuse specialist Judith Trowell states that it wasn't until the late 1970s and early 1980s that childhood sexual abuse began to be widely recognised as damaging.

This is not to condone Cuthbert Worsley's fumbled attempts to mature sexually with the help of his pupils. But it is interesting that child molesters like him, moral and tortured souls, were less constricted by the social – if not

* The age of consent in UK (for heterosexual sex) was raised to thirteen in 1875 and sixteen in 1885 for both sexes. It remains at fifteen in many European countries, including Germany, today, though newer international law offers protection against exploitation and abuse to 'children under eighteen'.

the legal – rules in the 1930s than today. Further, there was almost nothing, in literature or psychology, then to say what we now take as obvious: that teenagers could be harmed by sexual contact with adults, even if that was consenting. None of this can have helped the Worsleys to conquer their inclinations. And, as we shall see, from their transgressions arose the next generation of criminal teachers – the adults who abused in my school and many others in the 1970s.

# 39. 'Boy-love'

There were a variety of seductive justifications for Worsley and others attracted to children. They came in forms both moral and intellectual, excuses polished by generations of emotionally and sexually confused teachers – 'the pedagogic pederasts', as one of my correspondents puts it. Education at the schools was chiefly in the classics, right up until the end of the 1970s, and so most boys by the time they were teenagers learned the stories of love between master and pupil, older warrior and younger.

Though there was some talk of their unsuitability, most Victorian publishers of the classical texts included tales with a homosexual edge, though they did censor much heterosexual love poetry. Herodotus, Plato and Xenophon all write of the practice of *paidarastia* (boy-love). Most commentators then thought it a significant social phenomenon, at least among the aristocracy of the Greek cities. The most important ancient philosopher, Socrates, was the lover (in some sense) of his student and comrade Alcibiades. Socrates' trial for 'corrupting youth' and his subsequent forced suicide by drinking poison is the dramatic climax of the work of Plato, another of Socrates' students. In Renaissance times, the Italian neo-Platonists held that the act of sodomy was the means by which the teachers of Ancient Greece physically transferred virtue or wisdom to their students, a notion the Renaissance men apparently practised (and publicised across Europe). The Victorian teachers whose job it was to prepare men for service in the cause of the Empire could not have ignored these tales. It helped their cause that the Greek stories did not just suggest homosexuality as an educational tool, they also told of the superior fighting abilities of men who were lovers.

'Greek love' remained a common euphemism for sodomy or male homosexuality for most of the twentieth century. Ganymede, Euryalus, Patroclus, Jonathan and Narcissus, the love objects of gods and soldiers in the ancient stories, appear again and again as code for younger lovers in the underground literature of homosexuality. For aesthetes and intellectuals like Oscar Wilde, there was an abiding belief that the love between men was superior to any other – both intellectually and physically. The Bible gave them support, too. 'I am distressed for thee, my brother Jonathan: very pleasant hast thou been unto me: thy love to me was wonderful, passing the love of women,' runs a line from King David's lament for his dead friend, in the second Book of Samuel.

Some female homosexuals shared the notion that love between those of the same gender was superior. Many of the female teachers at the women's boarding schools that were founded towards the end of the nineteenth century were educated in Latin and Greek like their male counterparts. They would have been aware that there was a grounding for the notion of lesbian love in classical times through the fragments of the poems of Sappho of Lesbos, though there is no evidence that the same teacher–pupil relationships were part of female aristocratic life in Ancient Greece.

But the vision of an era of tolerance and intellectually

sanctioned love between men inspired many homosexual teachers in the nineteenth and twentieth century: they had little knowledge of any other civilisation, and lauded the classical ones as superior to anything before Queen Victoria's. However mythic, this folk-history of paedophilia and its antecedents in a golden age provided an intellectual justification to those who might cast their sexual predation as the celebration of an ancient, beneficial teaching practice.

The tolerant atmosphere evaporated when the trial of Oscar Wilde, and other late Victorian court cases, revealed some of the realities of urban gay life. The general public stayed in the dark, but the privileged knew about the revelations in court of boy prostitutes and soiled sheets in seedy hotels. Wilde was given two years' hard labour; he lost his family and his life and career were essentially ended. Nonetheless, the academic interest in classical pederasty continued to grow in essays and books by schoolmasters who were themselves homosexual.

John Addington Symonds is the best known of these. He is considered an early hero of homosexual liberation because of a monograph he wrote in 1873 called 'A Problem in Greek Ethics'. Though only ten copies were published at the time, it became influential: it is the first positive account of classical pederasty. He also restored the male pronouns to Michelangelo's love poetry, outing the artist as homosexual four hundred years after his death. As a schoolboy he played a part in the downfall of the homosexual headmaster of Harrow, Charles Vaughan.

These cultured Victorian gentlemen called themselves Uranians, before the word homosexual was coined. (It refers to the goddess Aphrodite Urania, a female spirit created from the male god Uranus.) But the term is best known because of the Uranian poets, who produced and published a vast amount of classically flavoured sentimental poetry that went as far as it dared in sensual descriptions of young, beautiful men. J. A. Symonds was one of these: coy and cloying the poetry may be, but it is brave. In 'The Meeting of David and Jonathan' (1878), Jonathan embraces the young David: 'In that kiss / Soul into soul was knit and bliss to bliss.' Hardly shocking now, but it was written less than twenty years after the abolition of the death penalty for 'buggery'.

Other Uranian schoolmaster-poets are now more comic than tragic. One of the most prolific was John Gambril (or J. G. F.) Nicholson, who taught at a succession of minor public and grammar schools between 1884 and 1925. Each slim volume of poetry (and a memoir, *Love of a Choirboy*) was dedicated to a boy he had taught. *A Garland of Ladslove\** (1911) was dedicated to Victor Rushforth who, it should be said, ended his life a finance expert in the Indian Civil Service, married with children. Generally, the denouement of Nicholson's narratives is piercing disappointment – the love object turns shy of the older man's advances, leaving him to go on down his lonely path, sadder, wiser and yet more intensely awake to beauty.

Rather different was the Reverend Doctor Edwin Bradford, the most successful poet of boy-love. He published moralising public school tales alongside fruity, muscular verse. That takes the Uranian form from the delicate hinting of Edmund Gosse and Oscar Wilde to something that salutes Kipling and veers into the camp of *Carry On*.

The poems are earthy, but it is the heartiness that is most shocking now. *At Last!* is a chirpy account of a man

* Ladslove is a folk name for an aromatic herb.

out on an evening walk after church. His negotiations with a 'shy little fellow' he meets ultimately lead – there isn't really any other interpretation – to satisfactory sex in a woodland grove. Bradford published ten volumes of this stuff, starting, in 1913, with *Passing the Love of Women and Other Poems* and ending with *Boyhood* (1930). These were well reviewed, without any sideways remarks, in the mainstream press; Bradford continued his day-job as a Norfolk market town vicar until he died in 1944, aged eighty-four. Among his fans were the poets John Betjeman and W. H. Auden, though the unintentional comedy was surely what they enjoyed.

### The Call

*Eros is up and away, away:*
*Eros is up and away!*
*The son of Urania born of the sea,*
*The lover of lads and liberty.*
*Strong, self-controlled, erect and free,*
*He is marching along today!*
*He is calling aloud to the men, the men:*
*He is calling aloud to the men –*
*'Turn away from the wench, with her powder and paint,*
*And follow the Boy, who is fair as a saint . . .'*

The Uranians were not just poets and writers. One of the most famous was the society painter Henry Scott Tuke RA (1858–1929). He 'could do for boys' flesh what Renoir could do for women', says one historian, and did it for years, on a grand scale, specialising in pink and alabaster youths skinny-dipping in shallow water. (Tukes now sell for a quarter of a million pounds or more; Elton John owns eight of them.) Often his models are schoolboys – one

Etonian was taken to pose for Tuke by his own housemaster. One of Cuthbert Worsley's colleagues at Wellington in the mid 1930s had a large Tuke in his rooms at the school – 'a shimmering beauty of an adolescent lying naked in the grass' titled 'Summer Beauty'. The school's headmaster, invited to view it, said merely, 'Pretty: very pretty.'

Worsley slept with the Tuke-owning teacher, Roland Staines. He was 'obviously what we should now call a queen . . .' yet discreet while within school bounds, Worsley is convinced. He writes: 'Roland was a remarkably good teacher and thoroughly in control of his inclinations . . . It was his simple rule that while they were at school the boys were sacred. And he never deviated from it. But once they had left, it was another matter . . .' Staines had a large mansion near the school where he could indulge his ex-pupils and pursue his affair with Worsley. 'Since the boys he fancied had to be queer by nature, no harm was done,' Worsley happily concludes. It's not an uncommon view: my correspondence from ex-boarders is full of stories of teachers who tested the water with some form of physical pass. Finding the child not compliant they desisted, to try their luck elsewhere. But it is not always the case that an overt rejection was taken as final, or indeed that it had any effect on the predator at all.

Worsley left Wellington too, eventually, tormented by his unfulfilled lusts and his failures to resolve his moral qualms, one way or the other. The heterosexual colleagues with whom he feuded over the modernising of the school were increasingly suspicious: they called him the Red Teacher and were sarcastic about his romantic attachments to the boys. But, as Worsley said, they could never quite believe that someone so good at cricket could be so evil in other arenas.

He did eventually find his way into the bed of a thirteen-year-old he was tutoring, out of school. But though (he tells us) the boy was eager, Worsley failed to perform. Some – worse writers and worse men – might have pursued the bachelor schoolmaster's career, pouring their loneliness into bitter-sweet lyrics of unconsummated boy-love. But Cuthbert Worsley turned his frustration into action (after a few strange months at the newly founded experimental school Gordonstoun). Now thirty, he was at last growing up. He went off to pursue his awakening socialist beliefs and drove an ambulance in the Spanish Civil War. He started to write. His first book, *Behind the Battle* (1939), was about his time in Spain, his next three, including *The End of the Old School Tie*, and *Barbarians and Philistines: Democracy and the Public Schools*, called for the abolition of the schools and of the hypocritical moral codes under which he had fussed, unhappily, for so long.

The liberal British elite acknowledged and tolerated the homosexuality of male intellectuals right through to de-criminalisation in 1967. Havens were found for men who would be at risk in the wider world: not just in the boarding schools but men-only institutions like the colleges of Oxford and Cambridge, the Church and even some regiments of the Army (officers only). There's evidence that the female schools may have served a similar purpose. It's pointed out that unmarried schoolmistresses were just as much of a feature of the boarding schools as were bachelor masters. At the end of the nineteenth century 48 of 50 headmistresses of major girls' schools had not married; in 1975, only 2 of a sample of 19 were married. Many women went into education, as teachers or governesses, because Victorian Britain offered no other career to them. After the First World War, large numbers of women remained unmarried simply because so many possible partners had been killed.

The tolerance of homosexuality within the schools was completely at odds with attitudes in society at large. Homosexual sex was not just a crime (for men, not women), savagely policed and punished, but also completely unacceptable in most social milieux. It certainly appears to have been less acceptable than non-violent paedophilia. While it is important not to confuse the two issues, there is an ugly strand that surfaces in the copious underground and pornographic literature of homosexuality in and around the boarding schools, which suggests some men and older boys felt that sex with children was less important, less corrupting than the proscribed sin of homosexuality between adults. That thinking is akin to the moral justifications of the huge numbers of abusive Catholic priests who believed that homosexual or heterosexual acts with adults were more likely to send them to hell. The Bible is quiet on paedophilia.

Falling in love with and having sex with a child is a way to satisfy urges that the emotionally inadequate are unable to satisfy with adults – it is, according to psychologists of sex offenders, the primary motivating force of the most common type of paedophile. It is what Worsley wanted, and he is at his most dubious when justifying it. If only, he muses, in the aftermath of the night of failed sex with the thirteen-year-old he tutored, a trusted and admired man had 'with gentleness and love taught me the uses of my body' at the same age. 'It might have made all the difference. It would not have been an act of seduction, but one of education.'

As we've seen, men raised in this attitude of tolerance

were succoured by a philosophy cobbled together by notions of the ancient, licensed love between boys and men. When these damaged men left their colleges to enter an unfriendly world where illicit sex, heterosexual or homosexual, was not tolerated, a job in the private schools could provide a life-long haven. Even at severe and moralistic Wellington in the 1930s, Worsley found two fellow-masters who would welcome sex with him. He declares – as Evelyn Waugh does – that 'a majority of the Masters were clearly homo-erotic, to a greater or lesser degree, just as a majority were . . . bachelors'.

You have to leave the urbane pages of Waugh and Worsley – and the syrupy ramblings of the Uranian poets – to get an idea of what those bachelors were in fact up to when they preyed on the children in their charge. It is a complex story and it makes for harsh and distressing reading. A survey of the literature, both public and underground, of school-based sexual activity of the late nineteenth century and most of the twentieth century reveals very little in terms of suffering other than the pangs of unfulfilled love. But the unpublished testimony gives a very different picture. Most sexual contact between adult and child was aggressive and frightening to the child, however kind the adult thought they were being. Moreover it was and is often accompanied by threats or real violence. Genuine acquiescent encounters – if you believe a child can consent to such a thing – of the type prized by the Worsleys were not the rule but the exception. Far more common was coercion.

# 40. Counting the damage

After I first wrote about abuse at Ashdown and other schools, I made a database of all the allegations that I'd been sent. This would help me and the newspaper see what and whom needed investigating. It would also enable me to help people who wrote asking to be put in touch with others from their schools, often seeking allies to begin the process of complaint and redress.

I set to work cataloguing an initial 340 allegations of behaviour that seemed to involve a criminal act, ranging in severity from extreme violence and neglect to sexual assault. I didn't include disciplinary violence, like caning, which was legal until the end of the twentieth century, or mild neglect. Physical neglect of a child was illegal, but the law set a pretty high bar: it meant a failure to provide food, clothing or shelter. 'Emotional neglect' only became a criminal offence in Britain in 2015.

Most of those allegations specified a school; in all, 105 schools were named. But that average of over three allegations per school is a little misleading; some schools had many more, one of them had 21 covering 35 years. In total, I found about 250 allegations that constituted criminal sexual assault, evenly spread across three decades: 64 abuse allegations against adults in schools in the 1950s, 69 in the 1960s and 87 in the 1970s. There were just 16 from 1980 onwards.

The bulk of the schools have only one allegation, or a sole abuser. But there were many clusters of offences; in ten schools, the allegations involved four or five teachers in one period, usually in the 1970s. Often, one informant would name several teachers. So if, say, Jones said that at St Cake's the headmaster used to beat naked children until they bled, while the Latin teacher and the piano teacher both used to fondle them in private, that would count for three entries in the database.

But there are also hot-spots: schools with clusters of allegations, from many people concerning a number of teachers. Most of the accounts are new – I have not had many from schools where abuse has already been well-publicised and prosecutions have happened or are under way. Some are from people now in their eighties and nineties, so the events described date back to the late 1930s. The most recent was an incident in 2012, but I have had few accounts of events that happened after the mid 1990s. This does not necessarily mean that the schools began to be better run; there is a recognised tendency to delay reporting until later in life. Most of my correspondents only began to consider their time at school when children they cared for reached the age at which they first went. The great bulk of the incidents – 250 of them – came between 1950 and 1985.

Crunching the numbers produces other interesting details: 47 of the allegations came from women, 12 per cent of the total. Of those, 23 mention sexual abuse. Four of the abusers were female adults, two of them nuns in Catholic boarding schools. (National statistics claim that 5 per cent or less of sexual abuse of children by adults is done by women acting alone.) The other allegations from women often involve psychological abuse and neglect that seemed to cross the legal line and so became worthy of the database. One 'sadistic' nun in a famous girls' school would physically hurt the girls and humiliate them: one former pupil remembers being forced, aged eight, to carry her urine-soaked mattress down to breakfast and show it to the school. In another well-known school, a games mistress would physically check a girl to see if it was true that her menstrual cycle warranted being off games.

A woman who went at eight to a famous girls-only school in Kent in the 1980s told me how fear of a teacher there led to anorexia. Like many, she felt the lack of any comfort, even from the women in charge of pastoral care, the matrons:

> It would take too long to describe how awful the matrons were to us: making us wear the same knickers so they didn't need to wash our clothes, calling us little bitches constantly, reading our letters home so we couldn't complain (and telling us how we would upset our parents if we did), making us stand outside the dorms in our thin nighties at night (one made me stand in the bath) if we were talking after lights out. They never gave us the slightest bit of affection or care that we as little girls craved and needed . . .

She goes on:

> I experienced abuse by a teacher when I was about eleven or twelve and I wonder how much that also contributed to my feeling of being worthless and lacking control over my life. It was my games mistress Miss Harman Clark (now dead). It was a school joke how we would take it in turns to hold the door shut after swimming

so she couldn't come in to help us dress. She would be banging on the door.

One Sunday she called me out of the common room and took me to a dark cloakroom where we wouldn't be disturbed. She made me sit on her lap and tell her why I was so unhappy and what teachers I hated. I don't know if she touched me but I can't remember. What I do know is I felt it was wrong and I felt uncomfortable. I don't know if the abuse was sexual or not but she then went and told the very teachers exactly what I said about them. She made sure I couldn't tell anyone about that dark cloakroom because she made sure the teachers were angry at what I'd said. And I could never tell my parents because I had been taught at an early age we were never to say we were unhappy in case we upset them. So I retreated into my safe world where I starved and had some sort of control. They couldn't take that away from me.

Other patterns emerge. Only in roughly fifty of the reports of abuse, 15 per cent of the total, had any complaint been made to the police – and in only one of the girls' schools. Six of the schools were state boarding schools, often catering to Army or overseas civil service families, a system that still continues. The latter seemed to stand out for stories of particular horror. Here is one in the Home Counties that, like most, came with 'pretensions of being a traditional public school'. It mixed day and boarding children. My informant, 'Paul', was there from 1977 to 1984:

In my first year I was regarded as the lowest of the low by everyone boarding . . . about 120–130 pupils including the prefects who would humiliate, publicly embarrass, beat, beat up, batter and treat the lowest year as their personal slaves. Looking back it seems the teachers abdicated the responsibility of keeping discipline and turned a blind eye to the prefects' excesses.

Each breakfast and dinner, for my first four terms (year one and into year two), if I sat at a table with other boys they would leave the table to eat away from me. I ate two meals per day alone. Every day for ten weeks per term, for four terms. In nearly 200 mealtimes over 1977–79, I was the very last to be served as I was beaten, pushed, insulted, spat upon, poked and punched to the rear of the queue. The teachers who ate in the same refectory did nothing. The prefects did nothing to prevent the abuse and positively encouraged it.

I was beaten by prefects in their dormitory when summoned to make their toast, tidy their room, make their beds and cups of tea. Beaten with cricket bats, hockey sticks, studded rugby boots and fists, wetted twisted towels flicked whiplike . . . all of which caused great amusement to my tormentors. Because the older boys bullied me and got away with it, I became everyone's target. They broke me . . .

I wasn't sexually abused but they killed me psychologically, emotionally and assertively. I am cold-hearted, callous, find it hard to form an emotional attachment or cling to what I believe is an emotional attachment.

When I wrote back to Paul asking if I could quote from his letter, he gave me permission, but said that he'd been wrong when he said he hadn't been sexually abused. A photography teacher had used him and another boy at junior school to 'practise his caning' in the darkroom: 'we were fully dressed and if he did do something sexual as a result, it was after we'd left the room having had "six of the best" each'.

I suspect that Paul quite genuinely failed to mention this bizarre event because, in the landscape of his awful memories, it just did not loom very large. Yet the teacher's experiments on these two presumably consenting boys in the darkroom is, of course, the only issue he raises that could possibly have resulted in a criminal investigation. His account mirrors that of many: it gives a picture of an institution where violence, discipline, emotional torture and sexual abuse all merge into one never-ending horror for an unhappy child, planting the suspicion that this was the order of things as they were meant to be.

## Nests and rings

Once my database was organised, I went to see Andrew Norfolk. He is perhaps the only journalist in Britain whom you could call a child abuse specialist. Since 2012 he has been chief investigative reporter at *The Times*, but much of his time this decade has been spent investigating institutional sex abuse and organised cover-ups. He lives in the north of England, and there he came across stories of teenage white girls abused and prostituted in Rotherham and elsewhere by older Asian men. He detailed the grotesque failure of the authorities to investigate properly, or indeed see the abuse for what it was: an epidemic.

Norfolk is grizzled, chain-smoking, older-looking than his fifty years. When we met in Newcastle for an afternoon in summer 2014, I had only been in the business of sifting through first-person accounts of child abuse for a few months: Andrew had been at it for four years, and he looked exhausted. We talked a little of the burden of the stories, of the emotional effort that addressing each one required, of how limited our capacities for soaking up the tragedies were. He was having nightmares, too. His is a horrible, wracking job.

Our task was to compare notes. We wanted to get a sense of the scale of the scandal and of any gaps we might have that the other could help with. In *The Times*, he had already published a list of 130 independent schools, most of them boarding, where teachers had been 'implicated in sex crimes against children'. This covered the last fifty years, though the bulk of the cases were all much more recent, not least because of the rise in convictions of teachers for possession of indecent images. If you added in all the schools we knew of where there had been multiple allegations not acted upon, the number would rise to well over 200, approaching half of all the independent boarding schools in the country. Comparing his lists to mine showed surprisingly few overlaps: we were largely dealing with different people, not the serial complainers that journalists sometimes suffer. Once again, the scale was shocking. 'You know,' said Andrew, 'I'd be surprised if, in the end, just about every boarding school from the 1970s was not touched by this.'

We spent the bulk of the afternoon running through our red lists of schools. These were the ones where we thought an investigation was needed, because of clusters of complaints, or particularly horrific crimes or, most important, because the alleged abusers were still in a position to harm children. Between us we could identify 10 or more such schools – beyond those which already had police investigations going. But we both knew that the capacity and the interest of our organisations were limited. 'Child abuse does not sell papers' was a line I had heard more than once.

I had thought we might be able to track a single teacher across the years. A serial offender, a Grimes, riding his luck and progressing from school to school, Borstal or care home to grand college, pursuing children at will. There were many examples in the stories of child-molesting teachers sacked by a school, only for their victims to find them working at another establishment. This occurred so often it was as though it was prescribed in the manual of how to run a boarding school: calm the parents down, send the chap on his way with a reference. And it had happened in my own case. Mr Keane, the violent maths teacher who gave me a sweet in return for permission to put his hand in my shorts, had left the school shortly after my mother made her complaint. 'Terrible man, shouted a lot, didn't stay long. Expect we got rid of him,' another Ashdown teacher from the time told me when I asked about Keane years later.

But in the *Ashdown House Bulletin* for July 1970 there was more information. 'Mr Keane,' it said, in a list of boys and staff departing, 'will be taking up a post at a boarding school in Bournemouth.' This was a shock: it was compounded when Sussex Police found Keane's death certificate, dating from 2005. His profession was listed as 'secondary school teacher'. He had been forty-four when he taught me, when I was aged eight and nine. He had jobs at two more schools, at least, I later learnt. This meant that my – and my parents' – failure to report him had left schoolchildren, many of them vulnerable, to a violent sexual predator for twenty more years. So, I had more than a journalist's interest in trying to track an abuser through the years. Further, I was fascinated by how this could have happened, the culture of tolerance that would permit a man to go on committing this crime, one whose reverberations could cause misery for so long. I wanted to chart it, to understand it.

But the data – both mine and Andrew's – was not giving. There were examples of men who had progressed between two or three schools, but generally their careers had ended. They either went to jail, or just disappeared. Others – and this I came to realise was more amazing than the sackings – never left the school where they offended. In some schools I had reports of teachers with a known, mild predilection – taking photos in the changing rooms is a common story – who had survived in place for decades. Such men were usually at the cluster schools, ones where violence, sexual, physical and emotional, was so common that – you had to imagine – run-of-the-mill non-violent paedophilia simply did not get noticed.

# 41. A bad school

I'll draw a picture of one such school. It can't be named here because, though it closed some years ago, a legal investigation continues around it. It was a standard prep school. One hundred or so boarders aged six to thirteen lived in a grand old country house in Britain's Midlands. The curriculum was classical, the project entry to the big-name public schools. It had been in existence since the mid-nineteenth century and had a reputation for attracting the aristocracy, people who'd been dispatching their children to such places for generations. People who knew the drill.

The school – let's call it the Castle – got both Andrew Norfolk's and my interest because it made a big, attention-grabbing mess on the spreadsheet. I had twenty separate testimonies from it, but the biggest cluster of complaints all came from one period in the mid 1970s. Six different teachers were named and the offences all scored 4s and 5s on the 1–5 scale I use in the database (5 means regular sexual contact from adults with coercion and violence). In a prep school of that type, there would not have been more than a dozen full-time teaching staff. So half of them were, if the accounts were to be believed, criminal paedophiles. The worst of the alleged abuse, which cannot be detailed at the moment, centred around the school's hockey team.

I interviewed a teacher from the school and asked him how, in that tiny closed society, cut off from the outside world, he had failed to notice what had happened. Blithely he replied that, well, of course no one had had child protection training then. It didn't come in until the late eighties. 'If I'd known back then what I know now . . . well, I'm sure I would have acted sooner.' I looked back at him, dubious. This man had taught at the top private schools for forty or more years – he was a father himself. Some of the victims said they had told him what was going on. More than half the male staff were abusing their charges. 'You never spotted *anything* amiss?' I asked. 'Well,' he said, with a rueful grin, 'it was the best hockey team we ever had.'

Eventually, far too late to prevent lasting trauma to twenty or more children who had been drawn into their circle, two teachers were sacked. One disappeared, but the other, the coach, went off to teach at a boarding school abroad. Three of the other six continued to teach at the Castle until they retired or it closed. For thirteen years ex-pupils have tried to get police investigations or civil compensation cases going. So far, they have had no result.

The key figure in this story, the headmaster who first employed these men, will never be investigated. He died twenty years ago. But – let's call him Conrad – he is the person who makes the Castle stand out on the spreadsheet. Conrad ran the school for more than thirty years. There are many accounts of him in the correspondence: he was a violent and terrifying alcoholic 'and a truly great teacher', as more than one ex-pupil put it. He beat children as they did in the Victorian age, with immense energy and obvious delight, for offences both absurd ('using too much toothpaste') to tragic ('crying in chapel'). Conrad beat children for failures of discipline and failures of intellect. An inadequate test paper was as likely to earn the cane as was talking after lights out.

He beat particularly savagely for lying – a crime that from Victorian times onward was always met with the severest punishments. He would beat when drunk and angry, or in cold blood with cruel deliberation. Boys preferred the latter. The beating hurt either way and usually drew blood, but when drunk his aim was scarily erratic: he once cut a child's ear with a wayward cane-stroke. But the sober rages could be more terrifying. One remembers: 'Conrad carried a cane down his trouser leg into class. He once beat the desk of a hapless pupil with such ferocity that splinters flew up in his face. The pupil vomited over Conrad out of sheer terror and was dragged out and sent off to the San.'

On several occasions he beat all one hundred boys in the school in an afternoon. He used bundles of birch twigs, until Eton abandoned this in the 1960s, and then bamboos, like most headmasters. He also had a range of sporting goods: leather riding crops, cricket bats, billiard cues – 'I remember our delight when he broke his favourite one on X's backside' – a five-iron golf club and the bat from the paddle-and-ball game Jokari. 'Did he really use a golf club?' I asked. 'Well, he was a noted amateur golfer,' one correspondent told me, 'always practising his swing.' Another said yes, he did use the golf club, but reversed, hitting the boy's backside with the handle end. There were marks in the plaster of the low ceiling of Conrad's study from where he'd swung the weapons too energetically.

When he was a young man, Conrad had been lovable, several correspondents assured me – 'magic', 'inspiring', 'charismatic' – despite being handy with the cane. Being taught by him provided one writer, a well-known

publisher, with the happiest days of his life. But by the
time he was in charge of the Castle, shortly after the
Second World War, Conrad seemed to have settled into the
self that most of the accounts would agree on. That was 'a
gin-soaked, screaming beast', 'vast and tall . . . physically
intimidating and always utterly unpredictable' – phrases
like these come up often in the accounts – liable to lose his
temper at the smallest provocation – a misplaced verb, a
giggle in the chapel, a sponge on a floor. Nonetheless, he
was clearly a good headmaster in the ways that mattered
to parents (there were no governors or trustees): the school
thrived over the next thirty years, doubled pupil numbers
and built a sports hall and swimming pool. The Castle held
records for the numbers of academic scholarships awarded
by public schools. It excelled at hockey and other sports,
in the endless matches held against the other prep schools
nearby (though not, of course, the state ones).

He was sole proprietor of the business and he must have
been a good salesman. Conrad's clientele appears to have
become more and more smart. In the fifties the school was
a resource for the children of local professionals – solicitors'
and doctors' sons, and, as ever, Army kids – but by the late
sixties there were German aristocrats, many titled Britons
and the children of the new financial elite. Its prospectus
and entries in the published guides to British independent schools of the time show that its output was targeted
firmly at Eton and Winchester and its fees were higher
than most.

He made favourites of the most beautiful and clever
boys, but there's no anecdote of sexual fumbling attached
to the memories of Conrad I was sent. It is hard to imagine
a man so grand making himself so vulnerable. He was
married and his wife, a fearsome figure to the children, was

closely involved in the building's management: it would
have been impossible for her not to have known what happened, even behind closed doors. The way he delivered
his punishments, though, is indicative of something more
than simple flagellomania. The extended ritual around
these events was a complex sadism.

Conrad, like all his type, was a product of the high age
of private boarding schools. His discipline system, like his
other mechanisms of management and the classical curriculum, was copied from the Victorians. Quasi-judicial,
long drawn out, Conrad's punishments were dramas that
occupied the whole school for days. The accused might be
beaten immediately, if Conrad's rage was uncontrollable,
but the process more usually took as much as a week. A
crime was discovered, the accused found and pronounced
guilty in public, and then Conrad would retire to deliberate
over the punishment. A choice might be offered – usually an invidious one. A long boring detention, or a short,
painful episode with the cane? Did you want six strokes
with pyjamas on, or three on the naked buttocks? Three
strokes over separate nights, or three all at once? These
riddles in the lore of pain were much discussed among the
boys. Conrad would certainly publicise which road had
been chosen: and 'cowardice' – like taking the detention –
was a prime sin. At the morning assembly Conrad liked to
tell the school the story of the night's disciplinary action:
'Smith and Jones took it like gentlemen, but McTavish
blubbed like a baby.' Cruelties like this were many, and to
those who reflect now they seem more important than the
beatings.

Conrad would bully his teachers, too. One man's stammer was endlessly mocked, sometimes in Ancient Greek.
He would attach pejorative nicknames to both adults and

boys he disliked – 'chicken' or 'maggot'. He'd endeavour to get the school to use them, deleting the child's real name. Sometimes his cruelties seemed born of stupidity. A disabled child was due to arrive, and before he did Conrad briefed the whole school on the nature of his disability. He went on to say that if anyone insulted the 'spastic' or failed to be friendly they would be beaten. When the child turned up, no one would go near him.

Conrad is a real figure. He could be a composite: it's striking how many other headmasters – and some head-mistresses – operated and even sounded just like him. The psychological cruelty and the stupidity – as in that last example – is the most common factor. There is a stock emotionally abusive teacher, who starts with Squeers and runs through the fiction and the fact of school history for a hundred years and more. Elaborate plots to undermine and break a child are their trade, and they live a double life that fools adults, though children can see through them. Violence, licensed and unlicensed, was one of the tools of these sociopathic figures, just as public humiliation was.

I've read dozens of accounts of these demonic men and women. Many of them revelled in their Jekyll and Hyde existences: the way they abused children seems almost a celebration of the astonishing power and freedom they were permitted. The combination of urbane charmer of parents and violent abuser was most succinctly expressed to me by one of the survivors of Caldicott School in the 1970s. He told how his mother came to the school to meet with George Hill, the deputy headmaster, for tea and assurances of her eleven-year-old's health and happiness. 'She left, and he was raping me while I could still hear the sound of her car going down the drive.'

It is too simple to believe these men simply hated

children and happiness. They were more complex. Many
ex-boarders who became writers, including Roald Dahl,
Ian Fleming and Anthony Horowitz, created the most
vivid adult monsters out of their schoolteachers. It is no
surprise that the chief villain of J. M. Barrie's *Peter Pan*, a
story of war between adulthood and childhood as much as
it is of one between adults and children, is based on a sadistic prep school headmaster. He is 'cadaverous . . . bearded
and black-avised', a 'devastator of [Kensington] Gardens'.
Barrie may have met the models for Captain Hook when
he went to board, at eight, at Scotland's first private school
on the English model, the Glasgow Academy. He later
said Hook was an Old Etonian. But in the pirate, with
his childish malevolence and his swashbuckling charis-
ma, Barrie caught something of how these monstrous men
could bewitch and hypnotise – their staff, their pupils, the
parents.

They were impressive leaders, often sole traders who
combined management skills with salesmanship that
could convince parents to spend enormous sums on their
children's education. Conrad looms large in the memories
of his ex-pupils, many of whom still wryly admire him
while some seem almost in love. This is not uncommon.
Cicely Wilkes, Connolly and Orwell's headmistress at St
Cyprian's, was as manipulative, dishonest and cruel as any
in memoir or fiction. But the authors' published accounts
of her inspired ex-pupils to leap furiously to her defence.

Perhaps this is unsurprising. Another feature of that
prep school management manual was the system of favourites and bugbears. Conrad was adept at that: like many of
the teachers, he had his special boys and his villains. The
former would be buffed and flattered, drilled as scholarship
boys and cricket stars, the latter declared liars and cheats,

predestined failures whose future was to be what they were at the school: cannon fodder. It was another preparation for the wider world's hierarchies.

Most of his pupils who have bothered to consider it think he was sexually inactive. His marriage, to a woman whose savings helped fund the school, seemed to be a convenience. There was clearly a strong emotional attachment to his favourites, in the traditional pattern laid down by the Victorian pedagogues. One of his pupils from the 1950s writes:

> I think [Conrad] wrestled with his paedophilia, which probably made him that much worse. He was drunk far too often. His passions for certain boys (including [a future headmaster of the school]) were intense and obsessive. His temper, never far from the surface, erupted unpredictably and often. I sat for three years in his class. For him to beat – 'flay' would be a more apt description – the entire class for some trivial misdemeanour of one, occurred at least once per term. I recall him lunging across his enormous desk in a fury to grab a boy by the hair and pull him out of his own tight desk, and hammer him with whatever was to hand.

At least five of Conrad's favourites returned to teach at the school immediately after they had finished university, one of them with disastrous consequences. In his dominance, his tyrannical exercise of unquestioned power, in his considered and careful crushing of the spirits of children he didn't like, some strange lust was at work. But none of the psychologists of sexual aberration have any notion of what it was. The psychopathology of absolute power has a sexual element, of course. But, from my own searching in the thin academic literature of the psychology of child sexual abusers, I could find nothing to explain the Conrads.

Conrad must have been conscious that he was employing sexual criminals. Extraordinary numbers of them – so many, indeed, that at periods (and I only have accounts of parts of it) in his reign half of the staff are accused of criminal sexual assaults. Even in the idyllic wartime school, evacuated to Scotland, there was a teacher who 'interfered with the boys and one morning just wasn't there'. In the late 1960s and early 1970s there were a dozen full-time teachers, two of them women: six of the men are accused of acts ranging from fondling children's privates to penetrative sex. When, forty years later, police started investigating the mounting accusations against the school, one of the men had forty different accusers. In the early 1960s three teachers 'would now be considered paedophiles', as one correspondent puts it. ('Conrad wasn't one, just manically sadistic,' he goes on.) At one point in the late 1940s and early 1950s, four of the staff are accused of being violent sexual predators; one of them, I was told (though I have found no confirmation in court records), was jailed at that time for indecent assaults on boys. These were not pupils, but children living in the nearby village.

Another teacher features in all the accounts of the Castle, usually as an afterthought. He was the French master. He liked to hang around the games changing-room and indulge his habit of 'slipping his hands up your shorts to check if you were wearing underwear'. This strange duty was a career-long task for the master in question. I have accounts from men who went to the Castle from the early 1950s until the late 1970s who had the same underwear inspection done by the same French teacher. Did no one ever complain because the teacher was married with children?

Or because, unpleasant though the intrusion was, it was not actively frightening? Or because, compared with the rapes and the floggings, this was so mild that it just passed everyone by? The Castle employed a man who was organist in the chapel and provider of music lessons and a fill-in maths teacher, too: he fondled the boys during piano lessons or while doing algebra for thirty years or so, never questioned, never admonished. He also punished the child of one of my correspondents by sticking a pencil into the muscles of his thigh, every time he made a mistake.

This sort of behaviour – sexualised but unthreatening and so easier to ignore – went on throughout the prep schools and indeed many of the secondary ones. Among the most common stories sent me are ones telling of teachers who were photographers. Often they were the kindest and best liked (or least feared, at any rate). The fact that they lurked by the showers or in changing rooms to photograph children undressing was noticed, but not thought odd until my correspondents grew up. Sometimes the photographers enticed children to pose naked. Sometimes this was licensed by the school. One of my sisters, all of whom boarded from age eight at Windlesham House, a well-known 'progressive' prep school in West Sussex, was shocked when, thirty years later, a man she met at a party said, 'Oh, we've got a photo of you naked on our kitchen wall.' The teacher sold copies of his portraits of the smiling, undressed children to the visitors at the school's Sports Day. It was a more innocent time: this seemed harmless, charming, even to the parents. But the children knew better: they called the man Randy Andy.

At many schools, including the Castle, naked swimming was a rule. David Hare says that at Lancing College the boys were ordered to swim naked 'on the unlikely pretext that if we wore trunks the fibres from our garments would clog up the pool's filters'. Visiting clergymen watched the boys in the pool from a balcony.

The culture of tolerance is hard to dissect. The extent of the abuse is enormous and the failures of the authorities, in the schools and outside, so extraordinary it is hard not to assume some guiding malevolence. It is not surprising that many of the survivors of sexual abuse at the schools, just as those from state care institutions, assume conspiracy. But I think crimes of a lower order are behind the bulk of the stories. Incompetence, misplaced loyalties and a criminal failure in sense of duty, of the real job of properly caring for the vulnerable, explains most of them.

There is not a clear pattern of abusers being deliberately handed from school to school. It certainly happened, but when you examine the cases the whiff is of failed systems and laziness rather than conspiracy. Even today paedophiles get jobs where they have access to vulnerable children (and any child not in the care of its parents is vulnerable): the stories appear frequently in the press. In 2014 William Vahey, a teacher at the private London International School, was revealed to have drugged and then sexually abused sixty children on school trips, taking photos of them. Numerous complaints had been made about him at that and other schools. He had a conviction for child sex offences in California and his name had been on a list of known child pornographers given to the British police by another force, but they had not had the resources to investigate. When Vahey left the school, before he was exposed, the headmaster had written him a glowing reference.

Incompetence, lack of resources, lack of care and interest are all common, tawdry crimes but that doesn't lessen the suffering they brought. Idle headteachers or school inspectors – when they appeared – assumed the best of the adults, and so allowed great harm to happen. As the stories from schools and institutions run by the Catholic Church make clear, predatory paedophiles thrive where the rules are lax and human good nature is taken for granted.

It might appear that cover-up was normal across the private school system in the nineteenth and most of the twentieth century. That does carry the taint of conspiracy or extraordinary, stupid self-interest. It is as if the schools were all in turn being burgled by one clever criminal, yet the embarrassment was enough for them never to report it. Certainly it was very rare for sexual assaults to be reported to the police. My mother came up against this practice: bullied by the headmaster's wife out of insisting that action be taken against Mr Keane, the angry maths master who liked to put his hand down our shorts.

In the 1990s one parent was given a letter by Gordonstoun's bursar, promising him that a predatory teacher who liked to drug children before fondling and photographing them would never teach again – the quid pro quo for an agreement not to prosecute. In all the cases in the database where parents or the school authorities became aware that a teacher was abusing children in a criminal way, less than 5 per cent resulted in a report to the police, and usually only because parents insisted. (Most cases reported to me come from complaints filed years later). In the Gordonstoun case the same man was twice reported to the police for assaults against children at the junior school, but both times Gordonstoun appears to have arranged that no prosecution should happen. Often, as in the Caldicott case, when attempts to prosecute did go ahead, they failed on technical grounds. In Scotland such cases are almost impossible to prosecute, because Scottish law demands a second witness to corroborate an accusation.

It's not hard to see why the schools did all they could to avoid prosecution. Such publicity and the loss of a few fee-payers could close a school: many were unstable financially. So the common solution, when faced with a Captain Grimes, was to placate the parents with assurances and threats ('How's it going to be if your little boy is dragged through the courts?' – went the argument; 'It'll be his word against Mr Jones's, and the Press will be there too') and pack him off, with a good reference, to pursue his career and interests. In my database I have around fifty cases that were 'dealt with' in this manner. At the Castle, all these things happened. In its 140 years of existence no teacher was ever arrested, let alone prosecuted, for an offence committed against its children, though I have credible allegations against more than twenty. Even today, schools have no duty to report an allegation against their staff to anyone beyond their walls.

In the Castle and several other private schools, in some of which the legal mill is still turning, it is hard not to believe that the worst-possible scenario was what actually happened. 'Sexual abuse on an industrial scale' is the journalist's cliché: there is truth behind it. Some twentieth-century child-care institutions, many of them religious-based, were organised, self-perpetuating paedophilia machines. Not only was the culture of child abuse endemic and tolerated, but it was repeated down the generations. Abused children could return and find a place to abuse – this awful cycle appears to have played out in the case of Peter Wright, the Caldicott headmaster jailed in 2013 for multiple abuses. He was himself at school there in the 1940s, when sex between children and predatory behaviour by adults was common. Another Caldicott teacher, John Addrison, was in 2013 convicted of six offences against children who had been his pupil. Addrison was a nineteen-year-old student teacher: only six years earlier he had himself been a pupil there. He told the court that convicted him that he had been abused as a child. Other victims have reported that Addrison was abused by Wright at the school in the early 1970s.

What is most extraordinary is that the Castle, like Caldicott, was a family school — family-run, and family-patronised. Apart from Conrad, all the other headmasters brought up their own children at the school. Generation after generation of local families sent their children there. The descendants of two nineteenth-century headmaster-proprietors were pupils there in the 1970s. It's hard not to conclude that adults who had been sexually abused there sent their own children into the same horror.

This is more common than seems possible. One of Vyvyen Brendon's interviewees tells her of his school, Allen House. This notorious Surrey prep, which closed in 1986, had a number of paedophile teachers over the years: unusually, one has recently been prosecuted. Among the sexually abusive teachers the interviewee knew was the headmaster, who liked to touch the boys 'inappropriately' at bathtime. (A group of the parents eventually persuaded him to leave on an extended holiday.) But the victim's dominant nightmare derives from the fact of his father having attended the school, under the same headmaster. 'That his father might have known what was going on . . . is what bothers him most about the experience,' writes Brendon. It is a worry many of us who know our fathers or mothers suffered at their schools share.

A survivor of one of the prep schools where habits of physical abuse were repeated over generations told me his own story of traumas and violence, long suppressed. Like many of my correspondents, it was only in middle age that he'd come to acknowledge and understand what had happened, after the breakdown of his marriage had brought him to psychotherapy. He talked of his own father's undoubted misery at school, which he could now see was very like his own. He ended this grim story thus: 'Despite everything, I sent both my boys off at eight. They were miserable too. We never learn.'

# PART SEVEN

# Meeting the Vampires

I should have realised that headmasters, despite the gowns and mortars, are far from being saints. Did you hate yourself or those you flogged while you flogged? Did you love them? – that would have been really sick. Did you believe you were helping them? Did you play the guilty memories back in your damaged head at night?

The novelist David Benedictus writes to the headmaster of
Eton and Fettes, Anthony Chenevix-Trench

# 42. Understanding paedophiles

On a golden afternoon at the end of Edinburgh's brief summer, I sit down to watch some paedophiles explain themselves. From the beginning of this project, I had wanted to interview an offender: to meet a man who had used his power to violate children and ask him questions.

Finding a paedophile isn't so easy, even if you believe, with the government's Children's Commissioner, that 225,000 children in Britain are sexually abused every year. I don't know the work-rate of the average child abuser, but that stat must mean there are more of them than there are GPs. (The English police estimate child pornography users alone at 50,000–60,000, annually.) As a journalist, I know well enough that people asked in the right way will – more often than not – talk. But first I had to find out how to get near enough to a sex offender to put the questions.

My motives for this search were quite clear, but I was not entirely comfortable with them. Many of the accounts of unhappy schooldays I was getting made it clear that physical and even sexual abuse were usually not the most important issues in the grander picture of psychological damage done by the boarding experience. The traumas, the ones that led to lifelong harm, were emotional – the warping caused by separation, loss of safety and privacy, by bullying and by the crushing of the spirit that seemed a deliberate part of the regime at so many schools. But, until the Serious Crime Act of 2015, 'emotional neglect' and psychological cruelty to children was not a crime in Britain.

So, to an extent, looking at sexual abusers in the schools was a side-track. It wasn't as though there was any need to prove to the public that it had happened, and on a large scale. Nor that the crimes had largely been covered up, quite methodically, almost as though that job was covered in the *How to Run a Boarding School* manual. The reason I wanted to meet an abuser, I had to admit, was because they fascinated me. It took no great leap to imagine myself as one of those sad men whose own miserable childhoods, bedevilled by cruel and perverse adults, had, by the most tragic irony, turned them into adults, incapable of finding love and happiness. Some became predators. By what twist of psychological good fortune had I escaped that fate? One ex-boarder friend, married, refuses to consider fathering a child, so great is his fear of what the world, or he himself, might do to it.

The men who abused us physically at my own schools were not available for my tape recorder. Four teachers — one at Eton, three at my prep school — had touched me in a way that satisfies the minimum definition of a sexual offence against a child. They were all, I now knew, dead. This was a pity: the egotistical journalist in me quite fancied a door-step show-down with Mr Keane. Stripping his soul in interview would have been my kind of revenge, and pretty good copy, too. But, a month earlier, the detective superintendent in charge of the Ashdown House investigation had rung to tell me they'd traced Keane and found he had died five years ago. She apologised for not coming to tell me this 'distressing news' personally. I was disappointed, not distressed. But I already knew how bitter such news had been to some survivors, denied for ever not just their day in court but any hope of revenge.

Seeking a paedophile, I went to people who work in re-habilitation psychotherapy for a lead. But none of them could help: 'For a start, patient confidentiality rules out passing you a name. And then, can you imagine a practi-tioner deciding that getting a sex offender client to talk to a journalist might be beneficial?' Eventually, I arrived at Donald Findlater. I should have gone to him first. Badger-haired, bouncy and bright-eyed, his life's work has been in the treatment of sex offenders, at the Wolvercote Clinic and with the Lucy Faithfull Foundation. Donald is open and interested in addressing the institutional prob-lems and the policy culture that allows those who want sex with children to operate. He's well known as an opin-ionated and controversial debater on children's safety and the policing of sex crime. He likes to look you straight in the eye and ask – for example – if you're really sure about what you've just said. He challenges: 'But does the family offer all the solutions for good child raising?' Find-later is exercised, on the day I meet him, with work he has been doing in Queensland with aboriginal communities. There, incestuous child abuse is so ingrained a problem it seems hard-wired into the anthropology of that damaged society.

I've become used to psychology academics' and practi-tioners' eyes glazing as I tell them I want to talk about boarding schools – 'posh kids' abuse' – but Donald is in-terested. He can see – at least, he agrees politely – that what happened in the child-care institutions of the elite must have a bearing on the crimes and failures of the in-stitutions that look after all British children, and indeed those in all the countries that aped the Victorian school system.

But, as in all areas of social work, he is overwhelmed. Online child pornography is the subject of the current Lucy Faithfull campaign,* and rather more pressing than my quest to look into the eyes of a historical abuser. It's estimated that 70–85 per cent of child sexual abuse happens in or around the family – 'incestuous abusers are just lazy paedophiles', he says, quoting a colleague's remark. He cites a recent European report that suggests one in five children in Europe have been victims of some form of 'sexual violence'. (Most studies of child sexual abuse use 'inappropriate touching' as the base definition.) One researcher, Dr Kirsty Hudson, took a sample of 22 convicted child abusers for her fascinating study, *Offending Identities*. Only one had assaulted a child unknown to them. Eight had assaulted a relative.

Abuse around the home is, necessarily, the greatest part of Donald's casework. He and his colleagues, I begin to understand, face an elemental problem with human sexuality, whose awful effects are a growing problem today. 'So, if only one in nine cases is getting reported,' says Donald, 'what's happening to the rest? Shouldn't that be top priority?' Of course historical researches are not a priority. I am close to confessing that the real reason I want to meet a paedo is because I'm unprofessionally fascinated; I think he suspects it anyway.

Part of Donald's work is educating people who may employ sex offenders. So today he sits me down to watch some videos he shows to Catholic bishops. He and his colleagues have taped their interrogations of paedophile

* Donald Findlater has since left the Lucy Faithfull Foundation.

priests, some of them ex-teachers. The men had only been admitted to the rehabilitation programme because they had accepted that they had committed crimes – a step 30 per cent of convicted sex offenders never take.

In the depths of an empty restaurant, sunlight blasting through the outer windows, Donald sets me up with a laptop, headphones and a pot of strong coffee. I wonder if I am being tested: my reaction to this material may dictate what access I get to more. 'Are you sure you want to do this?' he asks kindly. I'm not sure what he means, for a moment, then I understand: confessions of child abuse are difficult to hear.

I realise that, in my eagerness to meet an abuser, I haven't thought this through. Only last week I was in tears as I re-read some of the accounts of bad times at school sent me by readers of my articles – jolted not by any particular detail, though there is vivid anguish in all the stories, but by the accumulation of misery and injustice. I'd been reading them, making notes for this book, for three days and it had become too much. 'I'm a researcher,' I tell Donald. 'I know when to stop.'

# 43. Fred and Colin

The first video starts. The defrocked priest is grandfatherly. His Irish accent, soft, kind, smoothed for sickrooms and confession boxes, is reassuring. It is a physical shock when, suddenly, I catch something ungodly in his eye, in a drop of his jaw: a *moue* that's both self-deprecating and flirtatious. He is talking of his remorse. I feel nausea rise and a pricking in my eyes. I realise Findlater is by the sofa, bending over me, and so I remove the headphones, pause the video.

'Are you OK?'

'This one is . . .' I don't want to seem unprofessional. 'It's making me too emotional.' Donald nods. 'And I'm confused by the empathy I feel. The truth is, I can imagine my teachers' heads on their shoulders.' I can: I'm entertaining the idea of Billy Williamson being filmed; I can see him, like these elderly Irishmen, contrite, old man's hair side-swiped across their baldness, savouring their self-abasement as they tell all in the same patient, authoritative voice they might use to brief a parent about a difficult boy.

Watching the videos, there's a disturbing sense that they are performing in a scene of their own long life story, that this latest turn provides another outing for their egos. The predictable workings of my sympathy gland, so uncritical, so suggestible, disgust me. I am being groomed into emotional collaboration. I write in my notebook: 'A shabby old defrocked Irish paedophile manipulates me like Hannibal Lecter.'

The first video features 'Fred', a man well into his seventies, thin white hair precisely combed, his face with its blotches of pink and red like a map of the British Empire. Quietly he tells the camera how useful a school is to paedophiles: 'Teaching gives enormous access to children . . . You're trusted, you're working in a classroom situation, one hundred to one hundred and fifty children pass through your room in a day and you've access to the child as an individual.' He might be describing the opportunities you get using a hide when wildlife-spotting.

He goes on to detail his modus operandi. He begins with identification of vulnerable children, ideally with an absent or alcoholic father. Then there's the offer of help with school work or exam revision, patient grooming of the needy mother. 'I would do the very best to help the family, but unfortunately not for the reasons she thought.' The adverb, the 'unfortunately', is the only grit in his bland tale of the chase and the capture. Was that an apology? The blip comes again: 'I would make the boy a friend, dependent on me: a lot of the boys I abused, sad to say, were poor boys . . . I was like a dad to them.'

'Sad to say'? Who is sad? These notes ring falser when, in a short moment where he seems more alive, Fred tells us what sort of boys he sought – though no one asked him the question. 'Good-looking, slim, vulnerable. I like boys with a gentle smile on them.' But, those moments aside, the five-minute narrative is colourless. It comes to an end with an equally bland account of the sex acts the priest forced his pupils to perform – anal, oral and mutual masturbation, posing for photos – and the statistics: seven victims over thirty years of abusing, seven victims, no convictions. You are left with a sense of a husk-man, drained of shame, of lust and pride: his crimes, his career and his life done.

The second interviewee, 'Colin', is much more potent. Though he's as drab as his predecessor, pinned by the camera like a moth to a sheet of card, he is alive and still fighting. There's a coy knowingness and a flash in his eyes that says he's still ready to coax, flirt and manipulate. He makes me shiver.

His confession goes on for eight minutes. It's not unlike the first priest's – the same tale of targeting the vulnerable, and then of careful grooming. But, here, the voice is alive. Colin takes delight in laying his schemes out for us. You get a sense of an issue I've been told about, that for the 'preferential paedophile', the construction of the snare and the luring of the child is as much a part of the excitement as any other act. Seduction is the game, and among its tactics are dissembling and cover-up. Intelligent criminals may give themselves away because their ego demands that someone admires their work.

At one point the interviewer says that he wishes to put a question asked of all the priests who face this camera: How did you reconcile the abuse with God? Colin is ready with his answer, confident:

The bottom line would be, this was a weakness in me – and God really understood it. But look at all the hard work, and all the good people were getting. I used to struggle with it some of the time, other times I would let it roll on . . . Even in those struggles, I would be able to identify with the pain of other people's struggles: I would be able to empathise. If I wasn't in this situation and if I hadn't been through these struggles I wouldn't be able to empathise with them. God was using me as a broken reed, really. God knows me, he understands where I'm coming from. It's up to him to do everything and me to do nothing.

Self-pity stains his large eyes. But this is a layer over his arrogance. Colin reckons – and there was no indication that he'd ever questioned this – that his sexual abuse of children made him a better priest. And God agreed. Not just that his struggles to control himself made it easier for him to understand his parishioners' struggles with – what? blasphemy? fornication with consenting adults? – but that the good things, 'all the hard work', he did to establish himself in the community and access children – the camping trips, the boxing club – counted as mitigating circumstances. It was as though he was giving himself his own character reference. The question I wanted to ask was, does God still believe in you? But the tape was over.

Donald's purpose in showing me the videos was, he'd said before I started, that I should begin to understand the different types of paedophile sex offender. These he divided into three: preferential, opportunistic and situational. 'The primary interest of the first is sex with children. This is a thoughtful, anticipatory person who creates the opportunity to do that. The opportunistic paedophile is anti-social, not necessarily interested in sex with children, or it's not their sole interest, and they will commit different types of crime for thrills. The end of that spectrum is psychopathic, but only about 3 per cent of crimes have that aspect.'

An example of a situational offender is Jeremy Forrest, a schoolteacher who in the summer of 2015 became a tabloid sensation when he ran off to France with a fifteen-year-old female pupil he was 'in love with'. 'He had a back story,' says Findlater, 'an ordinary guy, relationship going wrong, life an emotional mess, obsessed with the pupil and receiving a level of reciprocation of emotional interest. He's thirty-five to forty, he knows the normal boundaries, normally aware, but commits a gross, self-harming act.

'Most of the situational offenders want relationships, they want acquiescence,' explains Donald. 'They want to feel that the good they do overrides the offence. Typical is the type of offender who's had a job with children from the street. "I was rescuing kids, what I do is about love and care and much better than what they come from," is the excuse.'

It is a shock to hear that 30 per cent of the sex offender prison population is in denial. They believe either that they are innocent, or that what they did should not be seen as criminal. Many talk of having been in love, as though that were a mitigation.

When the videos were finished and Donald and I talked, I had to ask him if, in the classification of paedophile types, anyone had looked at the specifics of offenders who operated in child-care institutions where violence was a regular event. What about those flogging headmasters, licensed to hurt children 'for their good', who recruited staff who would procure for them, perhaps paedophiles themselves? My correspondence was full, I told him, of accounts of masters who clearly were getting sexual satisfaction from the act of flogging. They seemed to cross the boundaries of the paedophile types – both preferential and opportunistic. And, most important, they did not look for consent, unlike the greater part of the paedophile spectrum – including the priests I'd just seen. Donald agreed, there seemed to be a gap in the research – the licensed abuser in an institution.

That is not the only gap. The issue that brought me to
Donald was something we had all seen – from the Kincora
Boys Home to the private schools of my correspondence
– evidence of child abusers who worked in rings. Simon
Hackett, a professor of criminology with a specialisation
in the maltreatment of children, called it 'the recruitment
issue' when we spoke of this. He first came across it while
investigating, as a social worker in the 1990s, the North
Wales children's homes scandal. It is a feature of closed or
isolated institutions: one dominant male had arrived and
very quickly recruited other paedophiles. 'But the thing
is, these generally were young men with no previous whatsoever. Interviewed after arrest, they'd tell you, "I had a
girlfriend, I was just normal, I'd never thought about kids
in that way in my life. But he was so powerful, you just
could not say no. He made it something exciting, a gang,
a secret we all could share."' The key to the alpha male's
group-forming strategy was not just that having colleagues
helped with security and procurement of children, but that
the recruitment and initiation were part of the thrill. But,
as Kirsty Hudson confirmed, there was very little academic study of child sex abuse in institutions, and what there
was looked at individuals, not groups of offenders. Despite
public hysteria about rings of paedophiles, the consensus
was that – with pornography-sharing an exception – such
things were very rare.

I realised, as I formulated my questions for a follow-up
talk with Donald, that I was going a little bit mad. The
warning signals were there – the bump in the lower chest,
the feeling of nausea. This was not research. I was busying
myself to classify and pigeonhole the abusers like a col-
lector trying to apply Linnaean principles to a new batch
of exotic insects. Donald Findlater, Stephen Smallbone,

Kirsty Hudson, Simon Hackett and all the other researchers and practitioners had good cause to do it, because they needed to understand the types in their search for effective treatment and better protection for children. But I was just doing it because, like all the victims, the obsessive survivors gathering evidence for trials, the campaigners for legal redress and public inquiries, I needed to get reason on my side, at last.

The search for truth can become a mania. It was easy to see a survivor's autism in many of my correspondents and interviewees. Behind the drive to amass the facts of their abuse, and its circumstances, was an avoidance of the need to repair the damage. Inevitable, perhaps, and the detective work was engrossing, certainly. But productive? I'd known and read enough of survivors in anguish at the collapse of their court case, or distraught because some long quest for retribution or an apology had come to nothing. Survival of child abuse is a tale illustrated with box files, card indexes and all-night search engine binges. Move on, move on, played the song in my head.

So, to bring this quest to a conclusion, I started writing letters to recently convicted men who had assaulted children in boarding schools. There was no shortage of candidates: another case of historic abuse in an institution popped up via my Google News alerts two or three times a week. Most of my letters I sent to Her Majesty's Prison Whatton, the Northamptonshire jail where since 1990 low-risk sex offenders have been housed. Others who had been released or received suspended sentences (not uncommon with the older ones) I tried to contact by blanket-mailing all possible home addresses that came up in Internet searches. It was a slow fishing expedition.

But one of the letters paid off. In a court report in a Surrey newspaper, I'd come across a serial abuser, a man with three previous prison sentences, all for offences against children. These included a sexual assault on a ten-year-old boy and 'media offences' – prosecutor-speak for possessing, making or distributing illegal images. In the most recent case, he had been hauled up for multiple offences at a boarding school in the 1970s and 1980s, an averagely rackety place I'd already heard about from several ex-pupils. The man, now in his seventies, had been given a suspended sentence. To the disgust of the prosecuting counsel and the police, the judge had concluded that serving more time might damage his 'good progress' as a rehabilitated sex offender.

# 44. Maurice

Maurice, as I'll call him, emailed back the day he received my letter. He said he felt 'honoured' by my approach. Indeed, sex in boarding schools was something that he was writing about himself, with hopes of publication.

> This particular subject matter has been of great interest to me for a number of years, and having been a schoolmaster myself for twenty years, but now retired, I naturally have every reason to pursue this from many angles. As with a great many boys who attended a boarding school: be it preparatory or public school, etc., I was sexually involved with not only other boys, but also with a number of masters, hence my reason for regarding this a wholly important topic.

I phoned him and we agreed to meet the following week in a Yorkshire seaside town. Maurice said he'd cook me lunch: he sounded quite thrilled. But it wasn't to be so easy. He got cold feet. He changed the meeting place and then he postponed it indefinitely. He had, he said, sent some of my journalism on boarding school experiences to well-placed friends: they advised him not to trust me. These friends, one of them a QC, thought I was bitter about my own experiences, seeking revenge and clearly cashing in, too. Perhaps I was cross, they said, that I couldn't afford to give my own children the same great education from which I had so clearly benefited. What's more, my writing on boarding schools was 'facile' and 'ungrateful'. In other emails he showed a kinder face: in one he said he didn't want to tell me about his boarding school experiences because he thought I might find them too distressing.

I felt quite a bit of sympathy for him in his hesitation. You don't have to be a cynic to work out that a convicted child molester's chances of getting a fair hearing from any journalist are limited: their chances of being able to see what they want to in print are close to non-existent. As we all know, only the dead are less of a libel risk than convicted child molesters. Further, a convicted serial child abuser living under a false name in the community has lots to fear, especially one who is seventy-four and not physically well. In unforgiving modern Britain, in a time of public hysteria about children's safety, Maurice's social status was certainly lower than a drug dealer's, perhaps nearer the level of the retired Nazi concentration camp guards who pop up every now and then. Maurice would be stupid or singularly unaware not to be nervous at the prospect of talking to a journalist, especially one like me, a self-declared survivor of abuse at school.

In the end, having expressed his many doubts, Maurice tells me he has decided that I am sincere and he isn't going to listen to his friends. Indeed, he says, talking to me might help him with his own literary projects, which include his autobiography and a full-length fantasy book for children. So, one afternoon we have the conversation – or rather, for three and a half exhausting hours, he pours it out on the telephone while I listen. We get straight down to it; his tone is plain, sometimes legalistic, rarely emotional.

'In terms of my own experiences in terms of what's loosely termed sexual abuse, my life in that vein began when I
was eight years old. Not with men, I hasten to add. It was
with older boys. Just past my ninth birthday I did become
involved with a man, a schoolmaster – I suppose it could
be called mild sex abuse. No more than fondling, that kind
of thing. He would call me to extra reading lessons, and he
would slip his hand up inside my shorts and . . . he fondled
me. I found it pleasurable, I didn't object in any way. I was
I suppose his star performer.

'I had similar experiences in the cub scouts. And in the
scouts . . . But then when I was ten, my grandfather found
a termly boarding school in Roehampton, a very exclusive
place. It only held forty boys. Two buildings joined together by a long corridor, with the older boys in one side
and the younger in the other. Next door was a very wealthy
man, a German who was a pornographer, specialising in
boys only. He would let us use his swimming pool. And of
course in those days, you all swam naked, and so I became
involved with him when I was eleven . . .

'Not long after I became a boarder at this school, I
made a friend, Jack. I'd only been there a few weeks. He
introduced me to one of the masters there who took us
for French, and ran the stamp club and formed a choir.
Quite coincidentally, very similar to the situation when
I was at [the first school he worked at as an adult] . . .
It was a very cunningly planned ploy, to indulge certain
boys in his proclivities, which were, at night in the dormitory when we were in bed, he would come in to make
sure we were warm enough, which entailed him putting
his hand under the sheets and blankets. We wore pyjamas,
traditional ones that fastened with a cord, and he would
slide his hand in, run his hand over our bodies, and then if

there were no objections, and he registered compliance, he would slide his hand up inside our pyjama top, on to the bare skin of our chest and stomach and, again, with nothing to deter him from going further, he would then slide his hand down inside our pyjama bottoms. This went on almost every night . . .'

The story spills from Maurice with steady deliberation, like bricks being set upon a wall. His slow, flat voice has an occasional edge of old-fashioned posh. The recital is hard to interrupt. Not that it is new. It is perhaps the most common boarding school abuse story, the trusted teacher's calming hand coming to soothe in a parody of parental good-night rituals, then slipping beneath the sheets, probing, testing to see which child is responsive. It's been told to me by adults as terrifying, weird and humiliating: some talk of lying in the bed frozen, pretending the intrusion isn't happening, even of leaving their bodies and watching from above the bed. A few talk of finding it exciting, stimulating. There, of course, the shame and confusion begins: 'How could I call it abuse, if it was pleasurable?' But Maurice says he had no confusion.

You were ten, I say. How did you feel when this was happening?

'I loved it. I know it sounds daft . . . But I loved it. I am going to put this to you quite candidly: I cannot remember throughout my boyhood when I had what could be termed a bad experience.' He pauses. 'Except for once, when I was eleven. I was actually raped, by three much older boys on Roehampton Common . . .' How horrible, I say, poor you. 'Yes, it was traumatic . . .' The voice is still bland. 'I'd had numerous sexual experiences from an early age, but . . . This is what boys do. It's a progression from "I'll show you mine, you show me yours," sort of thing.

What made it worse was that I didn't know the boys. I'd never seen them before.'

The story goes on: awful and dreary. It is credible in its detail, though Maurice's assumptions – like the one that a boy's evolution from playing doctors and nurses to gang rape is quite natural – are eye-popping. But the narrative is smoothed by many tellings. Maurice makes friends with a teenage male prostitute, who protects him and gets the rapists beaten up. The pornographer next door to the school takes photos of the little boys. The French teacher who likes to feel under the blanket introduces Maurice to the special thing he does with Jack in his study.

Do you feel you were ever coerced? Do you feel that you agreed to these adults' invasions?

'Agreement isn't the word. Consent, maybe.'

I'm not sure of the difference – does he mean he was bribed, which is what Mr Keane did at my school?

'There was no bribe.'

You told me, I say when he pauses, that you were an unloved child. Rejected by your mother. (Maurice has told me she was a 'prude', disgusted by his childish nakedness – she preferred his younger sisters.) 'Some would say you would welcome this sort of attention from teachers because you craved physical warmth and affection?'

He agrees: 'Absolutely, and you're not the first person to suggest that. Every child needs love and affection. When their parents are incapable of giving that to their offspring, then the child will turn to someone who is able to do so. Hence my devotion to my grandparents, especially my grandfather. And, if a man, a schoolmaster, or Akela in the cubs, is friendly and accommodating and helpful, a child will naturally become drawn to that.'

I can't help but think of the story John Peel told in his

memoir, of the Shrewsbury school monitors who were the only source of help or kindness for a lonely thirteen-year-old, and had to be paid with sex.

This is why people worry about early boarding, I say. It can make the children vulnerable to adults. 'Oh yes,' he says. 'Of course it does. Jack, my friend, never mentioned his parents. He lived with an uncle and aunt and he was a termly boarder. He'd been involved with the French master, known as Gerry, from the age of eight. He was a very good-looking boy and this master took a shine to him and offered him whatever . . .'

What? I ask. Love? Safety?

No. 'Stamps,' says Maurice. 'Gerry ran the stamp club. And for favours granted he would give a boy some fairly rare stamps. In fact, my collection grew as I grew, and I was there three years. I got my first Penny Black.'

Maurice would go to Gerry's study after his bath, in his dressing gown, and choose some stamps. 'He would undo the dressing gown and, you know, things would happen. That was fine. I always came away with a reward. It might be a rare stamp, or two or three not-so-rare stamps. And the same applies to Jack.' There's a pause. 'It wasn't until I was eleven years and four months old that he buggered me. I knew he buggered Jack a great many times, because Jack told me.'

The school was busy with paedophiles. Gerry was having sex with other boys, and so were two other masters. The deputy headmaster liked to slipper the boys on their naked bottoms for discipline – never hard enough to cause pain. Afterwards, he would caress the boys where he had hit them. Then there was the school gardener, who liked boys and watched them swim naked in the child pornographer's pool. The senior boy in charge of the dormitory would summon the younger ones into his bed. ('That's just boys flexing their muscles.') But, Maurice insists, there was no coercion, ever. He didn't like the other men, so he didn't have sex with them. The only violence or compulsion he ever encountered, in his sexual growing-up, was the rape on Roehampton Common.

So the school, which the headmaster and Gerry had started in the 1930s, was effectively run for men who wanted to have sex with children? I ask. For the first time, Maurice sounds peeved. 'That's the dichotomy people don't understand, when a boy needs love and affection he will turn to a master. Nice kids need that to grow up, properly. But, in some people's terms, the child is going to be abused.'

Maurice is insistent that the relationships he had were a just exchange. Sexual favours in return for parenting. Gerry was kind and decent, children's first recourse for anything, from having spilt something on a jumper to someone stealing tuck. 'If you had any concerns, any problem, you'd go to him. I was hopeless at French – but if you went to him saying I can't translate this sentence, he'd say, "Don't worry, come up to my study and we'll work it out." He wouldn't fondle me, and I'd leave knowing how to translate the sentence. The thing is, Alex, everybody loved him. Nobody had a bad word to say about him.'

And how would you feel about him if you met Gerry today?

'I would love to meet him again. I'd invite him to dinner, have a good old chin-wag, reminisce, thank him for all the help he gave me, and so on. I have no feelings of animosity about him.'

But he took a very wrong advantage of his position. You don't hold that against him?

'Not at all. He made my stay there a happy one.'

He could have done that without having sex with you.

'Of course he could, but as far as I was concerned that was part and parcel of it. He didn't hurt me or cause any discomfort or pain. And I had a friend, Jack, who had already been having sex with him for two years when I arrived. He had enjoyed it so much, it was probably the reason he introduced me.'

What happened, I wonder, to Jack? Maurice doesn't know. Friends tend to disappear from his life, though he is still in touch with the boy prostitute who had organised the beating up of the Roehampton Common rapists. We return to the theme of whether he feels any anger against Gerry.

'There was I, a young boy, deprived of love and affection from my parents, deprived of a decent home life, with a three-year-old sister that was taking all the attention away from me, and suddenly planted in an establishment where somebody had the decency to take me under his wing and give me love and affection. How could I possibly complain about that?'

We pause for a second.

'But when I think about it,' he starts again, 'now, sixty years on . . . You're quite right. He did take advantage of me, and of Jack, and the others. Whether or not I can truthfully say that he took away my innocence . . . no, I can't say that. Yes . . .' He is halting now, and his voice sounds old. He has talked non-stop for an hour. 'It is arguable to say that I was a victim. I didn't feel that I was, naturally. And when I left the school, I was very sorry to be parted from him. I've often thought of him, over the years. I don't know what happened to him. The chances are he was found out, that he fell from grace.'

I push him a bit. Are all the memories of his early

schooldays happy? He'd referred, in one of his letters to
me, to traumatic events. 'Very few and far between. Or,
shall I say, that I don't remember them or I don't want to
remember them.

'The only down side of it all,' he says, in the tone with
which you might mention a mild skin rash, 'was when I
became an adult, teaching. I was doing what was done to
me. There was no buggery, anything like that. But it was
the other side of the coin. I was taking advantage of the
situation . . . which obviously should never have happened.
They were my victims. They didn't go to school to be mo-
lested, they went to school to learn. They had trust in me
and I abused that trust.' His tone is flat as he says the last
sentences, as though he is repeating a lesson.

You say that about the boys you abused, I venture, but
you don't, I think, feel that about yourself. 'No, I don't,' he
says, firmly. 'It's bizarre, isn't it?'

I say it's interesting. He thinks for a little.

'While I was in prison, and I was on these courses, I met
naturally other sex offenders, some for boys, some for girls,
some for women, the whole spectrum. But of all the ones
who were in for boys, most of them had had relationships
as children with schoolmasters or men. And not one of
them, not one, said, "Oh, it was horrible! A terrible time."
They all felt that, so far as they were concerned, it was beneficial, it was rewarding, it was pleasurable, there were no
negative views, it was all very positive. Now, whether they
were trying to hide the truth, that they might have been
traumatised, I don't know. But they all said that one of the
reasons why they went on to abuse was because they had,
in inverted commas, been abused themselves. They had
enjoyed the encounters and therefore, as did I, assumed
that other boys would enjoy it in the same way.

'I know now that that's not always the case, that there are naturally people abused as children who hated every minute of it, but they were afraid to do anything about it. To me that's terrible, that a child can't express their feelings, and they can't go to somebody and say this man touched me.'

I told him that I had been written to by men, more than a few, who had decided that the sex adults introduced them to at school had not harmed them. But I thought the fact that the men had written to me showed something important: time had led them to acceptance of the events as a way of living with themselves. Not as a healthy response, just the only one that was feasible, in an environment that offered no safety, no trustworthy adults, no reliable love. They had been traumatised: many had spent lives tainted by the memories. But Maurice wasn't having it.

'I have only ever met one man who was genuinely traumatised by what had happened to him at prep school [he names a famous Catholic one]. Because the abuse was violent: it was forced on him.'

Maurice left the Roehampton school in 1955, aged thirteen. His own 'fall from grace' was still twenty years away. His father was now in prison (for selling stolen goods) and so he went to live with his grandparents. He failed his common entrance exam to public school, and so he had a private tutor for two years, 'a very nice man' who lived in the nearby village. It is no surprise to hear that the tutor began a sexual relationship with Maurice which went on till the boy was eighteen.

His grandfather, a major general in the British Army, knew something of this: the young Maurice had told him that the Akela, the scout leader, had fondled him. His grandfather did nothing – 'it wasn't buggery, or anything, so it wasn't important enough'. He explained 'Greek love' to his grandson – and later told him that at public school he had had affairs with older boys. 'It was normal for a pretty thirteen-year-old to be jumped on by the seventeen-year-olds,' he said, and Maurice took comfort from it.

Did he really think that that was generally the case? Oh yes, he tells me. He's seen it, researched it, talked to lots of people. In all the schools, sex between boys, between adults and boys, was rife. A ten-year-old selling himself to thirteen-year-olds for tuck, teachers with a string of young 'favourites' they used for sex. 'Traditional.'

Maurice went on to a minor public school in Oxfordshire and to Oxford University, where he got a degree in English. He knew he was homosexual (he does not like the word 'gay'). But apart from one student affair, his twenties were sexless, he says. He wanted to be an interior designer, but wasn't able to get started, so he made his living as a private tutor to children. 'There was no sexual interest, I was very good. Nothing happened.' This went on until, aged thirty-two, in 1974, Maurice got a job at a well-known school, now closed, near Woking. He says he had never considered having sex with a child until then. But he arrived at an institution where, just as at his Roehampton prep school, adults having relationships with the children was quite normal.

'It took me back to my childhood. It was rekindled, my sexual interest in boys. When I first went there I took over the role of teaching English, Scripture, Latin and History from a young chap in his early twenties who was asked to leave because it was discovered that he was having an affair with one of the very attractive eleven-year-olds there.

I discovered that from the boy himself, though we were just friends. But [the boy and the young teacher] had been having a sexual relationship. The teacher got himself teaching at another prep school just outside Leatherhead, he was kicked out of that for the same reasons, he then got another job, at another prep school. No questions were asked. Another master at the school had had the same thing just before I arrived. Nothing was ever said to any of the parents. We had another master while I was there, he was resident, he had a room at the school where he would entertain boys. He would be there completely naked, smoking a cigarette, when the boy came up to see him. He was sacked, but not for that. He was sacked for giving a boy a cigarette.

'When I went there, no questions were asked by the headmaster. Nothing about my life, my experience, no background check. I had only been there for a few months when I learned that the deputy headmaster who had been there since before the war was entertaining his favourites in his study, to bugger them. The boys talked about it, I knew it, because I had my spies. The boys trusted me, they knew I was a sensible and intelligent person, who wouldn't blab. They told me things that no boy should ever tell a master – which boys were having clandestine activities, and who with. But who was I to tell on anyone? And the boys were happy.'

Maurice's voice has risen a tone. He is outraged that it could be so simple for a man with an interest in children. 'It was so easy. So unbelievably easy for any man, any Tom, Dick or Harry, to get a job at an all-boys school, boarding, without any questions being asked. You didn't need a reference. And it's only after a length of time, when suddenly his proclivities have come to the fore, that he is sacked.

That's all, sacked! The headmaster, obviously, fearing that this will get out, that the parents will take their offspring away, will give an excuse – a death in the family, something like that. Parents don't want to see what's going on, it's the old ostrich syndrome.'

So you felt licensed to do what you liked at the school?

'More or less. I assumed the boys liked me as much as I liked them. I was giving them as much love as I could, in the proper way – forget the other side of things. I literally loved them and they loved me. I was like an uncle. One boy came up to me one day – I'll never forget it – and said, "Sir, I wish you were my father."'

In addition to covering half the syllabus, Maurice took school camping trips and taught art, photography and sport. At one time he was warned not to be too physically friendly to the children, not to give them piggy-backs.

'They love you too much,' the headmaster told him regretfully. 'I was afraid to even pat them on the head. Of course at the same time, perversely, I was abusing them. Work that one out! It's bizarre! If someone had come up to me and said why, I'd have said, I haven't got a clue! No idea!' Maurice laughs.

The chosen boys were invited to a space – in court it was called a 'secret room' – he had built in a loft at the school. There he would give them cider, take photos, 'letting what might happen, happen – no buggery, though'. When he was finally tried for these crimes, thirty-seven years after his arrival at the school, the charges included feeling a child's penis. Witnesses said that he performed sexual acts and made them reciprocate. Maurice won't tell me how many of the boys he had sexual relationships with. But one of the men whose evidence later brought him to court said the sex and cider sessions happened weekly.

Why does he think he did it?

'Since then, over the years, with all the courses, and psychologists, help from friends, other professions, I now understand why I was doing what I did. Because of the positive side of my involvement with it when I was a boy, hoping in some way to extend it, so that they would enjoy that sort of relationship. But how naïve can you get? I was naïve!' And the boys at the school had consented? Not in so many words: 'I did always make quite sure that they were not adversely affected by my wanting this type of relationship with them, and not one of them was not happy about it. Quite the opposite, in fact.'

Maurice, long a shy loner, bloomed at the school. He was the cool, sports-car-driving young teacher, liked by the school parents, with lots of friends. He was an active Young Conservative, attending conferences: he met Margaret Thatcher. He socialised with other men who liked boys, meeting to dine and swap photographs and film of naked children. At one of these parties he met a minor BBC celebrity and two Eton masters, one of whom, Raef Payne, was my housemaster there. (Payne was as openly 'out' a homosexual as was possible at the school at that time.) Maurice was not out, but his life was idyllic; he was fulfilled in his work, socially and sexually.

As our conversation goes on into its third hour, he contradicts himself more and more: the sex was wrong, the sex was harmless, the sex was beneficial. After we spoke, he emailed me 'Further thoughts', a rambling document where he reveals just how much sexual activity there was at the school. He tells of witnessing a thirteen-year-old having sex with four ten-year-olds in a hop-picker's hut on a school camping trip – and just how harmless he then thought that was. 'I did not consider that what was taking place there was of any real danger to the boys, for there was never any moment of apparent fear, disquiet, emotional unbalance or unhappiness. At least, none that I could easily recognise.'

Again and again he tells me how 'deprived' these children were – of normal family life, of love. He suggests the schools tacitly tolerated the relationships because they knew the children had emotional needs that had to be satisfied. Given that, what he and the other men did was OK, but there were limits. Forced sex and anal sex are wrong; masturbation and oral sex are all right. So is bribery.

Maurice is angry about many things, as the average seventy-four-year-old man on the edge of society will be. Politicians, psychologists, journalists, social workers, the police are all incompetent and dishonest, 'evil'. As you'd expect, a particular sore is the injustice of current law. 'Take a child, you develop a friendship, things are engendered, and eventually the friendship becomes intimate, it's a shared intimacy and the man touches the boy's penis. The boy enjoys it because it's immensely pleasurable, nobody can deny that, and they enjoy it, so much it happens again, and again. The friendship develops, they are happy – the boy can't wait to see his friend, he's doing well at school, everything's fine. Then the man is caught. He gets, say, six years in prison. OK: same scenario, but the man's a nasty man, he kicks a boy, inflicts a real injury, breaks a bone, the man goes to court, he gets two years. You can inflict pain on a child, that's almost acceptable. Yet you can give love and affection to a boy with minor sexual attachments and you're a beast, a fiend, an evil man. We're going way over the top in dealing with this matter, making a mountain out of a molehill. We need some common sense.'

*

Maurice's happy time at the Woking school came to an
abrupt end in 1984. He fell. 'I had become very close to
a boy, an eleven-year-old. We loved each other, put it that
way. Despite what people say, young boys are just as capable of loving as others are. But . . .' – and I hear the sex
offender's coursework kicking in – 'it was a wrong influence. He was a boy and I was a man. He was not able to
comprehend, or cope with that sort of situation.'

But a child, by definition, can't consent to sex with an
adult, I say.

He acknowledges that he now – post-rehabilitation –
realises that. At the time he believed that the children had
given 'silent consent' – just as he had, as a boy. Or more:
'I most certainly encouraged it when I was a boy, and so
did a great many others I have encountered over the years.'

What followed was a repeat of what happened to Maurice and his mate Jack at eleven years old. The love-object
brought along his friend, slightly younger. Maurice
'touched' him, and this boy, 'quite happy with that situation', started coming to Maurice regularly. Then disaster
struck: another teacher hit this child. When he next went
home he told his parents about that, and added, 'By the
way, Mr [Maurice] touched my willy.'

The parents complained. Maurice was asked to leave immediately. 'It was the end of my world.' The headmaster
and his deputy were regretful; they offered help. Parents
telephoned and sent letters of commiseration and support.
At Christmas, the headmaster sent him a card with a white
dove on the front. Maurice became an interior designer,
and then a private tutor. One of his subsequent prosecutions concerned a child he was tutoring.

Eighteen years later, according to Maurice, one of his

'closest friends' from the school, a former pupil who, he confides, 'couldn't get enough', went public. He gave a statement to the police alleging abuse, but the investigation petered out. Another eight years passed: in 2010, the same ex-pupil and two others made further complaints. Maurice was tried and found guilty on twelve counts of assault and having sex with children. 'Thank God, the judge was intelligent,' says Maurice. 'He said, considering that you've done the courses, and pleaded guilty, and you've been to prison before, I am going to give you eighteen months, suspended for two years.' According to court reports, the judge said that the pre-sentence report was 'unusually favourable', stating Maurice was a 'changed man and presented a low risk'. Maurice in fact got two eighteen-month sentences, and walked free.

The records show that he has been prosecuted four times and in prison twice after losing his job at the Woking school, serving six years in total. In 1988, he was prosecuted for sexual assault on a boy and taking photographs, and served two years in prison. Then in 1994, there was a sexual assault on a ten-year-old whom he had been coaching, for which he was sentenced to ten years, and served four. The next prosecution, in 2003, was for possession of DVDs of child pornography. For that, as part of the probation order that was his sentence, he had been enrolled in a project to rehabilitate sex offenders. This was not the first he'd attended, but the previous one had been run by prison officers and 'silly schoolgirls who had only just left uni with a psychology degree . . . a complete and utter waste of time'. This time, though, the programme had been very good. It helped him 'break through my long-lasting barrier of obstinacy' on the issue of whether children can genuinely give consent. Had the course made him happier?

'Oh yes, absolutely,' he says with certainty. 'I can live with myself.'

I asked him what he would do today, with his knowledge, to protect children better. He is firm: 'We need people, people with common sense, to go to the schools and explain to the children that there are people called paedophiles who are dangerous . . . Tell them to notify somebody if there's a man pestering them, a man who's staring at them. They've got to be told that for a man to sexually or physically abuse them is going to damage them for the rest of their lives. Children can't be expected to understand that.' This all sounds very sensible. The NSPCC would agree that children need more than encouragement to speak up.

So you must now accept that your life was damaged by men who preyed on you, I say. 'No, I can never say that. I was not critically injured; I was not hurt in any way. People need to understand that there are those who, like me, were subjected to these things and, well, look, I've not just overcome it, but I've accepted it for what it was.' It is, I can't help but think, the purest iteration of the principle of stiff upper lip, of turning adversity into triumph.

That night I dream that I am standing in our local shopping mall, in an upper gallery, leaning against a railing and watching the crowds below. For some reason I'm wearing a pyjama top but no bottoms; as I become aware of this I realise a security guard is staring at me, aghast. He can see my penis and he starts yelling. Next, I am bolting through the mall's corridors, slipping at corners, bouncing off walls, still half-naked, chased by a crowd of young teenage boys in white shellsuits: they want to kill me, the paedo. They are pulling at my sleeves and I am shouting as hard as I can for help. I wake up, sweating, still shouting. My wife, half asleep, stretches out an arm and tells me it's all right.

# PART EIGHT

# The Product

# 45. The aftermath

We are often told that they taught us nothing at Eton.
That may be so, but I think they taught it very well.

General Herbert Plumer, addressing a dinner of Old Etonians
in 1916

Between 12,000 and 17,000 young men and women
emerged from the boarding schools each year from the
late 1940s until their popularity started to slide in the
1980s. That leaves alive today around one million people
who have had experience of British boarding schools. Since
2000 boarder numbers have been stable at around 70,000,
down from a probable peak in the late 1960s of around
155,000. Even now, more than half of the parents entering
their children for boarding school have had the same sort
of education themselves.

For wealthy Britain and for increasing numbers of
foreign parents, the system works: it provides entry to
jobs, universities and influential networks, as it always
did. The statistics on the schooling of those who rule –
judges, politicians, senior officers in the military, bank
directors, journalists – show that the private schools fill
those seats just as they always did. For broken families,
single parents, the career-driven, or people overwhelmed
by their children's needs and problems, boarding remains
the off-the-peg solution it always was: socially acceptable

residential care for kids. The enormous difference today is that boarding costs, in real terms, about three times what it did when I was at school, and when my grandfathers were – more than £30,000 a year at many boarding public schools. (When I went to Eton in 1974, the annual fee was £861 – the equivalent of £10,300 today; in 2017 a year at the school costs £32,000 before extras.)

So the boarding school is now, for the first time in modern history, out of reach of much of Britain's ordinary professional class. Increasingly children are recruited from the newly wealthy of Russia, Africa and China: foreigners account for 30 per cent of all boarders. This is a brand-aware clientele. Eton, according to the *Financial Times*, is Dolce & Gabbana. But that school maintains entry requirements, including a requirement for good English, which will put off some Russian and Asian students. Others have been forced to adapt, start remedial English classes, and accept that foreign students are becoming the bulk of their business. Stowe, Charterhouse and Wellington are among the famous names with large numbers of foreigners. Foreign nationals recently made up 50 per cent of the student population at Roedean, the clifftop home of the 'blue-stocking' British woman hardy of body and steely of mind. At another smart girls' school, Cobham Hall, the proportion is 40 per cent among the younger years and 60 per cent at sixth form. Both the schools, though, have seen their overall numbers halve. Some schools have had to pledge to reduce the number of overseas students. The overseas parents are not happy if their children aren't mixing with proper British ones; one agency for German and Italian parents only recommends schools that can promise the children are a minimum of 80 per cent real British.

But the business of farming foreign children in British

boarding schools brings in approaching £1 billion a year; so valuable is the trade that Harrow, Repton, Marlborough and others have franchise schools from Kuala Lumpur to Kazakhstan. There are half a dozen British public schools in the United Arab Emirates alone, and fifty-two overseas members of the elite club, the HMC. 'Floreat Etona', goes the motto – 'Let Eton flourish'. It does, and, as the new millennium goes on, its rivals and clones do too.

There are still thousands of Britons rich enough to send their children away. They know the risks. They always did. According to Vyvyan Brendon's survey of 100 ex-prep school pupils, a third remembered the time as very unhappy, and a third as both good and bad. People are perhaps more forthcoming with me than they might be with the ordinary researcher, because I am of the tribe. Most ex-boarders I speak to outside those who have come to me with a story of abuse will say, as one did, 'mainly boring, some times of great fun, and some that were absolutely dreadful'. I suspect that about 60 per cent now see their experience as, overall, less than positive. Whatever the statistics, the experience of boarders seems to be significantly different to that of the general population, about half of whom remember their schooldays as the happiest of their lives.

Most ex-boarders who got in touch with me did so because school went wrong, for them or their loved ones. But even from the worst experiences, they drew diverse and complicated conclusions. These people are usually articulate, funny and often adept at self-criticism. They are quick, too, to doubt their memories, to dilute their remembered pain with irony and equivocation. This is a tribe of schooled Victorians, for whom naked self-expression is an offence, who use self-deprecation and wit as clothing, covering up what should not be shown to outsiders, or even to those closest to them. 'Mustn't fuss' is still the motto, and sometimes you grow impatient with the stories, desperate for an astringent to wash away all the crusted evasions and caveats.

I left my prep school at thirteen with nothing but relief: it was the end of a jail sentence. At eighteen, when I turned my back on my last public school, it was with joy: full of lust and hope. Like many I was not ready to deny or object to the experiences that, however bad, seemed at the heart of what was me. I felt like a rebel, and I liked that – the schools had made me angry against systems that I considered were unjust, or arbitrary. I was going to go out and prove Billy Williamson, my first headmaster, who told me so often how useless I was, just how wrong he had been. There is ample evidence that many people from all sorts of schooling emerged with the same sense of release. At last their lives, for so long hemmed and regulated by bullies and fools, would begin.

In my life as it followed over the next twenty or so years, I did things that, later, I was to realise were quite common among ex-boarders, and not only those who had left school angry. I was an addict, of stimulants and narcotics, of adrenalin and laughs, and sex too. I was certainly an addict of love, in a way that I knew was troubling – I wanted to know that women wanted me, would pledge themselves to me, and as soon as I had certainty of that, I would move on. I hated this destructive tendency in myself but I tried to ignore it. Like many, I sought thrills and danger in my work. I became a war correspondent. I also suffered more and more from depression and anxiety. I found work in organisations difficult, unless my boss was a woman – I could not accept male authority. Sometimes when women rejected me, I found the pain almost unbearable, something I didn't understand at all.

When I at last met a woman I could love properly, and we had a child, I realised I had to work out what had made me the person I was. It was then, too, that I found there were many others – men and women – carrying the same baggage. To outsiders, many of us appeared self-confident, arrogant, careless of others and poor empathisers. That is sadly typical – our accent alone flags those traits to other Britons. But, however shiny the surface, inside was a man hobbled by the self-doubt and confusion drilled in during the years from eight to thirteen.

For most ex-boarders, decades pass before they begin to pick apart what happened at school. Relationship problems, or having children reach boarding school age, triggers such analysis. The collapse of a career may do it: the abrupt loss of status and ejection from an institution is something the boarding school class is ill-equipped to handle. When people look for explanations of the flaws they see in themselves or others, it is to the beginnings they turn. Sometimes that is triggered by counselling. Psychotherapists in the 'boarding school syndrome' field write of how often a patient will appear to discuss anxiety or depression, and only after some time will the issue of having left home early to board surface. People whose relationships are in trouble have often been led by the self-examination that follows to wonder if their – or their partner's – emotional development went wrong. New mothers and fathers who read child-care manuals learn, perhaps for the first time, about the over-arching importance of healthy 'attachment' to a loving, secure and stable caring adult – and so they question their own attaching.

There are other shared themes in the stories I've heard. Often those who wake up to what happened see an emotional deficiency in themselves. Several letters from older men who've read my articles start with accounts of the success they have made in life, in material ways. Then there's a protest that what happened to them wasn't really abuse – there had been nothing sexual. They'd just been bullied and unhappy, but it had toughened them up, prepared them for the challenges of a cut-throat business world. Then comes a half-admission of disappointment about their personal lives. 'Of course, on the marital front, I haven't done so well – three wives, three divorces, lots of mess. Now I realise, a little sadly, I am better off alone.' This sort of survivor, Nick Duffell writes, 'lacks sympathy for himself'. Another therapist I know talks of an ex-boarder in his sixties, a successful businessman, confessing, 'I don't know who I am.' He ascribes this emotion to the habit of a vulnerable and anxious child developing a 'false self' for protection. Rediscovering the true self can be the work of a lifetime.

Many have decided that loneliness as an adult was a fair price to pay. 'Boarding school teaches self-sufficiency, not whining. Even if this instils in me some characteristics I so dislike. (As we were taught at school – "love no one, trust few, always paddle your own canoe"),' wrote one man. Often there is deep and life-eroding anger. But some wrote just to insist that they are all right. Here is an unusually frank one:

> So it was at the age of eight or nine or ten I learned the world was a wonderful place where cunning and deceit could outflank, outfox and eventually outgun everybody and the higher the profile of the target the more

vulnerable it was. It was an attitude which stood me in
good stead in journalism, then law and then business.
Expect no quarter and give none.

My female correspondents are usually less overtly angry,
but their assessment of the damage is just as frank. 'I've
realised I don't miss people,' a woman who went to board
at thirteen told me. 'If my children are away, or my husband is, I actively don't miss them, at all. I realise now that
I taught myself that, at school. Taught myself not to feel
hurt or pain – not to need people.'

   She would not, I think, see any good side to her boarding
school life. But ambivalence about the experience is very
common. Even among those who suffered most – on objec-
tive evidence – I've found people still wondering whether
it wasn't all for the best. The belief, which goes back to
the eighteenth century, that a blemished childhood may be
the most productive still lingers. 'Happiness is beneficial
for the body, but it is grief that develops the powers of the
mind,' wrote Marcel Proust, adding his note to a theme
running in Western thought for four centuries.

   The schools had implanted a fatal doubt in many of their
product. It was that they should not trust their own judge-
ment. That their elders and betters would inevitably know
best. After all, their parents had made the decision to send
them away, for their benefit and pleasure. So while they
thought they were unhappy, they might well be wrong.
Perhaps if they'd bucked up and tried a little harder? Or
perhaps there was something wrong with them. Once this
doubt had taken hold, all was to be doubted. If a teacher
was to put his hand on their genitals, perhaps that was
right? Bullying the weak and unattractive might be right
too, if you'd been bullied in your turn. Often the lesson

learnt is that, if you suffered, it was because you had earned it. That proves hard to shake off.

All of it leaves a lot of guilt. Guilt at what you did, which now as an adult seems plainly wrong. Guilt at having let your parents down, who'd loved you and made sacrifices for you to go to school. Guilt at what you failed to do. Recently I received a moving letter from a man, a reader of my articles, apologising for bullying me at our prep school. He said, carefully, that I didn't have to accept the apology, or even respond, but added: 'If you wish to see me, face-to-face, then I am available to you.'

I had never heard of him. He had confused me with someone else. But I got in touch, thanked him, and explained. He told me his story, how he had been bullied, and had become a bully in turn. It was plain to see that he really needed to get an apology himself. Guilt is long-lived and cuts in many ways.

Misdirected reactions are terribly common. Here is an excerpt from an account by a man who suffered at a badly run school, in a way that has warped his life. Yet his anger is dissipated into self-criticism:

> I am sent the [school magazine] and in one issue I read that the teacher who made that hesitant attempt at abuse only recently retired after a lifetime's teaching career. At least I think I did – I can't be sure I've remembered his name right. But I feel profoundly guilty, not knowing how many more boys or girls he might have abused. Should I have spoken out? It's too late now, I think – my memory is no longer fresh enough to give evidence to the police.

Another common theme is the pain that the boarders

may cause to those around them, who try to love people whose capacity to accept and benefit from that may be very limited. Here lie some of the saddest stories – tales from sisters, mothers and ex-partners picking over the causes and effects of suicides and wasted lives. Stories of much-loved little boys and girls who went away one September morning and never wholly came back; at least, not as they had been known.

Suffering is gluey, an Old Etonian friend wrote, it smears and sticks to many things, for many years. Here's one story, which starts with a visit to the old prep school, a smart Home Counties one now notorious for serial mental and physical abuse:

My former partner took me back there once and showed me round. As he showed me the little dormitories I asked him whether *he* had ever been bullied or abused there. The reason I asked was that at the time (he was then about thirty-five) he was already showing signs of the alcoholism that was later to blight both our lives and that of his beautiful daughter, whom he never sees.

He denied it, but he did tell me that he had run away twice; once getting as far as the town where his mother lived before being re-captured. I remember being aghast when he told me that his mother *had never been informed by the school that he had run away*. To this day she doesn't know. The headmaster apparently scolded and threatened him with all manner of punishments if he revealed it. I remember thinking firstly – 'why on earth didn't they tell her – you must have been so unhappy' and then . . . 'your mother lived a few miles away and didn't work – why were you even at boarding school in the first place?'

Anyway, I used to think that he was lying when he denied that he had been abused or bullied and that his terrible drinking must have its roots in some nameless, buried incident. He would binge for three weeks at a time and end up in A and E, from where I would receive a phone call and have to rescue him. It was wholly unbearable for us both. He was never a 'social' drinker. He always drank joylessly, straight from the bottle, as though he wanted to die.

Now I have read your article, I think that there may have been no 'incident'. That the damage was more subtle. That the lack of safety or trust there, the brutal response to his act of distress in running away, and many other incremental incidents, left their permanent mark.

He told me, with a little swagger, during the visit to the school that in fact, so far from being really homesick, he had been precocious enough to 'pretend' to feel homesick so that the attractive young woman in charge of his little dormitory would come and give him an extra hug before bed. He was about ten. Ten years old and desperate for a hug and having to pretend to himself, and to me, that it was sexual precocity that made him ask for it. How does one even begin to unpick that? At the time, I was prim and shocked and censorious. Now, it makes me cry for him.

Anyway, we are still in touch but no longer together. He does not work and for the last six years he has lived on disability living allowance; a full-blown alcoholic in a wheelchair who occasionally panhandles for change in the town centre.

He was *loved*. His daughter loved him. I loved him very deeply. But *he can't love*. He is less capable of love than any other man I have ever met and I now know in

my heart that his experiences at the school were partly,
or wholly, to blame.

If I put aside the letters that are unresolvably angry –
which often looks like a pretty reasonable response – I find
most of the rest are coloured with self-doubt and eagerness
to find something good from the experience. That perhaps
is a healthy reaction. But sometimes, reading them, I ache
for the child whose real and rightful needs went unrecog-
nised, unfulfilled, even by the adult who emerged. Again
and again people strive to rationalise and excuse. Parents
are absolved: they were divorcing, they were unwell, they
did important work abroad. Often you hear that a mother
or father, or both, had died, and so of course the best solution was to send the grieving child to boarding school. Joy
Schaverien writes of a patient for whom the school was an
escape from an intolerable situation at home. 'At least at
boarding school you knew where the punishments were
coming from.' One correspondent told me once that 'obviously' he had to go at six, though he was miserable, life
at home was impossible: his mother was an alcoholic and a
depressive who often failed to get out of bed or feed him.
Besides, his father had been to board. Then he added: 'Perhaps I've got it back to front: perhaps she was depressed
because I'd gone away.'

The anger, ever present, diffuses in different ways. One
woman told me she was convinced that she loved her parents more, because of going away to school when she was
six; 'for a start, they didn't have to deal with my nasty teenage me'. And so, on the same principle, she'd sent her own
children to board. An elderly couple told me how cross
they were at how much they had missed of their children's
childhood, a gap they understood now as they saw their

day-schooled grandchildren. 'Why did we do it? What on earth were we thinking?'

Another woman told me how she was sexually abused at her school, but her anger was not against the teacher, but her parents: 'I told them. They did nothing. I find that impossible to understand, to tolerate, even now, thirty years later. Especially now I have children of my own.' For many, the pain involved in accepting their parents let them down is so bad that it is easier to move the blame to something amorphous – the schools, the culture, the government.

# 46. Making sense of it

Some people strive for nuggets of good amid this wreckage. It seems urgent to find them, beyond the normal ex-boarders' ambivalence. Self-pity is a sin as great as disloyalty, under the code. So the school was hell, but there were comic moments. Many were saved by the friends with whom they bonded in adversity, and who are still with them. A headmaster's whimsical brutality led to a lack of respect for invested authority and spurred a lifetime of political activism. The education was random, and antiquated, but the discipline of Latin prose and scholarship-getting was far better than anything children get today. A 'loner' tendency that grew out of solitude and friendlessness at school has led to an extraordinary life of self-reliance and adventuring. 'Would we have George Orwell or Roald Dahl – or John Cleese and Stephen Fry – if they hadn't been unhappy boarders?' runs a popular argument.

Lord Robert Cecil, another generation would point out, was dismally unhappy at Eton, continually bullied, withdrawn after five years at the school in physical and nervous breakdown. The experience left him a depressive who believed 'human nature was essentially evil', according to his biographer, Andrew Roberts. Until the end of his life he would cross the road rather than encounter an Old Etonian. Yet – look! It made him three times prime minister, as Lord Salisbury.

There is another side to these supposed positive blemishes. A spouse whose reaction to a family problem that requires loving engagement is to start planning another solo sailing trip across the Atlantic. A man with the habit, if faced with a row, of storming out and cutting down a tree: 'We don't have many trees left round the house!' says his partner. An inability to be happy or relaxed with anyone except those old school friends 'who understand me'. Horror at telling an outsider of a problem or a weakness – and so ruling out any help like marriage counselling. Leaping to the defence of the hated institution, if any but someone who also suffered there should dare to criticise it. 'He was allowed to complain about Mummy, but no one else was,' says a friend of her ex-partner. 'Mummy?' 'That's what I called his school. For him, that's what it was, and always would be.'

George Orwell is perhaps the most complete boarding school survivor. There is a cold irony in the fact that someone who made such great use of the oppression of boarding school also personifies so many aspects of those who were damaged by it. One of those is the driven man, the one who can never relax (for the devil makes work for idle hands . . .), who must always find another job, another chore. He was successful, extraordinarily hard working and prolific. Yet he never believed it. Here he is writing after the triumphs of 1984 and *Animal Farm*, just a few months before he died of tuberculosis, aged forty-six:

It is now 16 years since my first book was published, & abt 21 years since I started publishing articles in the magazines. Throughout that time there has literally been not one day in which I did not feel I was idling,

that I was behind with the current job, and that my
total output was miserably small. Even at the periods when I was working 10 hours a day on a book, or
turning out 4 or 5 articles a week, I have never been
able to get away from this neurotic feeling that I was
wasting time . . . As soon as a book is finished, I begin,
actually from the next day, worrying because the next
one is not begun, worrying even that there never
will be a next one – that my impulse is exhausted for
good and all. If I look back and count up the actual
amount that I have written, then I can see that my
output has been respectable; but this does not reassure
me . . .

Whether through this sort of 'workaholic timetabling',
as Nick Duffell puts it, or through other strategies for
avoiding the past, most people find ways to keep themselves intact in the life-long crisis that can start from
unhappy schooldays. The more self-reflective adults will
recognise the habits, and the trouble they bring. But they
tend to despair of being able to alter themselves. So when
the notion that a boarding school past came with known
and treatable psychological symptoms took hold in the
1990s – largely because of the work of psychotherapists
like Duffell and Schaverien – many leapt for the idea, as
for a lifebelt in a shipwreck. Being a 'boarding school survivor', Duffell's phrase, was a new club, another fraternity,
a safe way to explore the experiences and the after-effects
without, God forbid, being alone or disobeying the code.
The change could be dramatic: one ex-boarder describes
being still 'a buttoned-up schoolboy' at the age of thirty.
Then he underwent psychotherapy, and was at last able to
cry over the death of his father. The only positive side of

this story is the lesson that talking about it really seems to help.

You might conclude from the twentieth- and twenty-first-century commentary on the public school system that most people believed it to have been largely a disaster, for Britain and the world the British establishment touched. Perhaps 90 per cent of the writing is against them. Defenders of the system who don't work in it are few. As we've seen, public school product of the orthodox type are not very good at expressing passionate belief. The major twentieth-century writers who did believe in the system, like Powell and Waugh, are too determined to layer their enthusiasm in irony to be of much use. Those who were sceptical, or against it, are often careful not to appear too starkly judgemental. After all, that might risk being taken for a zealot or a bore – very un-stiff upper lip. Peregrine Worsthorne, ex-boarder and ex-editor of the *Sunday Telegraph*, is one of the few vocal defenders. But his argument that a 'democracy needs an elite' and that government should support the schools because they are the best providers of that has never gained much traction. (In any case, the state does significantly support the schools by letting them have the tax advantages of charitable status.)

Many who hated their school will noisily defend the principle of it from any assault by the unentitled outsider. The journalist George Monbiot, criticised for his own account of his boarding school experience, wrote: 'Because private schools have been so effective in moulding a child's character, an attack on the school becomes an attack on all those who have passed through it. Its most abject victims become its fiercest defenders. How many times have

I heard emotionally-stunted people proclaim "it never did me any harm"?'

To the psychoanalysts and therapists who tackle ex-boarding school pupils, none of this is confusing at all: it is normalisation, the process by which someone comes to terms with the memories of painful or traumatic events they've been through. What they need to do is edit them to appear less damaging, or turn them into something that can happily be lived with. How much easier – especially for those left low in self-belief by the experience – to decide the system was right and you were wrong. Rejecting it is so much harder: it means rejecting everything that made you, including your parents' good intentions. The ultimate – and common – normalisation process in ex-boarders is to decide that their experiences, however unhappy, were so normal and useful that their own children should be put through the same process. (This explanation, while logical, makes it impossible for anyone who went to a boarding school to defend it to the boarding school syndrome practitioners: they are just normalising.)

One of the effects of normalisation is an anger, sometimes excessive, at those who disagree. Often, when *The Times* or *Daily Telegraph* print critical articles, the reaction is furious. In 2015 a painstaking interview with the psychoanalyst Joy Schaverien appeared in *The Times*, under the provocative headline 'Does boarding school harm you for life?' The comments broke down, roughly, into 70 per cent pro and 30 per cent anti-boarding. The latter were mainly quite reasonable, the former often frothing: 'I say mind your own business. Keep your communist opinions to yourself,' went one. Schaverien was not only wrong but 'perverse and partisan' and dishonest. Others made better points:

The chap [a patient mentioned in the article] should be grateful. If he hadn't gone to boarding school, he'd probably not have done as well in life and as a consequence been unable to afford to see a psychotherapist. He should thank his lucky stars.

'But it's all changed, right?' nervous parents and reminiscing ex-boarders ask me. The answer is no: a lot has changed, but not everything. They are still boarding schools.

# 47. Today

Today, at the best-run modern prep schools, the potential damage of separation may well be taken seriously. The fact that boarding is no longer the six- or twelve-week sentence that it used to be must be significant to the child. A weekly boarder who knows that only five days separate him or her from home is different from one who knows that half-term is unthinkable numbers of weeks away. The ISC said in 2016 that of the 4,809 children boarding in junior schools, slightly fewer than half were full boarders – the rest were on flexi or weekly boarding.

Another important change is in communication. Parents, once told to stay away, are now less timid. Children can easily telephone or FaceTime home now. But there are those who still 'dump' their children, to quote a housemaster at one of the smartest schools. 'Sometimes I think we're just child care for the rich,' he told me. 'There are parents who use us who should not have had children at all.' Such things cannot of course be said to those who need to hear them.

The other area that is different is the number of criminals the schools employ. As we've seen, in the second half of the twentieth century, in hundreds of schools, there was an incredible laxity over recruitment. But the changes brought in by the Children's Act of 1989 – which came about because of the scandal around Crookham Court school, bought and run by a known paedophile for his and his friends' pleasure – made real differences. After decades of resistance, the private schools were subject to proper inspection and forced to take what had become known as 'child protection' seriously.

In 2004 a further Act introduced minimum standards for boarding schools, addressing issues like mental health, 'wellbeing', confidentiality and – how my old headmaster must roll in his grave – children's rights. The code even asks that pupils are enabled to make complaints and that their bedding be 'clean and suitable, and sufficiently warm'. There are stipulations on the use of 'restraint' – an awful echo of what used to go on in the old approved schools – and on ensuring child prefects do not abuse their positions, and that 'Staff actively search for boarders who are missing'.

Institutions, almost by definition, keep secrets and cover up information that might damage them. Children are still at risk from those who would harm or prey on them, not least because the code of not speaking out, not sneaking, keeping the stiff upper lip, is still in place. A recent freedom of information request by the BBC revealed that 5,500 sexual offences at school, including 600 rapes, had been reported to the police in England between 2012 and 2014 – 20 per cent of these were by children on children. If you believe the figures for how many such events are not reported, the true figure is at least three times higher.

In the private schools, a huge additional problem remains. The Department of Education's current standards for boarding schools are vague and contradictory on relationships between pupils and adults. There's a stipulation that 'Any boarder access to staff accommodation is properly supervised and does not involve inappropriate favouritism or inappropriate one-to-one contacts between staff and boarders', but nothing on how that should be policed or reported. There is no requirement for teachers or carers to have had any training beyond an induction by the school. Indeed, Conservative education ministers have for a while been pushing for unqualified teachers to be allowed into all schools: they are already permitted in academies.

More seriously, there is no more duty now on a private school's headteacher to report an allegation of sexual or physical abuse than there was when I went to school. As Tom Perry, founder of Mandate Now! and a survivor of abuse at Caldicott School, puts it:

> The fundamentals of child protection have not changed in fifty years because the failed model of 'discretionary reporting' of alleged and known abuse remains unchanged. While it does, no assurance which claims child protection 'is all different now' that is made by any Head or Chair of Governors, no matter how well regarded they might be, can have reliance placed upon it because it is incorrect.

The key thing that has changed is the economics of the boarding school: the vast fee increase means they can afford to be more selective about the staff. Online pornography (and cheap foreign travel) has provided paedophiles with new ways to satisfy their needs. The Internet also allows would-be teachers to be vetted more thoroughly, though criminals still slip through. But the codes and the motivations – the desire to avoid embarrassment or expense – that permit cover-up are still in place at the schools. The all-party campaign to bring the necessary changes to the law* needs support if we are ever to properly protect children in institutions, whether they are boarding schools or football clubs.

There's a luxurious crunch in the gravel surrounds of the grand schools. They lay it deeper, you suppose. For an ex-boarding school boy like me, arrival at such a place is no easy thing. The heart rate goes up. I start watching, listening very carefully. Vigilance is safety. It is the first day of the summer term at Fettes College, the Eton of the North, the gravel is noisy with SUVs and taxis returning children from the holidays, and the air is infused with the scent of cut grass from the cricket pitches and generous lawns. Sounds and smells – anything from boy sweat to floor polish or the chatter of those lawnmowers – tweak the memory. I know people who have panic attacks just driving past their old school.

Inside the vast oak doors of the central building – Victorian, but in the style of something built five hundred years earlier – is a notorious child abuser. He's bespectacled, twinkling, almost cuddly in a rumpled tweed suit. His portrait hangs in the school's polished entrance hall in a gallery of much sterner past headmasters – if you were to choose one of them all to take charge of your child, this would be the man. Appearances deceive. Anthony Chevenix-Trench was a drunk and a vicious flogger: many of his victims were certain he got sexual pleasure from the act. He was sacked by at least one other public school. Dozens of men still alive had their lives warped by him. This school was warned not to hire him – but it did. He

* More details on this can be found at this book's website, www. stiffupperlipbook.com.

died while serving as headmaster. And today, despite the complaints of ex-pupils, his portrait still greets every visitor.

There's no beating now: the boarding schools have changed. For a start, 83 per cent of those in the self-selecting elite of the Headmasters' Conference boast of in-house counselling services. I'm here for a seminar, organised by the school and given by an ex-boarding school housemaster turned motivational speaker. His topic today is 'How to develop a confident child'. He is called James Shone and with his charity, I Can and I Am, he tours the nation's private schools lecturing teachers, pupils and parents on 'how to build self-esteem'.

It isn't a topic you would think was of much concern with the privileged children at one of the country's most expensive schools. But then, most of the parents gathered for the lecture in an upper room in the great neo-Gothic building are about to leave their children, once again, for several weeks or months. That's a subject I'm going to bring up as soon as Shone's PowerPoint ends. That and the fact that even the HMC's own stats show that the pressure to succeed is greater than ever before and children are suffering. The Conference's research shows that two thirds of heads of the elite independent schools are worried about their pupils' mental health. Self-harming, eating disorders, depression and cyber-bullying are all of increasing concern. 'How do we inflate the golden balloon of self-belief?' Shone asks the audience.

There is a cruel threat to self-belief that wasn't there in my day: if you don't do well enough in exams the school reserves the right to kick you out. That is entirely, teachers have told me, because of the pressure on the school to score well in the exam league tables, and that pressure is because, if they don't, the parents will go elsewhere. How does Shone think being expelled for under-performing might affect a teenager's self-belief? I can feel my pulse beginning to race as I psych myself to confront the old enemy, the master at the blackboard.

The presentation starts. We watch some YouTube video of women running around an athletics track until one of them trips, falls, and then bravely gets back into the race. 'The lesson, guys, is it's not the falling over, but the getting up,' says Shone. I have to squint to see the screen now, because the spring sunshine is doing a laser show through the Gothic windows. Shone rambles on: he doesn't deserve my long-simmered anger. The parents are lapping up the aphorisms. I feel itchy: what are we doing in here on the loveliest day of the year so far? My son and daughter are playing football nearby. Many of these people won't see theirs for six weeks, perhaps twelve. When are they going to get a chance to apply Shone's advice to their offspring? An hour has gone: I slip out before questions and go to play in the park with my children while the sun is still out.

# Acknowledgements

I am very grateful for the support, advice and help of many people over the three years of research and writing that brought this book about. Some cannot be named. I am particularly in debt to Bella Bathurst, Petra Cramsie, Nick Duffell, Robert Dalrymple, Philip Eade, Jock Encombe, Samantha Fergusson, Bea Hemming, Florence Ingleby, Lucy Juckes, Lucinda McNeile, Ed Marriott, Gill Moreton, Simon Milne, Ruaridh Nicoll, Andrew Norfolk, Simon Partridge, Karolina Sutton, Francis Wheen, many people at the *Observer*, at Weidenfeld & Nicolson, and of course all my lovely family, including Ziggy.

# Bibliography

Further footnotes and full source references by page can be found at stiffupperlip-book.com

I am especially grateful to the authors and publishers of these books:

Jonathan Gathorne-Hardy, *The Public School Phenomenon* (Hodder & Stoughton 1977 and Faber Finds 2014 (e-book)

Jeffrey Richards, *Happiest Days: The Public Schools in English Fiction* (MUP, 1988)

J. R. De S. Honey, *Tom Brown's Universe: The Development of the Public School in the 19th Century* (Millington, 1977)

Vyvyen Brendon, *Prep School Children: A Class Apart over Two Centuries* (Continuum, 2009)

Royston Lambert with Spencer Millham, *The Hothouse Society* (Weidenfeld & Nicolson, 1968). Rights for use of this material are held by Peters, Fraser & Dunlop.

George Orwell, *Collected Essays, Journalism and Letters Vol 4* (Copyright © George Orwell, 1970) and 'Such, Such Were the Joys' (Copyright © George Orwell, 1952) are reprinted by permission of Bill Hamilton as the Literary Executor of the Estate of the Late Sonia Brownell Orwell.

### Introduction

*The Public Schools from Within: A Collection of Essays on Public School Education mainly by School Masters* (Sampson Low, Marston, 1906)

Royston Lambert, *The Chance of a Lifetime* (Weidenfeld & Nicolson, 1975)

Jill E. Korbin (ed), *Child Abuse and Neglect: Cross-cultural Perspectives* (University of California Press, 1981)

### Part One – Leaving Home

Andrew Birkin, *J.M. Barrie and the Lost Boys* (Yale University Press, 1979)

Auberon Waugh, *Will This Do?* (Arrow Books, 1991)

Rupert Everett, *Red Carpets and other Banana Skins* (Little, Brown, 2006)

Vyvyen Brendon, *Children of the Raj* (Weidenfeld & Nicolson, 2005)

John Chandos, *Boys Together: English Public Schools 1800-1864* (Hutchinson, 1984)

Winston Churchill, *My Early Life* (1930)

Vyvyen Brendon, *Prep School Children* (Continuum, 2009)

J. A. Mangan (ed), *Benefits Bestowed: Education and British Imperialism,* particularly Donald Leinster-McKay's essay on the nineteenth-century prep school, p. 56.

Hugh Montgomery-Massingberd, *Daydream Believer* (Pan Macmillan, 2001)

Desmond FitzGerald, *Many Parts: the Life and Travels of a Soldier, Engineer and Arbitrator in Africa and Beyond* (The Radcliffe Press, 2007)

Christina Hardyment, *Dream Babies* (Harper & Row, 1983)

Ian Gibson, *The English Vice: Beating, Sex and Shame in Victorian England and after* (Duckworth, 1978)

Joy Schaverien, *Boarding School Syndrome: The Psychological Trauma of the 'Privileged Child'* (Routledge, 2015)

Nick Duffell and Thurstine Basset, *Trauma, Abandonment and Privilege* (Routledge, 2016)

Robin Balbernie, 'Foundation years and the UK Government's life strategy', www.pipuk.org.uk

Heledd Hart and Katya Rubia, 'Neuroimaging of child abuse: a critical review', *Front. Hum. Neurosci.*, 19 March 2012

William F. Cornell (1988), quoted in William F. Cornell, Anne de Graaf, Trudi Newton, Moniek Thunnissen (eds), *Into TA: A Comprehensive Textbook on Transactional Analysis* (Karnac Books, 2016)

Valerie Sinason, Introduction, V. Sinason (ed), *Memory in Dispute* (Karnac Books, 1998)


**Part Two – Settling in at Prep School**

C. S. Lewis, *Surprised by Joy* (1955, HarperCollins edition, 2002)

Royston Lambert and Spencer Millham, *The Hothouse Society* (Weidenfeld & Nicolson, 1968)

David Limond, 'From a position of prominence to one of almost total obscurity: Royston James Lambert and Dartington Hall', *Journal of Historical Biography*, Autumn 2012

Adam Sisman, *John le Carré: the Biography* (Bloomsbury, 2015)

Vyvyen Brendon, *Prep School Children* as previously cited

Roald Dahl, *Boy: Tales of Childhood* (Random House, 2012)

Victor Lytton, *The Life of Edward Bulwer, First Lord Lytton* (Macmillan, 1913)

Daphne Rae, *A World Apart* (1983)

Selina Hastings, *The Red Earl* (Bloomsbury, 2014)

T. C. Worsley, *Barbarians and Philistines: Democracy and the Public Schools* (Robert Hale, 1940)

Colin Luke (dir), *Forty Minutes*: 'The Making of Them' (BBC TV episode, 1994)

Andrew Roberts, *Salisbury: Victorian Titan* (Weidenfeld, 1999)

A. N. Wilson, *The Victorians* (Random House, 2002)

Claudia Nelson, *Invisible Men: Fatherhood in Victorian Periodicals, 1850–1910* (University of Georgia Press, 2010)

Joy Schaverien, *op cit*.

George Orwell, 'Such, Such Were the Joys'

Jeremy Lewis, *Cyril Connolly: A Life* (Random House, 2012)

Arthur Marshall, *Whimpering in the Rhododendrons: the Splendours and Miseries of the English Prep School* (Collins, 1982)

Evelyn Waugh, *A Little Learning: the First Volume of an Autobiography* (1964)

Harry Thompson, *Peter Cook: a Biography* (Hachette UK, 2011)

Jeffrey Richards, *Happiest Days: The Public Schools in English Fiction* (MUP, 1988)

Jeremy Lewis, *Cyril Connolly: A Life* (Random House, 2012)

Po Bronson & Ashley Merriman, *Nurture Shock* (Ebury Press, 2009)

Julie Beck, 'When Nostalgia was a Disease', *The Atlantic,* August 2013


**Part Three – Growing up at Public School**

J. R. De S. Honey, *Tom Brown's Universe: The Development of the Public School in the 19th Century* (Millington, 1977)

Kathryn Tidrick, *Empire and the English Character* (I. B. Tauris, 1992)

A. N. Wilson, op. cit.

Derek Gillard, *Education in England* (2011), www.educationengland.org.uk

T. C. Worsley, op. cit.

Alice Renton, *Tyrant or Victim? A History of the British Governess* (Weidenfeld & Nicolson, 1991)

Leonard Woolf, *Sowing: an Autobiography of the Years 1880–1904* (Hogarth Press, 1960)

Mark Peel, *The New Meritocracy: A History of UK Independent Schools 1979–2014* (Elliott & Thompson, 2015)

Simon Raven, *The Old School* (Hamish Hamilton, 1986)

David Turner, *The Old Boys – the Decline and Rise of the Public Schools* (2015)

Grahm Greene (ed), *The Old School* (Jonathan Cape, 1934)

Raymond Chapman, *Forms of Speech in Victorian Fiction* (Routledge, 2014)

J. A. Mangan (ed), *Benefits Bestowed: Education and British Imperialism,* particularly Donald Leinster-McKay's essay on the nineteenth-century prep school, p. 56.

John Horne, Alan Tomlinson, Gary Whannel, *Understanding Sport: An Introduction to the Sociological and Cultural Analysis of Sport* (Taylor and Francis, 1999)

Karl Heinz Abshagen, *König, Lords und Gentlemen* (Stuttgart, 1938; English translation published 1939 by William Heinemann)

John Wakeford, *The Cloistered Elite: A Sociological Analysis of the English Public Boarding School* (Macmillan, 1969)

Julian Barnes, *The Sense of an Ending* (Jonathan Cape, 2015)

Erving Goffman, *Asylums* (Anchor Books, DoubleDay 1961)

Stephen Fry, *Moab is My Washpot* (Arrow Books, 2004)

Herbert Asquith, *Moments of Memory* (Hutchinson, 1938)

F. Anstey, *Vice Versa: a Lesson to Fathers* (1882)

Thomas Hughes, *Tom Brown's School Days* (1857)

Claudia Nelson, *Invisible Men: Fatherhood in Victorian Periodicals, 1850–1910* (University of Georgia Press, 2010)

Jeremy Lewis, *Cyril Connolly: A Life* (Random House, 2012)

Evelyn Waugh, op. cit.

Po Bronson & Ashley Merriman, *Nurture Shock* (Ebury Press, 2009)

Julie Beck, 'When Nostalgia was a Disease', *The Atlantic*, August 2013


**Part Four – The Uses of Violence**

Ian Gibson, op. cit.

R. Bosworth Smith, *Life of Lord Lawrence* (1883)

Alexander Waugh, *Fathers and Sons* (Hachette, 2016)

Edward Lockwood, *Early Days of Marlborough College* (1893)

Rictor Norton, *Homosexuality in Eighteenth Century England*, a source book, http://rictornorton.co.uk/eighteen/bits.htm

Deborah Lutz, *Pleasure Bound: Victorian Sex Rebels and the New Eroticism* (W. W. Norton, 2011)

Donald Sturrock, 'Roald Dahl's Schooldays', *Daily Telegraph*, 8 August 2010

A. Hay Tod, *Charterhouse* (1900)

Helene Adeline Guerber, *The Story of the Greeks* (1896)

Stephen Spender, *World Within World* (Hamish Hamilton, 1951)

Graham Greene (ed), *The Old School*, op. cit.

Daphne Rae, op. cit.

Ysenda Maxtone Graham, *Terms & Conditions: Life in Girls' Boarding Schools, 1939–1979* (Slightly Foxed, www.foxedquarterly.com, 2016)

Various, *The Assistant Master Speaks* (Kegan Paul, 1938)

Elizabeth T. Gershoff, Andrew Grogan-Kaylor, 'Spanking and Child Outcomes: Old Controversies and New Meta-Analyses', *Journal of Family Psychology*, June 2016.

Alec Waugh, *The Loom of Youth* (1917)


**Part Five – Sex and Some Love**

Tim Card, *Eton Renewed: a History from 1860 to the Present Day* (John Murray, 1994)

J. M. Wilson, *Morality in Public Schools and Its Relation to Religion* (Macmillan, 1882)

Y. Maxtone Graham, op. cit.

William Acton, *The Functions and Disorders of the Reproductive Organs in Childhood, Youth, Adult Age, and Advanced Life* (1862)

Florence Tamagne, *A History of Homosexuality in Europe*, Volume 1 (Algora, 2007)

Cyril Connolly, *Enemies of Promise* (Routledge and Kegan Paul, 1938)

T. C. Worsley, *Flannelled Fool* (Alan Ross, 1967); *Barbarians and Philistines: Democracy and the Public Schools* (Robert Hale, 1940)

J. A. Hadfield, *Childhood and Adolescence* (Pelican, 1967)

Alisdare Hickson, *The Poisoned Bowl: Sex and the Public School* (Duckworth, 1996)

John Chandos, op. cit.

Dean Farrar, *Eric, or Little by Little* (1858)

A. K. Boyd, *The History of Radley College, 1847–1947* (Blackwell, 1948)

Christopher Hitchens, *Hitch-22: A Memoir* (Atlantic Books, 2011)

John Peel, *Margrave of the Marshes* (Bantam Press, 2005)

Lord Rothschild, *Meditations of a Broomstick* (Collins, 1977)

Alec Waugh, *The Loom of Youth* (1917)


**Part Six – Captain Grimes and Captain Hook**

Evelyn Waugh, *Decline and Fall* (1938), *A Little Learning*

Auberon Waugh, 'Suffer the Little Children', *Spectator*, 30 September 1977

Philip Eade, *Evelyn Waugh: A Life Revisited* (Weidenfeld & Nicolson, 2016)

Richard Meinertzhagen, *Diary of a Black Sheep* (Oliver & Boyd, 1964)

Brian Garfield, *The Meinertzhagen Mystery* (Potomac Books, 2007)

Nick Duffell, *The Making of Them* (Lone Arrow Press, 2010)

A.W. Richard Sipe, 'Secret sex in the Catholic system', *National Catholic Reporter*, 28 March 2010

David Turner, op. cit.

Colm Tóibín, 'After I am hanged my portrait will be interesting', *London Review of Books,* 31 March 2016

David Hare, *The Blue Touch Paper* (Faber, 2015)

Eileen McGinley and Arturo Varchevker (eds), *Enduring Trauma Through the Life Cycle* (Karnac, 2013)

Matt Cook et al, *A Gay History of Britain* (Greenwood, 2007)


**Part Seven – Meeting the Vampires**

J. Brown, 'Preventing child sexual abuse: towards a national strategy', NSPCC (2015)


**Part Eight – The Product**

Andrew Roberts, *Salisbury: Victorian Titan* (Weidenfeld & Nicolson, 1999)

Derek Gillard, op. cit.

Headmasters' and Headmistresses' Conference, 'First data on mental health trends', October 2015; http://www.hmc.org.uk/

# Index